PARENTAL RIGHTS AND RESPONSIBILITIES

Analysing social policy and lived experiences

Harriet Churchill

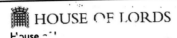

First published in Great Britain in 2011 by

The Policy Press
University of Bristol
Fourth Floor
Beacon House
Queen's Road
Bristol BS8 1QU
UK

Tel +44 (0)117 331 4054
Fax +44 (0)117 331 4093
e-mail tpp-info@bristol.ac.uk
www.policypress.co.uk

North American office:
The Policy Press
c/o International Specialized Books Services (ISBS)
920 NE 58th Avenue, Suite 300
Portland, OR 97213-3786, USA
Tel +1 503 287 3093
Fax +1 503 280 8832
e-mail info@isbs.com

© The Policy Press 2011

British Library Cataloguing in Publication Data
A catalogue record for this book is available from the British Library.

Library of Congress Cataloging-in-Publication Data
A catalog record for this book has been requested.

ISBN 978 1 84742 090 9 paperback
ISBN 978 1 84742 091 6 hardcover

Cover design by Robin Hawes
Front cover: image kindly supplied by www.alamy.com
Printed and bound in Great Britain by TJ International, Padstow
The Policy Press uses environmentally friendly print partners.

Contents

List of figures, tables and boxes

Figures

Tables

Boxes

Acknowledgements

I am indebted to many for their help and support in completing this book. I would like to thank my colleagues at the Department of Sociological Studies, University of Sheffield for their support, encouragement and assistance. I'm very grateful for the constructive comments received from anonymous reviewers and hope to have done justice to their engagement with the book. Much appreciation goes to The Policy Press team for their incredible support. Thank you especially to Leila Ebrahimi and Karen Bowler. Last but not least, thanks to friends and family for their encouragement.

List of abbreviations

BSA	British Social Attitudes Survey
CB	Child Benefit
CSR	Comprehensive Spending Review
CTC	Child Tax Credit
CYPP	Children and Young People's Plan
CYPU	Children and Young People's Unit
DCSF	Department for Children, Schools and Families
DfES	Department for Education and Skills
DH	Department of Health
DIUS	Department for Innovation, Universities and Skills
DSS	Department of Social Security
DWP	Department for Work and Pensions
EEC	Early Excellence Centre
ESA	Employment and Support Allowance
EU	European Union
EYDCP	Early Years Development and Childcare Partnerships
FACS	Families and Children Survey
FC	Family Credit
FCS	Family and Children Survey
HBAI	Households Below Average Income Survey
HFEA	Human Fertilisation and Embryology Authority
IB	Incapacity Benefit
ICs	Incapacity Claimants
IS	Income Support
JSA	Jobseeker's Allowance
LA	local authority
MCS	Millennium Cohort Study
NAPP	National Academy of Parenting Practitioners
NCS	National Childcare Strategy
NDLP	New Deal for Lone Parents
NDYP	New Deal for Young People
NESS	National Evaluation of Sure Start
NFPI	National Family and Parenting Institute
NMW	National Minimum Wage
NNI	Neighbourhood Nurseries Initiative
ONS	Office for National Statistics
PSA	parent support adviser
SETF	Social Exclusion Task Force
SEU	Social Exclusion Unit
SML	Statutory Maternity Leave

SMP	Statutory Maternity Pay
SSLP	Sure Start Local Programme
TFR	Total Fertility Rate
UNCRC	United Nations Convention on the Rights of the Child
WERS	Workplace Employment Relations Survey
WFTC	Working Families Tax Credit
WTC	Working Tax Credit
YJB	Youth Justice Board

ONE

Introduction

The focus and aims of the book

This book engages with debates about parental rights and responsibilities. From a legal perspective, the Children Act 1989, Section 3(1) defined parental rights and responsibilities as 'all the rights, duties, powers, responsibilities and authority which by law a parent of a child has in relation to the child and their property'. The Children Act 1989 and Children (Scotland) Act 1995 clarified that parents and families have primary responsibility for children and that parental responsibilities are lifelong (persisting if married or cohabiting parents separate and divorce). This legislation made child welfare 'the paramount consideration' in family–state–child relations. Parental rights (the rights and freedoms granted to those with parental status and responsibilities) were revised as 'rights that enable parents to fulfil their responsibilities for children and promote child welfare' (Children Act 1989). This principle attempted to balance parental and children's rights to public support with more traditional 'liberal' notions of parental rights to non-interference from the state (Eekelaar, 2006; Bridgeman et al, 2008).

This book examines notions of parental rights and responsibilities informing recent social policy developments. The focus is primarily on policy developments in England (where policies are devolved) and the UK. The book analyses what Daly (2004) referred to as 'welfare state support for families':

> policies covering cash support to families, provisions for working parents, services for families with children, and benefits and services for higher need families. (Daly, 2004, p 136)

These entitlements and provisions entail social, economic and employment rights; provide support and services for 'in need' families; and encompass state intervention to promote child welfare, 'family functioning' and wider societal objectives. Social policies are informed by assumptions and ideological perspectives about the role of families and children in society, and divisions of responsibility for children, young people and social welfare within the state, and between the state, parents, families, young people and communities. The book focuses on five policy areas: welfare-to-work measures, financial support for families with children, childcare policies, statutory family-friendly employment rights, and family and parenting support services. The book does not include an in-depth assessment of mainstream education, health or family law policies (although it does review children's and family services reforms under the responsibility of the former Department for Children, Schools and Families [DCSF] and the Department of Health). To contain the scope of the book, there is a focus on families with children aged 16 and under, rather than older teenage young people or children residing in state residential or juvenile settings. Alongside this focus on welfare state support for families, the book examines other aspects of public policies for families, such as government inaction and the discursive construction of 'family', 'parent' and 'child'. The analysis focuses on the radical developments in family policies since the late 1990s under New Labour and the changing family/child and social policy agenda that characterises the early months of the new Coalition government. Policy agendas, developments and impacts are evaluated against:

(1) empirical and theoretical debates about child, family and social well-being in the UK
(2) human rights, family support and egalitarian principles
(3) social research on parental and service-user perspectives and experiences.

Informed by these critical social policy and sociology literatures, the book highlights the shifting and contested nature of parental rights and responsibilities, and assesses the social justice and social well-being implications of policy developments. The conclusion argues for social policy to promote child, adult, family and social well-being via more extensive social rights to family support and a wider public debate about parental rights and responsibilities.

Shifting and contested notions of parental rights and responsibilities

The 2010 General Election illustrated the changing and contested nature of parental rights and responsibilities. Economic policy, the rise in the public deficit and rising unemployment were major issues, but prominent themes were also claims of a 'social crisis', 'family and social breakdown' and social risks to children. The major political parties all supported the following policy agendas, objectives and initiatives:

- meeting the revised child poverty reduction targets
- sustaining investment in early years services
- extending welfare to work measures
- extending paternity leave, parental leave and rights to flexible working options
- expanding nursery provision
- improvements to health and education services, with an emphasis on citizens' rights, as consumer citizens, to involvement in services, better information and standards of service
- 'intensive' interventions for families with 'multiple and serious problems'

- child protection reform
- reforms to address the 'risks to children' from contemporary life-styles, such as internet safety
- new compulsory forms of community service and volunteering for young people aged between 16–19 years
- more support for couple relationships and couple and family mediation services
- family law reform aimed at promoting child welfare and fathers' involvement in children's lives
- community regeneration and citizen participation (Conservative Party, 2010; Labour Party, 2010; Liberal Democrat Party, 2010; Plaid Cymru, 2010; Scottish National Party, 2010).

These proposals reflected much continuity in policy themes, priorities and programmes, and took forward some proposals previously set out in independent policy reviews, government departments, think-tanks, interest groups and political parties. Further, many resonated widely with policy developments elsewhere and the priorities of influential international policy agencies (OECD, 2005, 2009; *Official Journal of the Council of Europe*, 2007).

These points of consensus indicate that the New Labour years will have an enduring legacy. New Labour's family and child policies sought to: reduce poverty among (deserving) low-income families; reduce long-term welfare reliance; promote employment opportunities and secure full employment; regenerate deprived neighbourhoods; reduce crime and anti-social behaviour; support parents; address 'serious family problems' and 'invest in children'. Some coherency across policies was discerned in terms of communitarian Third Way ideologies; notions of 'the social investment state'; and New Public Management ideas about marketisation and notions of 'network governance' (Newman, 2001; Dwyer, 2004; Jensen, 2006; Lister, 2006). Akin to the US, Third Way politics has particular resonance in the UK context, due to the dominance of two political parties historically aligned to more social democratic agendas versus neoliberal approaches to social policy (Bonoli and Powell, 2004). In the early 1990s, communitarian and Third Way perspectives not only pointed to a revised social democratic agenda whereby social justice 'ends' were to be realised via 'market means' and embracing economic globalisation, but included explanations for social problems which pointed to the role of 'culture' and social deviance as well as 'economics' (Etzioni, 1993; 1996; Blair, 1998; Dwyer, 2004). Communitarians raised concerns about 'excessive individualism', 'moral decline' and 'dwindling social responsibility' in contemporary society while also calling for governments to address the social injustices created by income inequalities, poverty and social exclusion (Deacon, 2002; Dwyer, 2004). Changing family structures and the shift to the 'dual earner' family were often the focus of concern. For example, Etzioni (1993) argued that society suffered from a 'parenting deficit'. 'Parenting deficits' were associated with dual earner families where both parents work full time; poor-quality childcare provision; and rates of parental separation, divorce, cohabitation and lone parenthood. For Etzioni (1993), cultural, economic and social policy factors were to blame. Factors included excessive materialism and individualism, and the 'unintended consequences of women's emancipation', whereby higher rates of maternal full-time working and more consumption-based life-styles meant that parents were not providing children with the attention, guidance and care they needed (Etzioni, 1993, p 20). Etzioni (1993) aligned these concerns with more traditional social democratic concerns about relative poverty and the stresses and strains of raising children on a low income and in deprived neighbourhoods. Overall, Etzioni (1993) called for the state to intervene 'on the side of culture and economics' via the following policies: more financial incentives for marriage; marriage preparation and education schemes; parent education initiatives; citizenship education; employer and state support for working parents; investment in quality childcare provision and early years services to support families with young children. Etzioni (1993) and other communitarian writers further pointed to welfare reform and the role of the state to promote active citizenship and parenting (Mead, 1997; Deacon, 2002). Drawing on US welfare to work programmes, the solution was to be more conditional social rights, whereby the state sought to change behaviour and attitudes via systems of benefit sanctions and financial incentives (Mead, 1997). Third Way perspectives informed New Labour's discourses of social exclusion. Levitas (2005) illustrated how New Labour viewed social exclusion as rooted in labour market exclusion and poverty, but also showed that discourses about a deviant moral underclass and family dysfunction were significant. These perspectives, on the one hand, meant welfare rights were enhanced for low-income (deserving) families (in or out of paid work) and – in some respects – all families with children. The support claims of working parents were recognised and Labour introduced policies to strengthen the statutory employment rights of working parents (mainly mothers). But on the other hand, Labour instigated a range of social policies which diminished the welfare rights of the 'undeserving poor', sustained social inequalities and divisions and sought to extend and enforce parental responsibilities for children, young people and social problems. New sites of family and parenting support developed – with significant investment in parent education and family-level interventions (Featherstone, 2004; Churchill and Clarke, 2009).

Likewise, coherency across policy objectives has been explained with reference to 'the social investment state' (Lister, 2002; Featherstone, 2004; Jensen, 2006). Here the overarching social and economic functions of the welfare state, in the context of globalisation, prompted policies aimed at 'high cost, low productivity' socially excluded groups and 'human capital deficits' (Jensen, 2006; OECD, 2009). Jensen (2006) found that European and international policy agencies promoted the social-investment state approach. However, Jensen (2006) argued that there were 'adult-centred' and 'child-centred' approaches. New Labour's child and family policies were aligned with a 'child-centred' social investment discourse although

Labour's third term in office saw the emergence of more comprehensive policies to address 'skills gaps' in the labour market among working-age people. In addition, New Public Management and ideas about 'joined-up governance' informed New Labour programmes for modernising the welfare state. Here there was emphasis on marketisation, managerialism, consumerism and governance via networks and partnerships (Newman, 2001). The marketisation of public services was well under way under the previous Conservative government, whereas the extensive use of networks and strategic partnerships returned to long-standing concerns about improving cooperation and coordination across government departments and public services. New Labour was infamous for extending the use of targets and performance-monitoring systems.

Following the financial credit crisis, and the emergence of the current period of economic recession and crisis, policies for returning to economic growth and reducing the public deficit dominated the 2010 General Election. Added to a sense of economic crisis, election campaigning was orientated towards addressing notions of social and political crisis, ideologically constructed in multiple ways in respect of concerns about widening social inequalities versus a growing social underclass or the need for political reform in the wake of political scandals such as the MP expenses affair. The 2010 Labour Party manifesto reflected much continuity in recent policy developments under the Labour government although in the new policy context there were to be major public sector efficiency gains and cuts in public spending. Political reform was on the cards, with proposals including plans to reduce the voting age to 16 years. Further, proposals were set out to further strengthen the rights of consumer citizens to involvement in public services, such as parental rights to have a greater say in relation to schools. Other proposals included: implementation of new legislation to allow parents to 'share' maternity leave and maternity pay rights; extending the right to request flexible working options; extending tax credits; a National Care Service for social care for older people; a National Youth Service to provide young people with community work and recreational opportunities; benefit reform and a review of family law (Labour Party, 2010). These proposals championed young people's political rights and rights to recreational opportunities, parents' rights as consumer citizens in relation to schools, fathers' rights and older people's rights. They reflected concerns about parental responsibilities for children in the context of parental separation and divorce, and young people's community involvement.

The proposals of the Conservative and Liberal Democrat Parties reflected the emergence of alternative overarching social and economic policy agendas, although these parties also concurred with New Labour in some areas of policy. Both fashioned an alternative 'Third Way' based on rebalancing 'rights with responsibilities', promoting active citizenship and seeking 'social justice ends' via 'market and community means' (Lister, 2010). Conservative Party policies were informed by a programme to reduce 'costly and ineffective' welfare state support for families developed under New Labour (Conservative Party, 2010). Further, to address the economic crisis via reductions in public spending and levels of public debt, the Conservatives set out policies to reduce state bureaucracy and 'waste in the public sector', and to promote the role of the private sector in public services. An additional discourse was that of promoting the 'Big Society', which addressed issues of economic, social and political crisis via more community responsibility and involvement in neighbourhood regeneration and the commissioning and delivery of public services. Investing in children did not appear as such a strong theme, beyond recognition of the significance of early years services and early education provision. The Conservatives' social policy agenda was dominated by cuts in public spending and a new era of public service reform. The latter agenda sought to dismantle 'big government' (Conservative Party, 2010). The Conservative Party's campaign emphasised 'personal, family and community responsibility' and sought 'the 'Big Society' by promoting more social responsibility and community action (Conservative Party, 2010). Its election campaign was informed by the pre-election 'Broken Britain' campaign (Kirby, 2009). A pro-marriage stance was central to this synopsis of social problems, and alternative family formations were aligned with 'dysfunctional families' (Duncan Smith, 2007; Cameron, 2009). To 'fix the broken society' the Conservatives sought to 'favour married couples in the tax and benefit system', 'strengthen personal and family responsibility', 'do more to reduce welfare dependency' and 'stop the Government from doing things which undermine the family' (Cameron, 2009). By 2010, the 'Big Society' was aligned with localism: 'a redistribution of power and control towards individuals, families and communities and away from politicians and bureaucrats' (Conservative Party, 2010, p viii). This agenda entailed proposals for more self-help initiatives, more community and voluntary sector involvement in public services and citizen involvement in the running of public services, such as parental management of 'free schools' – although the degree to which these measures involved devolved funding and budgetary powers was unclear. In addition, the Conservatives set out proposals to reform the benefits system, invest in employability schemes and introduce a National Citizens Service for young people aged 16 years. In respect of parental social and employment rights, the Conservatives planned to extend policies developed under Labour that were viewed as compatible with raising economic productivity, addressing human-capital deficits and promoting child welfare, such as:

• rights to flexible working for parents with a child under 18 years old
• a flexible approach to parental leave so that parents could share maternity leave and pay rights
• more free, part-time nursery provision for pre-school children.

However, the Conservative Party's proposals differed from those of the Labour Party and Liberal Democrats in respect of: (1) the pro-active support for marriage; and (2) the return to more targeted welfare state support for families with children.

The Conservatives promoted tax and benefits reforms which sought to favour married couples, and reductions in state-provided financial support for less needy families with children (those with average and higher than average levels of household income). Sure Start Children's Centres would be reorganised towards delivering more targeted support and services aimed at the most 'disadvantaged and dysfunctional families' (Conservative Party, 2010).

The Liberal Democrat Party presented different discourses and agendas. To some extent, in comparison to the Conservative agenda, the Liberal Democrat Party manifesto was more critical of the market, called for more regulation of the banking system following the financial credit crisis, and highlighted the dangers of 'the commercialisation of childhood' (Liberal Democrat Party, 2010). There was a greater emphasis, in line with Labour, on children, particularly 'children's rights' and 'risks to children' from normative contemporary life-styles and parental separation and divorce. Further, the Liberal Democrat Party embraced family diversity and did not promote an overt pro-marriage stance (Clegg, 2010). Gender equality issues were also to some extent more on the agenda. The Liberal Democrats set out proposals to encourage men to work in the childcare sector; extend fathers' rights to time off for antenatal visits; extend rights to parental leave akin to maternity leave rights; and tax cuts for low-to-middle income families. The emphasis on fathers' rights was translated into policy as more equal rights for mothers and fathers in several areas, such as in statutory maternity and paternity employment rights and rights to 'equal access' post divorce (Liberal Democrat Party, 2010). More universal pre-school provision was on the cards – with proposals to provide 20 hours of free nursery childcare to all children over 18 months old. The Liberal Democrat Party claimed that it would take forward Labour's 2009 Children Bill, which sought to make the UN Convention on the Rights of the Child part of domestic law. There was a stronger focus on 'risks to children', namely from poverty, abuse, contemporary life-styles, commercialism and online internet safety (echoing policy concerns raised by the former Department for Children, Schools and Families).

Following the 2010 General Election a new Conservative–Liberal Democrat government took office. Since coming to office, the new Coalition government has announced unprecedented public spending cuts and initiated major reforms to the welfare benefits system, the education system, the NHS and local government services. Further, the Childhood and Families Task Force was established to review child and family policies in June 2010. At the time of writing, we await the Task Force report. In addition, a review of the family justice system is under way.

The analytical foci and approach

This book pursues a critical analysis of recent developments in child and family policies in the UK. It seeks to inform the current policy review via an analysis of: (1) empirical and theoretical research about child, adult, family and social well-being; (2) the social justice implications of revisions to parental rights and responsibilities; and (3) everyday experiences of parenthood and parenting.

Well-being studies offer an alternative perspective to one-dimensional and alarmist responses about social change and social problems (Williams, 2004a). 'Well-being' discourses have become increasingly significant to British social policies. The new Coalition government has stated a commitment to further develop social indicators to monitor and promote social well-being (HM Treasury, 2010). Well-being is a contested term, however, and a range of multi-disciplinary perspectives deliberate: What constitutes human well-being and universal human needs, rights and capabilities? What constitutes child well-being or family well-being? What social conditions promote universal child, adult and family well-being and sustainable socio-economic development? How are citizens faring in the UK, compared to other advanced industrial nations? In contrast to the more alarmist and general policy discourses about 'family and social breakdown', empirical research on child, adult, family and community well-being reports high levels of life satisfaction for many and some improvements over the past decade or so in respect of some social indicators of well-being (Bradshaw and Richardson, 2009; MacInnes et al, 2009). Since 1998/99, there have been significant reductions in child poverty and some deprived neighbourhoods have been significantly regenerated (Hills et al, 2009). Rates of property crime and violent crime have fallen, educational attainments rates have, in average terms, improved and there have been some improvements in health trends (MacInnes et al, 2009). However, on a number of social indicators (and in contrast to levels of national wealth) the UK performs badly in comparison to other European and OECD countries (Bradshaw and Richardson, 2009; OECD, 2009; Stiglitz et al, 2009). Moreover, where improvements were made in recent years – such as in employment rates and reductions in child and family poverty – progress has halted and some trends reversed (MacInnes et al, 2009).

Informed by multi-dimensional theories of well-being, well-being studies provide important insights from which to critically analyse social policies and social practices. With a focus on child well-being trends and policies, Bradshaw and Richardson (2009) analysed the statistical relationships between indicators of social policies and children's outcomes. They found that poverty and material deprivation most strongly predicted lower levels of child well-being across all life domains and that there appears to be 'a positive relationship between overall child well-being and levels of national wealth' (Bradshaw and Richardson, 2009, p 346). However, there also appeared to be a negative relationship between levels of income inequality in a country and overall levels of child well-being (Bradshaw and Richardson, 2009, p 347). A critical factor, in addition, was that national scores for child well-being were positively correlated with higher levels of spending on families in respect of services and benefits as well as higher levels of 'children's subjective well-being' (Bradshaw and Richardson, 2009, p 349). In contrast to the pro-marriage stance of the Conservative Party's family policies, Bradshaw and Richardson (2009) found the prevalence of 'new family forms' or 'broken families' (ie lone parent families, cohabiting-couple families or step-families) did not predict national child well-being scores. Bradshaw and Richardson (2009) pointed to the role of social policies and/or informal social support within families and communities 'to compensate for the negative effects of family disruptions and lone parenthood' (Bradshaw and Richardson, 2009, p 347). Policies that invested in children's and family services, supported families, reduced mothers' higher risk of poverty (associated with welfare reliance and part-time, lower-status work) and addressed gender inequalities in the domestic and public sphere are thought of as key measures in this respect (Millar and Gardiner, 2004; Williams, 2004a).

Critical social policy and sociology raise social justice issues. While critical social policy retains an interest in the 'details' of policy developments, institutional frameworks and the cost-effectiveness of particular initiatives, of paramount concern are issues of social justice, human rights and social equality (Williams, 1989). Critical social policy incorporates an eclectic range of political and theoretical perspectives, such as political economy, feminist, environmentalist, children's rights and anti-racist critiques of the welfare state, policy initiatives and policy studies (Pierson, 2006). While welfare states reflect to some extent the collectivisation of social risks and more extensive state provision, theorists critiqued the welfare state as an instrument of social control and inequality. From a political economy perspective, the development of welfare states in advanced industrialised countries reflected a revised labour–capital settlement and reorganisation of social reproduction in the interests of capitalism (Esping-Andersen, 1990; Pierson, 2006). What was critical to the social welfare and transformative potential of the welfare state was not the mere presence of social rights and collective public provisions, but the degree to which the welfare state reduced citizen reliance on the market and families (Esping-Andersen et al, 2002 ; Hantrais, 2004). Beyond a one-dimensional social class analysis of organised interests within and beyond the welfare state, social welfare movements and critical policy analysts have examined the relationship between social policies, social inequalities and social relations in relation to gender, age/generation, disability, 'race'/ethnicity and sexuality (Williams, 1989; Pierson, 2006). This book has been influenced by feminist and children's rights critiques of welfare state restructuring. Feminist critiques of the modern welfare state system highlighted the ways in which welfare states influence gender relations, and how social policies are shaped by gender norms assumptions and ideologies (Daly and Rake, 2003). Anti-racist feminist perspectives have examined the relationship between these gendered social processes and the institutionalised racism that operates within the welfare state and government policies (Lewis, 2000). Children's rights perspectives alert us to the ways in which social policies order generational relations and inequalities (Ridge, 2002).

The revisions in parental rights and social rights for families reviewed in this book raise social justice concerns. Part Two of the book examines the degree to which social rights enhance parental capabilities, resources and opportunities to promote their own, their children's and social well-being. A critical assessment of contemporary social rights involves critiques of the 'consumer-citizen' model (Clarke, 2005). The intensification of parental responsibilities further raises social justice issues. Firstly, the gendered division of care responsibilities and labour means there is a need to assess the gendered nature of policy developments and impacts (Lister, 2002). Secondly, when all families are measured against White middle-class norms, these developments raise concerns about the relationship between social class and ethnic inequalities, as well as broader interactions between social policies and social disadvantage related to age, residence, migrant status, educational attainment and disability (Gillies, 2007). This issue is related to the degree of public and citizen consultation, participation and engagement in policy processes. Thirdly, social justice implications are raised when policy objectives serve elite groups and sustain social inequalities rather than promote child, family and social well-being. Social policies that emphasise parental responsibilities for social problems can produce 'scapegoats' for entrenched social problems and contradictions. Fourthly, related to some of the points above, social justice concerns are raised when legal responsibilities place duties on citizens which are 'beyond their control' or for which they have 'limited capacity' to fulfil (Matravers, 2007). Lastly, social justice concerns are raised by the contradictory 'children first versus work first' principles informing social policy. Again, these have profound gendered implications and relate to a broader issue about the neglect of caring needs, labour and responsibilities within the British welfare state (Williams, 2004a). Parents, as adult citizens, are expected to put 'work first' and provide for children via the labour market. However, equally they are expected to put children first and provide intensive parenting.

The insights of well-being studies and social justice concerns regarding critical social policy and sociology are further developed in this book via an analysis of social research into everyday experiences of family life, parenthood and parenting. The concept of 'family practices', which refers to family, parenthood and parenting as a social practice (Bourdieu, 1990), is relevant. From this perspective, 'motherhood', 'fatherhood', 'parenthood' and 'parenting' are 'social practices and expectations that are historically and culturally situated, and [with shifting] meanings [that are] contingent upon broader social, political and economic exigencies' (Bainham, 1999, p 1, with author additions). The term 'parent' in this book is used in an inclusive way, for example, to include: birth and social parents; mothers and fathers; resident and non-resident parents; married/cohabiting/lone/ unmarried/same-sex and step-parents. However, there is also a need to be critical of the term and guard against 'adult-centric' notions of child-rearing which neglect children's agency and the significance of parent–child interactions in parenting (Bainham, 1999). The notion of 'family practices' highlights the different ways in which people 'perform and do family life' and allows for analysis of subjectivity-agency-structure dynamics to social action (Bourdieu, 1990). Family practices are constituted by, and constitutive of, interrelated social relations, differences, divisions and inequalities, such as in relation to social class, gender, generations and ethnicity (Ribbens McCarthy et al, 2000; Mayall, 2002; Gillies, 2007; Smart, 2007). Leaning towards qualitative research and grounded theorising, situated family-practices research highlights the diversity and complexity of family practices in the past and present; the 'gaps between family ideals and family experiences'; the different experiences of family members; the 'operating principles' that guide action in families and family relationships; and the new social risks and challenges associated with changing family structures and changing parenting expectations which challenge existing 'normative scripts' (Morgan, 1996). While being mindful of research findings generated from children's and young people's accounts and experiences of family life, the book contrasts policy discourses and developments against accounts of parenthood and parenting as a lived experience. This illuminates multiple discourses and meanings about parenthood and parenting, and some overlaps as well as many discrepancies between policy and parental perspectives. Overlaps emerge from widely held views that parents are expected to meet children's needs and take responsibility for children's care and upbringing. However, diversity and complexity emerges from different ideas about the respective responsibilities of different family members, and different ideas about children and children's needs. Moreover, parenting in practice involves negotiating the particular relationships, circumstances and situations that make up family life. In-depth accounts of lived experiences offer insights into how parents' perceive their rights and responsibilities, how they fulfil their responsibilities for children and the difficulties, challenges and pressures they face. It is recognised, however, that the analysis is based on the author's thematic analysis of social research and that researchers do not have 'direct access' to people's lived experiences. The literature in this area was systematically identified via searches of sociological and applied social research databases, social science search engines and Google Scholar searches. Ultimately, the analysis seeks to examine themes in this body of research and represent a diversity of accounts of parenthood and parenting experiences in order to pose policy-relevant issues and questions.

The structure of the book

The structure of the book relates to the three stages of analysis. Part One examines the broader social and political context to recent policy developments. Chapter Two reviews the concepts of child, family and social well-being, and Chapter Three turns to a critical review of social trends and social research debates. Chapter Four considers the historical development of parental rights and responsibilities in the UK context and compares the UK approach to other advanced welfare regimes. This chapter considers political perspectives on the aims and objectives of the welfare state, social citizenship and the respective responsibilities of parents, families and the state for children. The chapter additionally considers international trends in social policy and debates about Third Way policy convergence. Part Two of the book takes a more in-depth look at recent policy agendas and developments in the British context from 1997 to 2010. Three chapters analyse how parental rights and responsibilities have been reformulated. These chapters chart policy changes aimed at parents as paid workers, economic providers and child-rearers/carers. Part Three of the book examines how policy perspectives resonate with and differ from accounts of parenthood and parenting as a lived experience. Parenthood and parenting are not uniform experiences. These chapters aim to examine parenthood and parenting in different contexts. They identify everyday ethics of care towards children; contemporary 'moral dilemmas' within parenthood and parenting; and several insights from research into parenthood and parenting as a lived experience. The conclusion (Chapter Ten) deliberates the policy implications. There is a need for a more comprehensive family support agenda, underpinned by a more supportive relationship between the state, families and parents that engages in a genuine partnership with parents, families, communities, children and young people.

Part One
The broader context

TWO

Conceptualising child, family and social well-being

This chapter considers notions of 'child, family and social well-being' and sets out the social values and analytical approach informing the book. It argues for a combined analysis of child, adult, family and social well-being which draws on quantitative and qualitative social research to inform social policy agendas and critical debates about parental rights and responsibilities.

Child, family and social well-being: definitions and principles

'Well-being' is an inherently contested concept, defined relative to the purpose for which the concept is employed, disciplinary foci and social values (Jordan, 2007). Related concepts are equally contested, such as human needs, sustainable development, quality of life, life satisfaction and social quality (Stiglitz et al, 2009; Dean, 2010). The term is increasingly significant to British social policy debates. Part Two of the book examines the previous Labour government's child well-being agenda. Many recent policy reports utilise the concepts of child, adult, family and community well-being (MacInnes et al, 2009; Wollny et al, 2010). The new Conservative-Liberal Democrat Coalition government has pledged to develop national indicators of social well-being (HM Treasury, 2010). The shift from 'welfare to well-being' is associated with a shift in overarching policy objectives towards promoting higher standards of welfare and socio-economic development. For example, in 2006 the Department for Environment and Rural Affairs defined well-being as:

> a positive, social and mental state. It is not just the absence of pain, discomfort and incapacity. It arises not only from the action of individuals, but from a host of collective goods and relationships with other people. It requires that basic needs are met, that individuals have a sense of purpose, and that they feel able to achieve important personal goals and participate in society. It is enhanced by conditions that include supportive personal relationships, involvement in empowered communities, good health, financial security, rewarding employment and a healthy and attractive environment. (Quoted in Skilton, 2009, p 6)

Multi-dimensional notions of individual and societal well-being move social policies beyond one-dimensional perspectives (ie national well-being is not sufficiently measured in economic terms and neither is individual or household welfare, Stiglitz et al, 2009). Well-being promotes holistic, interconnected and democratic ways of understanding the lives of citizens, the nature of social problems and the overarching functions, aims and objectives of social policy.

However, there are limitations to the concept. It is linguistically and culturally specific. Bradshaw et al (2006) remind us that 'child well-being' is a popular term among English-speaking countries and agencies. Further, in some respects 'well-being' does not imply an imperative for state action in the same way as 'needs based' or 'rights based discourses'. The Children Act 2004, for example, defined child well-being as 'being healthy, keeping safe, enjoying and achieving, making a positive contribution and economic well-being'. These aspects of child well-being incorporate notions of children's needs, capabilities, rights and responsibilities (Bradshaw et al, 2006). The approach informing this book draws on:

- human and children's rights legislation, critical social policy, feminist ethic of care perspectives, situated family practices theories, the sociology of childhood, the capabilities approach and ecological models of human development (Bronfenbrenner, 1979; Doyal and Gough, 1991; Equality Commission, 2007; Williams, 2004a);
- empirical research on child, family and social well-being (Bradshaw and Richardson, 2009; Wollny et al, 2010; Stiglitz et al, 2009);
- a commitment to deliberative policy processes (Equalities Commission, 2007).

Conceptualising child well-being

The first issue in conceptualising child well-being is the question: what is a child? The 'welfare paradigm' often defines a 'child' in age-based and developmental terms (James et al, 1998). The Children Act 2004 stated a child was aged 0–18 years;[1] the UN Convention on the Rights of the Child (UNCRC) defined a child as 17 years and under, while other child welfare legislation defines a child as 16 years and under. These definitions are informed by child development theories. While human development is now thought of as a lifelong process, specialist child development knowledge constructs 'stages of development' (ie child development textbooks commonly include chapters on pre-natal development, infancy, early childhood, late childhood, adolescence and early adulthood). Child development research provides specialist knowledge on development processes, such as, stages of physiological maturity; cognitive development (ie how children develop speech and language, reading skills, motor skills or problem-solving skills; how children learn); theories of social and emotional development (ie how children develop social skills and emotional awareness; the importance of attachments to carers in childhood) and theories of adolescent development (ie which normalise adolescent 'risk behaviour' as denoting important developmental processes) (Heath, 2009). While early theories tended to point to innate developmental processes, since the 1970s researchers placed more emphasis on the dynamic relationship between physiological, cognitive and social factors (Bronfenbrenner and Morris, 1989). Moreover, child development studies shifted focus towards promoting developmental 'strengths' – children's 'assets, capabilities, relationships and resources' – in order to promote well-being – rather than merely researching 'developmental delays, disorders and problems' (Pollard and Davidson, 2001).

Sociological definitions of childhood provide an alternative perspective. James and James (2008) define 'a child' from a social-constructionist perspective:

> A child is a human being in the early stages of its life-course, biologically, physiologically and socially. It is a member of a generation referred to collectively by adults as children, who together temporarily occupy the social space created for them by adults and referred to as childhood. (James and James, 2008, p 14)

This definition recognises that children are 'in the early stages of the life-course' and that human development involves interrelated biological, physiological and social processes. However, childhood is viewed as socially constructed, which in turn reflects generational social relations. These researchers promote children's and young people's rights, recognise young people's unique lived experiences, monitor children's subjective well-being and seek to promote multi-cultural and holistic notions of a 'good childhood'.

Social indicators and empirical research on child well-being debates the relative utility of:

- the 'deficit approach' versus the 'strengths based' approach
- the use of objective and subjective measures of well-being
- approaches to children's participation in well-being studies and policies.

A recent report by the OECD (2009) defined child well-being in terms of six life domains:

- material well-being
- housing and environment
- education
- health
- risk behaviours
- quality of school life.

This report argued for governments to employ a 'deficit' approach (OECD, 2009, p 26), focused on improving well-being among disadvantaged children, 'children with problems, disabilities and disorders', and focused on addressing 'deficits in human capital' (OECD, 2009, p 24). Chapter Three links this approach with 'the social investment state' (Jensen, 2006). For data and policy relevance reasons, the OECD (2009) report did not review children's subjective well-being, citizenship issues, the quality of family and peer relationships or children's civic contributions.

Bradshaw and colleagues' framework is informed by the 1989 UNCRC, specialist knowledge on child welfare and ecological models of human development (Bradshaw and Mayhew, 2005; Bradshaw et al, 2006; Bradshaw and Richardson, 2009). Ecological models of child development are represented by Bronfenbrenner's (1979) model of human development. Informed by social systems theories, Bronfenbrenner (1979) conceptualised human development as shaped by interactions between an individual and interconnected systems. Individuals are recognised as having unique characteristics, abilities and dispositions and as actively shaping their development and 'external environment'. Figure 2.1 summarises Bronfenbrenner's model.

Figure 2.1: A representation of Bronfenbrenner's (1979) ecological model of child development

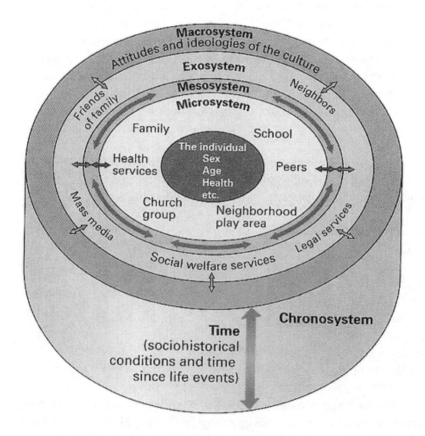

Source: Smith et al (2007, p 10).

Figure 2.1 places the child at the centre of four interrelated social systems: the 'microsystem, mesosystem, exosystem and macrosystem' (Bronfenbrenner, 1979). The 'microsystem' and 'mesosystem' include the relationships and settings children often interact with: a child's immediate family and kin networks, peer networks, places of residence, educational or care settings, communities of association and local neighbourhood. These relationships and settings are thought to have the most 'proximate' or 'direct' influence on child development (Fernstein et al, 2008; Heath, 2009). Individuals, 'microsystems and mesosystems' in turn interact with the 'exosystem'. In relation to child development, the exosystem has been defined as 'the societal context in which families live, including among others, parents' social networks, the conditions in the local community, access to and quality of services, parents' workplace and the media' (Bradshaw et al, 2006, p 9). These systems interact with the 'macrosystem' – another level of societal influences and individual–social interactions such as national social policies and laws, political ideologies, social norms, technological advances, cultural change, the quality of the physical environment and international trends.

While widely influential, ecological theory is not without its critics. Empirical research has utilised this theory to primarily examine micro-, meso- and exosystems, defining the 'micro- and mesosystems' in narrow terms as 'home, classroom, peer group and neighbourhood' (Churchill and Clarke, 2009). Further, the high level of abstraction and equal weight afforded to multiple contexts and interactions provides a comprehensive framework but is less suited to setting policy and practice priorities (Churchill and Clarke, 2009). Another concern is that social systems theories provide a limited critique on the prevailing social order and inequalities.

Bradshaw and colleagues' research is informed by the UNCRC (1989). The UNCRC is based on the construction of the family as the private realm and parents, families and their communities as primarily responsible for the day-to-day care of children. In this respect children's rights place obligations on parents and families as well as on states, and provide civil rights to minimal state interference in family life. State–family–child relations are regulated according to the overarching principle of the 'best interests of the child' (Art 3). The UNCRC promotes children's rights to:

- life, maximum survival and development (Art 6)
- care and protection for well-being (Art 3.2)
- a standard of living adequate for the child's physical, mental, spiritual, moral and social development (Art 27.1)
- live a life free from discrimination (Art 2)
- express their views freely in all matters that affect them and in accordance with their age, evolving capacities and maturity (Art 12.1)
- have their views taken into account in decisions made by public authorities which affect them (Art 12.2).

Some children are afforded special protections (ie adopted children; children with disabilities; children living in state institutions; refugee children and children from ethnic minorities).

Drawing on the 1989 UNCRC, ecological theories and available data, Bradshaw et al (2006) developed the child well-being indicators for the 2007 UNICEF report on 'child poverty among 21 advanced industrial nations'. Bradshaw and Richardson (2009) reported a revised framework for monitoring child well-being across the EU member nations which examined:

- health
- subjective well-being
- children's relationships
- material resources
- behaviour and risk
- education
- housing and the environment (Bradshaw and Richardson, 2009).

An additional domain developed by Bradshaw et al (2006) was the 'citizenship' domain. However, this was not included in the UNICEF report or the revised EU index, for data reasons (Bradshaw and Richardson, 2009). The revised EU framework sought to place more emphasis on children's rights, children's well-being in the now and children's subjective well-being (Bradshaw and Richardson, 2009).

It is worth summarising Bradshaw and Richardson's (2009) research. In the overall child well-being index the UK was ranked 5th from the bottom, 24th out of 29 countries, based on data for 2006. This was due to low ranking in the health domain (mainly due to poor immunisation rates and below-average scores in children's self-rated health); the material resources domain (due to high rates of child and family poverty and 'workless' households); the education domain (due to wide educational inequalities and relatively high rates of 16- to 18-year-olds not in education, training or employment) and young people's subjective well-being (Bradshaw and Richardson, 2009, p 324). Bradshaw and Richardson (2009) statistically analysed the relationship between domains, indicators and national child well-being trends. These researchers found that:

- levels of material well-being most strongly predicted national child well-being overall;
- there is 'a positive relationship between overall child well-being and levels of national wealth';
- there is 'a negative between income inequality and overall levels of child well-being';

- the prevalence of 'new family forms' or 'broken families' (ie lone-parent families, cohabiting-couple families or step-families) did not predict national child well-being scores;
- child well-being scores were higher in countries with higher levels of spending on families in respect of services and benefits, particularly 'in kind services';
- there was a positive relationship between 'children's subjective well-being' and a higher overall national score for child well-being (Bradshaw and Richardson, 2009, pp 346–9).

These findings have significant policy implications, which will be returned to later. There are many other influential frameworks in this field (Ben-Arieh and George, 2006). Ben-Arieh (2002) developed an international multi-disciplinary framework, moving beyond a focus on OECD nation states. Child well-being was conceptualised in terms of:

- safety and physical status
- personal life
- civic life
- children's economic resources and contributions
- children's activities.

This framework emphasises 'the child' as an active participant in personal, civic, economic and social life (Ben-Arieh, 2002).

Hanafin et al (2007) developed social indicators for monitoring child well-being in Ireland via consultation with young people, child welfare experts, parents, service providers and policy agencies. This initiative found, compared to experts' panels and adults, that young people placed greater emphasis on: formal and informal forms of social support to help them cope and achieve; the quality of their family and peer relationships; the importance of 'pets and animals' in their lives; having their own bedroom; having adequate rest and enough sleep; and having a range of 'things to do' (social activities and opportunities to participate in recreational, play and cultural activities) (Hanafin et al, 2007, p 91). Another model was developed by the Good Childhood Inquiry. Informed by interviews with children, young people, parents and carers as well as an expert panel and child welfare research, the Good Childhood Inquiry asked 'what do British children need to have a good childhood?' (Layard and Dunn, 2009). Layard and Dunn (2009) concluded that, most of all, children need:

- loving families
- friends
- a positive life-style
- 'solid values' (which give meaning to life and are acquired from parents, schools, the media, political and faith organisations)

- good schools
- good mental health
- enough money.

Conceptualising family well-being

The concept of 'family well-being' is less prominent in policy debates, although the Family and Parenting Institute. a government-funded child and family policy think-tank and research institute, has recently promoted the concept (Wollny et al, 2010). An immediate issue is how to define 'family'. The Universal Declaration of Human Rights (1950) talks of the 'human family', where all humans are of equal worth and have equal rights. In contrast, two common ways of defining 'family' are: (1) according to a range of characteristics such as genetic links, marital or legal ties, co-residence or the nature of family relationships; or (2) the social functions expected of families. Official statistics define families in terms of family household types and represent families according to factors such as co-residence, marital ties and couple or lone parent status. Families with children have diversified and are more complex, in comparison to the immediate post–war years. Major trends include the decline in families with children headed by married couples (Figure 2.2); increases in parental separation and divorce (Figure 2.3); increasing numbers of step–families and families headed by cohabiting couples, and the rise in extra–marital births. In England and Wales in 2008, marriage rates were at their

Figure 2.2: Marriages and re-marriages, England and Wales, 1950–2007 (thousands)

Source: ONS (2010a, p 20, Figure 2.11). Includes all first marriages for both parties and first remarriages for one or both parties.

Figure 2.3: Divorces, England and Wales, 1950–2007 (thousands)

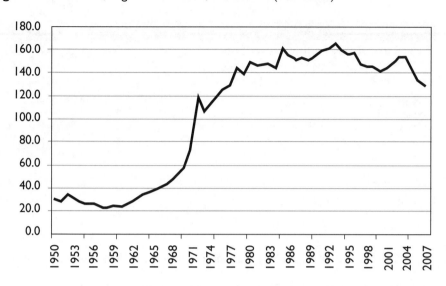

Source: ONS (2010a, p 22, Figure 2.15).

lowest level since records began, with 21.8 men marrying per 1,000 unmarried men and 19.6 women marrying per 1,000 unmarried women (ONS, 2010c). In 2008, 45 out of 100 married couples divorced (ONS, 2009). Cohabitation has become a more common experience, as a precursor and alternative to marriage. The decoupling of marriage, parenthood, reproduction and sexual relations led to rises in extra-marital births and the diversification of family formations. While 55% of registered births were to married mothers in 2008, 45% were to unmarried mothers (ONS, 2010a, p 24).

Adults and children experience more changes in family and living arrangements, with a higher incidence of solo living, parental separation, remarriage, re-partnering and step-families. Families with children are more diverse, due to greater recognition of same-sex relationships and the passing of the Civil Partnerships Act 2004, which enables same-sex partners to recognise their relationship as a civil partnership akin to marriage. Tables 2.1 and 2.2 summarise key changes in family type from 1971 to 2008/09. In 1971, 92% of dependent children lived in family households headed by a married couple, but by 1991 this had reduced to 81% of children. In 2001, 75% of children lived in families headed by a married or cohabiting couple. In 2008 this number had increased slightly, due to no further reductions in the percentage of children living in married-couple families and increasing numbers of children in cohabiting-couple families (ONS, 2010a). In comparison, the proportion of children growing up in lone-parent headed households rose from 8% in 1971 to 25% in 2001, due to the increase in numbers of divorced and single unmarried lone mothers. Table 2.2, however, shows that

Table 2.1: Dependent children by family type, Great Britain, 1971–2008 (%)

Family type	1971	1981	1991	2001	2008
Married couples (and cohabiting couples from 2001)	92	87	81	75	77
Lone mother	7	11	18	22	20
Single	1	2	6	10	11
Widowed	2	2	1	1	0
Divorced	2	4	6	7	5
Separate	2	2	4	4	4
Lone father	1	2	1	3	3
All lone parents	8	13	19	25	23

Source: (ONS 2010d, Table 3.6).

Table 2.2: Number of dependent children by family type, UK, 1997–2009 (millions)

	1997	2001	2005	2008	2009
Married couple	9.6	9.0	8.6	8.3	8.3
Cohabitating couple	1.0	1.3	1.5	1.7	1.7
Female lone parent	2.5	2.7	2.8	2.8	2.9
Male lone parent	0.2	0.2	0.3	0.2	0.3

Source: ONS (2010a, Table 2.5). Civil partnerships and same-sex couples included in the figures for married and cohabiting couples from 2008; dependent children are children aged 16 and under or 16–18 years in full-time education.

in the last 10 years or so the number of children living in lone-parent families has increased by 500,000 while the number in families headed by cohabiting couples grew by 700,000. These figures, though, reflect a static snapshot of family households with children and do not convey the complexity of family relationships beyond household residence.

Similar trends have been witnessed across European Union (EU) and OECD member states. In crude average terms, the EU marriage rate peaked in the 1980s and since then has been on a downward trend (Eurostat, 2008, p 46). Marriage rates fell in many Scandinavian countries in the early to mid 1960s, in several Western European countries in the late 1960s and 1970s and in many Southern European countries in the 1980s and 1990s (Eurostat, 2008). In 2006, the UK had slightly higher than average marriage and divorce rates compared to the EU27 and above-average rates of children living in lone-parent families and average levels of cohabitation.

Other legal changes have extended parental rights among same-sex and single unmarried adults. The Children and Adoption Act 2002 granted adoption rights to same-sex couples and single adults. Many families include adopted children, although numbers of adoptions in England and Wales fell from 21,000 in 1975 to 4,637 in 2007 (www.baaf.co.uk, accessed 4 January 2010). Additionally, the growth and use of fertility treatments has increased. According to the Human Fertilisation and Embryology Authority (HFEA), an estimated 14,057 women received fertility treatments in 1992, but in 2007[2] this rose to 36,648 receiving treatments. The use of egg and sperm donors, and artificial insemination techniques, enables same-sex couples to bear children together. The Human Fertilisation and Embryology Act 2008 introduced new rights for female same-sex couples and heterosexual couples to jointly register the birth of a child conceived using egg or sperm donors. From 2010, male same-sex couples could apply to access the same rights. Further, many children are under the responsibility of social services authorities. There were 60,900 children aged under 19 years registered with children's social care in England on 31 March 2009, 73% of whom lived with foster carers and 10% in children's homes (DCSF, 2009b). Definitions of 'parent', 'child', 'family' and 'family household type' need to be inclusive of these changes and complexities.

An alternative approach to defining 'family' is according to the roles and functions expected of families and family relationships. Function-based definitions evoke ideas about 'functional and dysfunctional families and family relationships'. Linked to the previous definitions, family functioning is often associated with particular family characteristics, such as family household type or parental employment status (Home Office, 1998). However, child and family welfare research more often conceptualises family functioning as differentiated by social values and situational contexts, and hence changing somewhat as society changes (Wollny et al, 2010). In classic functionalist terms, the family is defined in terms of the traditional family unit (Cheal, 2009). The family unit fulfilled the functions of social reproduction, as the primary social unit which provided everyday care (providing food, warmth, shelter, childcare, informal support, and care for sick or older family members), transmitting culture, language and values between generations and providing socialisation, and operating as a unit of consumption (Cheal, 2009). Changes in family structures have fuelled alarmist responses about the breakdown of the traditional family unit, which regulated these functions via gendered family responsibilities, adult and patriarchal authority and obligations to the marriage contract (Williams, 2004a; Smart, 2007). Other function-based definitions, however, do not align functionality purely with these characteristics. An alternative approach refers to the functions and qualities of 'family relationships' incorporating but moving beyond a notion of the traditional family unit. Motivated by the need for more in-depth qualitative research on everyday family values, the ESRC Care, Values and the Future of Welfare (CAVA) Research Group examined social values in 'alternative family and intimate relationships' (Williams, 2004a). Williams (2004a) argued that these studies found much evidence that family and personal relationships in alternative family and partnering formations were sustained by 'ethics of care'. Sevenhuijsen (1998) defined an ethic of care as: 'motivation towards, and sensitivities to the welfare needs of others'. Williams (2004a) reported how family and community ties and relationships are sustained under challenging and changing circumstances, due to everyday ethics such as 'being attentive to others' situations, accommodating one's own needs to those of others, adapting to others' changing identities, and being non-judgemental and open to making and receiving reparation' (pp 7–8). Research with children and young people additionally found that the degree to which children felt they were 'liked, loved, cared about and cared for' figured highly in their accounts of what matters in family, peer and social relationships (Brannen et al, 2000; Madge, 2006). Part Three will consider the everyday ethics of care within lay accounts of parenthood and parenting generated by qualitative research. Critical policy analysis offers another way of analysing the social construction of family. Part Two of this book will review legal and policy changes which reflect changing expectations towards parents, families, children and communities, and changing notions of normative parent–child relations.

There have been attempts to develop a 'domains and indicators' approach to monitoring family well-being (Babington, 2006; Wollny et al, 2010). In the context of Australian debates, Babington (2006) conceptualised family well-being in terms of five interconnected domains:

- physical safety
- physical and mental health
- supportive intra-family relationships, open communication and shared problem solving
- social connections outside the family, including within the local community
- economic security and independence.

For Babington (2006), family well-being was a 'shared responsibility'. Each Australian family was encouraged to 'take stock of their overall well-being' and negotiate issues such as 'how much time they spend together', whether all members have 'a good enough connection with family members not living with them' or if they 'encourage their children enough' (Babington, 2006, p 2). Governments, employers, trade unions, businesses, public authorities and services, community organisations, media organisations, political parties and academics were assigned major roles. Government responsibilities, at the very least, constituted monitoring and addressing the social problems of child abuse and neglect, domestic violence, crime and anti-social behaviour, substance misuse, suicide, homelessness, poor life expectancy, high infant mortality, educational under-achievement, low basic skills among the working-age population, unemployment, poverty and social exclusion, household debt, forms of discrimination, lack of physical exercise and trends in accidents and injuries. Governments were equally encouraged to review access to public services, educational and employment opportunities, wage levels, financial support for families and work–family pressures; and provide information, resources and services which promote caring families, mutual respect among family members, non-violent forms of resolving conflict and social support for families and children (Babington, 2006).

Conceptualising social well-being

This section will briefly consider 'social well-being'. Stiglitz et al (2009) argued that social well-being indicators should incorporate:

- more comprehensive economic indicators
- multi-dimensional quality of life domains and measures
- sustainable development indicators.

Quality of life frameworks seek to promote good overall quality of life and life satisfaction. At the very least, this involves the fulfilment of basic human needs, which Doyal and Gough (1991) defined as needs for physical health and personal autonomy. According to Doyal and Gough (1991), these basic needs 'must be satisfied to some degree before actors can participate in their form of life to achieve any other valued goals' (Doyal and Gough, 1991, p 53). Box 2.1 summarises Doyal and Gough's theory of basic and intermediate human needs, informed by an inter-disciplinary political economy and health perspective. Here, intermediate needs are 'broad categories which relate to how basic needs are

Box 2.1: Doyal and Gough's (1991) framework of basic and intermediate needs

Basic needs	Intermediate needs
Physical health	Adequate food and water
Personal autonomy	Adequate housing
	A non-hazardous work environment
	A non-hazardous physical environment
	Security in childhood
	Significant primary relationships
	Physical security
	Economic security
	Safe birth control and child bearing
	Basic education
	Critical autonomy

defined' and 'satisfied' in a particular society or group (Doyal and Gough, 1991, p 5). Doyal and Gough (1991) argued that societal well-being is diminished if basic and intermediate needs are not adequately met. However the process of 'needs definition' in policy making should be a participatory one, as needs are defined and 'satisfied' in culturally specific ways. Doyal and Gough (1991) argued that social policies should be informed by expert knowledge as well as the lived experiences of those at the target end of social policies and democratic processes of decision making. In addition, Doyal and Gough (1991) proposed 'a higher order human need' – that of critical autonomy – involving capabilities to 'compare cultural rules, to reflect on the rules of one's own culture, to work with others to change them and, in extremis, to move to another culture' (Doyal and Gough, 1991, p 187). These researchers argued that international human rights legislation promoted critical autonomy via democratic political processes and rights to asylum and migration.

Drawing on quality of life research, the Office of National Statistics (ONS) has recently defined social well-being in terms of nine domains:

- material living standards
- health
- education
- personal activities including work
- political voice and governance
- social connections and relationships
- environmental conditions
- insecurity (economic and physical)
- overall life satisfaction (ons.gov.uk).

The approaches reviewed so far have been informed by human rights principles. This was also the case for the Equalities Review team, which developed a capabilities approach to produce the Equalities Measurement Framework (Equalities Commission, 2007). This research drew on Sen's (1993) theory of human capabilities. According to Sen (1993), while income and material conditions are critical to human well-being, what is most important is to be and do the things we freely choose to be and do, with respect for others' rights and freedoms. Sen (1993) did not construct a list of fundamental human capabilities but called for deliberative policy processes to promote critical autonomy and substantive freedoms. Some, however, have criticised the capability approach for being politically amenable to sidelining anti-poverty agendas (Lister, 2004).

In response to these concerns, the Equalities Review (Equalities Commission, 2007) combined a human rights and participatory approach, developing a list of basic capabilities informed by: (1) international principles of universal social, economic, cultural and political rights; (2) deliberative public consultation exercises and (3) interviews with individuals and groups vulnerable to social exclusion and discrimination (Equalities Commission, 2007). This process generated some interesting discrepancies. For example, the right to join a trade union was identified in deliberative discussions only following the researchers' pointing it out and group discussion (Burchardt, 2008). The Equalities Review (Equalities Commission, 2007) developed an Equality Measurement Framework based on three forms of inequality: inequality of outcomes, of autonomy and of processes. The research generated a framework for monitoring inequalities across 10 life domains and capabilities:

- being alive
- living in physical security
- being healthy
- being knowledgeable, being able to understand and reason, and having the skills to participate in society
- enjoying a comfortable standard of living, with independence and security
- engaging in productive and valued activities
- enjoying individual, family and social life
- participating in decision making, having a voice and influence
- being and expressing yourself, having self respect and knowing you will be protected and treated fairly by the law (Burchardt, 2008).

Conclusion

This chapter has examined notions of 'child, family and social well-being'. It has argued that human rights perspectives, participatory approaches to policy making and a number of 'well-being' studies offer important principles from which to review social and family policies and encourage more holistic understandings of needs, capabilities, rights and responsibilities. The frameworks and theoretical approaches reviewed in this chapter offer comprehensive visions of child, adult, family and social well-being. However, there are political, methodological (ie the development of indicators and data) and theoretical (ie concept definitions and theorising the relationships between indicators and domains, social processes and outcomes) challenges to developing the well-being agenda (Stiglitz et al, 2009). The next chapter turns to an analysis of social trends, and empirical and theoretical research debates.

Notes
[1] Aged 24 and under in the case of disabled young people.

[2] These figures are estimations calculated by the HFEA based on figures reported by licensed fertility centres when surveyed annually, www.hfea.gov.uk/99.html, accessed 4 January 2010.

THREE

Socio-economic change and social well-being trends

Social and family policy debates respond to: (1) 'the new social risks and opportunities' associated with demographic and socio-economic transformations (Taylor-Gooby, 2004); and (2) child, family and social well-being trends (MacInnes et al, 2009). In recent years, social policy debates have been dominated by the economic crisis in the global financial system and how to minimalise economic recession. Politicians and the media further often point to the social risks and fragmentation created by 'family and social breakdown' (Cameron, 2009) and 'excessive individualism' (Layard and Dunn, 2009). Chapter Two, however, indicated that empirical studies on child, adult, family and social well-being refute alarmist views about 'social breakdown'. This chapter therefore reviews social trends and research debates.

Demographic change

Alongside the changes in partnering, family formations and living arrangements described in Chapter Two, the post-war era saw declining fertility rates, an ageing population and increasing ethnic diversity. In England and Wales, the Total Fertility Rate (TFR)[1] rose in the immediate post-war era, peaking in 1963 when, on average, women gave birth to 3 children each (ONS, 2009). Following this post-war baby boom, the TFR dramatically declined. By 1975 women on average bore 1.6 children each (ONS, 2009). Since then the TFR has drifted between 1.6 and 1.9 children per woman (ONS, 2009). Moreover, the age at which women first bear children has increased, as have rates of childlessness among women. In England and Wales, the average age at which women had their first child in 1971 was 26.6 years (ONS, 2010a). By 2009, this had increased to 29.4 years (ONS, 2010a). In the UK, around 9% of women born in 1945 did not have children, compared to 20% of those born in 1965 (ONS, 2010). The fall in fertility rates in the 1960s and 1970s was associated with a 'transformation in intimacy' (the 'decoupling' of sexual relations from reproduction, family formation and child-bearing) and more equal opportunities for women (Hantrais, 2004). However, there is concern that women now are unable to have as many children as they would prefer, as European social surveys suggest that most prefer to have at least two children (Esping-Andersen, 2009). Factors such as the growth in higher education participation and women's full-time employment; the extended period of economic dependence in early adulthood; rising house prices, living costs, debts and costs associated with raising children; and the disproportionate responsibility women bear in caring for children are related to delaying child-bearing and having fewer children (Esping-Andersen, 2009). The variation in fertility rates across social classes, ethnic groups and geographical areas indicates the significance of socio-economic factors. Women with higher educational qualifications are more likely to delay having children until their early 30s, while women with lower qualifications are more likely to have children younger in their mid to late 20s (ONS, 2009). In 2004, around 17% of White British family households with dependent children had three or more children, while in other ethnic groups this figure rose to 28% of Black African families; 20% of Indian families and 40% of Bangladeshi and Pakistani families (ONS, 2005). Compared to England and Wales, the TFR in Scotland reached a lower level of 1.48 in 2002 and stood at 1.7 in 2009 (ONS, 2010a). In contrast, Northern Ireland had higher fertility rates compared to England and Wales, with women bearing 2.04 children in 2009 (ONS, 2010a).

In comparison to other OECD countries, the UK has average fertility rates. France, Ireland, Norway, the US and Australia had equivalent or higher fertility rates in 2008 (www.oecd.org/els/social/family/database, accessed 5 September 2010). Additionally, many countries have recently witnessed slight upward trends in fertility rates. Comparative policy analysts associated these trends with work–life balance and family support policies (Gauthier, 2002; Hantrais, 2004), whereas others point to inward migration and higher fertility rates among migrant groups (ONS, 2010a). Although there is concern about population decline and an ageing population, early parenthood is recognised as being associated with multiple disadvantage (Holmes and Kiernan, 2010). The UK has relatively high rates of teenage pregnancies in EU terms. During the 1990s, the rates of conception among girls under 16 years and aged 16–19 years fell, but since 2005 rates have increased again. In 2007, 8 per 1,000 girls aged 13–15 years became pregnant (MacInnes et al, 2009, p 64).

The long-term increase in longevity, coupled with reductions in fertility rates, has led to ageing population profiles. In 1971, 25% of the UK population were aged 16 years or under, while 13% of the population were aged 65 and over (ONS, 2010a). By 2008, the proportion of the population aged 16 years and under had reduced to 19%, while the proportion aged 65 years and over had increased to 16% (ONS, 2010a). Forecasts state that the percentage of the UK population aged 65 years and over will rise to 22% by 2031 and the proportion aged 16 and under will fall to 18% (ONS, 2010a, p 4). The majority of European countries face similar trends (Eurostat, 2008), which have led to policies in many countries seeking to promote 'active ageing'; raise employment rates to sustain balanced 'dependency ratios'; reverse population decline; halt a rise in poverty in old age; restructure pensions and rethink the social care needs of a growing elderly population (Hantrais, 2004).

Patterns of migration and increasing ethnic diversity are two further aspects of demographic change. From the 1950s, inward migration to the UK occurred on a larger scale as migrants were sought from the former British colonies to fill labour shortages. A mixture of 'push and pull' factors have since borne upon international migration patterns, such as the 'pull' of economic and employment opportunities in the UK and the 'push' of limited opportunities, civil unrest or political persecution abroad (Reeve, 2008). European and international legislation facilitates cross-border migration and in 2004 eight Central and Eastern European countries joined the EU. However, several pieces of UK legislation restrict inward migration in particular circumstances. In 2008, net migration stood at 163,000 people (ONS, 2008).This figure represented a decrease of 70,000 people migrating to the UK, in contrast to 2007 figures, and an ongoing reduction in net migration since 2004 (ONS, 2008). Between the late 1980s and early 2000s the number of applications for asylum in Britain increased, peaking at 84,000 applications in 2002 (ONS, 2010a, p 8).The number of applications then fell until 2008, when there were 25,930 applications for asylum in Britain (31,315 when dependent children are counted), which reflected an 11% increase in comparison to 2007 (ONS, 2010a, p 8).The Department for Children, Schools and Families estimated 3,700 unaccompanied asylum seeking children were under the responsibility of social services in England in March 2009, 87% of whom were boys (DCSF, 2009b).

These trends lead to more ethnic, religious, linguistic and cultural diversity, and more cross-cultural influences. Although somewhat out of date, the 2001 Census recorded that around 84% of children were of White British ethnic origin, 7% were of South Asian or Asian British origin, while 3% were of Black or Black British origin, 3% were of 'mixed' ethnic origin and 3% were of 'other' ethnic origin (ONS, 2003).Table 3.1 shows the age profile of the population of Great Britain according to ethnic categories for 2008, illustrating the younger age profile of ethnic minority groups.

There are social differences and much inequality between ethnic groups (Barns et al, 2006; Equalities Commission, 2007). Disadvantage arising from direct and indirect forms of racism are compounded by other sources of disadvantage – such as those based on migrant and citizenship status, social class, gender, disability or social class (Phoenix and Hussain, 2007).Across ethnic groups there are different cultural traditions, such as in respect of gender and generational roles, and family and kin roles and responsibilities (Barns et al, 2006). Some research suggests a disparity between traditional cultural practices among some migrants groups and British social norms (Phoenix and Hussain, 2007).The popular media often promote a negative view of many ethnic minorities and new migrant groups. Concurrently, survey data suggests that many feel Britain is becoming more racially prejudiced, particularly following the events of 9/11 (Ferguson and Hussey, 2010). Analysing the 2007/08 citizenship data, Ferguson and Hussey (2010, p 29) found that 56% of respondents thought that the UK had become more racially prejudiced between 2002 and 2006/07, while 25% thought levels

Table 3.1: Age structure of the population by ethnic group and age, Great Britain (%)

Ethnic category	Under 16 years	16–64 years	Over 65 years	All people
White:				
White British	18	65	17	100
White Irish	7	68	25	100
Other White	14	75	12	100
Mixed	51	47	2	100
Asian or Asian British:				
Indian	20	72	8	100
Pakistani	34	62	4	100
Bangladeshi	36	61	4	100
Other Asian	23	73	5	100
Black or Black British:				
Black Caribbean	20	66	13	100
Black African	33	64	2	100
Other Black	37	57	6	100
Chinese	12	83	5	100
Other ethnic groups	20	75	4	100

Source: ONS (2010a, p 4, Table 1.4).

of racial prejudice remained the same over this period and 11% thought prejudice had reduced (some declined to answer). The 2007/08 Citizenship Survey further asked respondents about immigration trends, asking 'whether they thought the number of immigrants coming to the UK should be increased, reduced or remain the same'. As many as 79% thought immigration should be reduced, with 53% stating that numbers should be reduced by 'a lot' (Lloyd, 2009, p 16). In contrast, 16% of respondents thought the numbers should remain the same, while 5% thought they should be increased (Lloyd, 2009, p 16). Reeve (2008) argued that the spatial dimension of recent migration policies and trends is important in explaining these negative social attitudes, as new migrant groups often settled in deprived neighbourhoods with little history of ethnic diversity, a pattern shaped by immigration policies (ie the policy of 'dispersal'), demand for migrant labour and the availability of cheaper housing.

Official ethnic categories, however, do not capture the complexity of social identities. Phoenix and Hussain (2007, p 1) warned against essentialist perspectives, whereby an ethnic group is treated 'as if it had unchanging characteristics and as if all members of the group had to be the same'. Reviews of research on ethnicity and parenting call for more in-depth research within and across ethnic groups and generations (Barns et al, 2006; Phoenix and Hussain, 2007). Further ethnic identities are differentiated by other sources of personal and social identity (Phoenix and Hussain, 2007).

Economic well-being and labour market trends

Overall, GDP and household income rose substantially in the post–war period. Figure 3.1 shows that GDP per head had risen around 1.5 times at the end of 2008 compared to the end of 1980 and that real disposable household incomes had doubled over the same period. Annual economic growth, however, varied considerably. Major economic downturns and recessions followed the oil crisis in the late 1970s and occurred in the early 1980s and early 1990s, followed by the latest financial crisis and recession from 2008. The economy experienced negative growth from 1980 to 1983 and from 1990 to 1993, but continuous growth from 1993 to 2007. Between 2007 and 2008, GDP fell by 0.4 percentage points (ONS, 2010a, p 60). Table 3.2 illustrates that the UK continues to have above–average levels of GDP when compared to the EU27 nations and that the majority of EU27 nations experienced slower or reduced growth in 2007–08.

Figure 3.1: Gross domestic product per head and real household disposable income per head, UK, 1948–2008

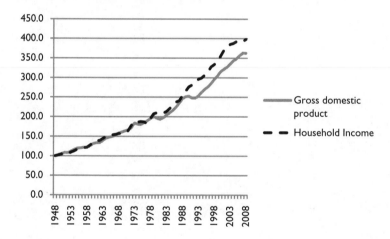

Source: ONS (2010a, p 60, Figure 5.1).

Economic cycles are reflected in employment trends. Figure 3.2 shows that the unemployment rate peaked to nearly 12% in 1984 and to just over 11% in 1993 (ONS, 2010a). From 1995 to 2005 unemployment fell to a historic low of 4.8%, but it rose back to 5.4% in 2008 and rose sharply to 7.8% in 2009 (ONS, 2010a). Concurrently, the employment rate fell to just below 68% in 1983, then rose to 75% in 1991, fell back to 70% in 1993, and then rose over a longer spell to reach 74.7% in 2008 – one of the highest employment rates in the EU (ONS, 2010b). However, in 2009 the employment rate stood at 72.7%, back at 1997 levels (ONS, 2010b). Less related to economic cycles though, over this period the economic inactivity rate remained at around 20–21% of the working-age population.

Table 3.2: Gross domestic product per head, EU27 countries

EU27	1997	2001	2007	2008
Luxembourg	215	234	267	253
Ireland	115	133	150	140
Netherlands	127	134	131	135
Austria	131	125	124	123
Sweden	123	121	122	121
Denmark	133	128	120	118
United Kingdom	118	120	119	118
Germany	124	117	115	116
Belgium	126	124	118	115
Finland	111	116	116	115
France	115	116	109	107
Spain	93	98	105	104
Italy	119	118	102	101
Greece	85	87	95	95
Cyprus	86	91	91	95
Slovenia	78	80	89	90
Czech Republic	73	70	80	80
Malta	81	78	78	76
Portugal	76	77	76	75
Slovakia	51	52	67	72
Estonia	42	46	68	67
Hungary	52	59	63	63
Lithuania	38	42	60	61
Poland	47	48	54	58
Latvia	35	39	58	56
Romania	-	28	42	46
Bulgaria	26	29	37	40

Index EU27 average = 100

Note: GDP per inhabitant at current market prices compiled on the basis of the European System of Accounts 1995 and adjusted to take account of national price differences.

Source: ONS (2010a, p 61, Table 5.2).

Figure 3.3 provides a more detailed picture of changes in household income, comparing trends for the top 10%, median and bottom 10% of household incomes. Disposable household incomes among the top 10% group grew at a much faster rate than among those on median household incomes, while median household incomes grew more than the household incomes of those in the lowest 10% group. Figure 3.4 shows that households in the lowest 10% of the household income distribution actually experienced a relative decline in average household income between 1997/98 and 2007/08 of 2.5%. Figure 3.5 shows trends in income

Figure 3.2: Employment rate, unemployment rate and economic inactivity rate, UK, 1971–2009 (% of working-age population)

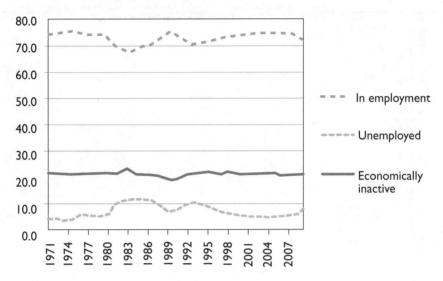

Note: Figures are for men aged 16–64 years and women aged 16–59 years, apart from the unemployment rate, which refers to people aged 16 and over.

Source: ONS (2010a, p 44, Figure 4.1).

Figure 3.3: Distribution of real household disposable income (equivalised household income before the deduction of housing costs), UK (Great Britain only for 1994/95 to 2001/02) (adjusted to 2007/08 prices)

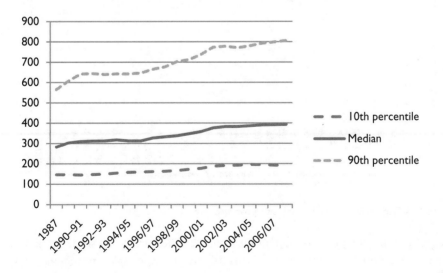

Source: ONS (2010a, p 61, Figure 5.3).

Figure 3.4: Changes in income across households in the income distribution, Great Britain, 1997/98–2008/09

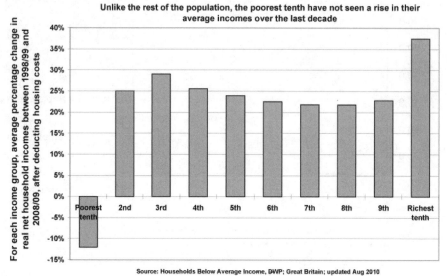

Source: Households Below Average Income, DWP; Great Britain; updated Aug 2010

Source: Guy Palmer (2010), The Poverty Site, poverty.org.uk,

Figure 3.5: The gini co-efficient measure of income inequality, UK, 1979–2008/09

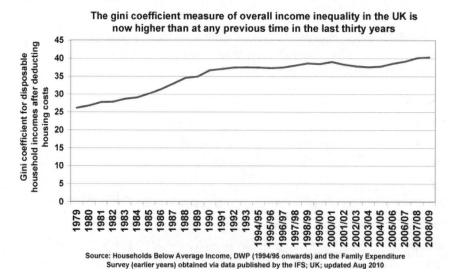

Source: Households Below Average Income, DWP (1994/95 onwards) and the Family Expenditure Survey (earlier years) obtained via data published by the IFS; UK; updated Aug 2010

Source: Guy Palmer (2010), The Poverty Site, poverty.org.uk,

inequality using the gini co-efficient measure. This measure shows some reduction in income inequality from 2000 to 2004/05 but increases again in recent years.

These trends are related to macro-economic restructuring and deregulation of wages and markets. The British economy is now 'post-industrial', with service sectors dominating the economy (Hirst and Thompson, 1999). By March 2008, 74% of male employee jobs and 92% of female employee jobs were in the service sectors (ONS, 2008). British manufacturing firms were more exposed to global market competition with the demise of economic management and corporatist policies during the 1980s, the introduction of legislation which reduced trade unions powers, privatised national industries, more deregulated markets, reduced state subsidies and new European and international trade agreements that sought to reduce cross-national barriers to free trade (Hirst and Thompson, 1999). While international trade and competition has long been important to the British economy (Hirst and Thompson, 1999), economic globalisation has generated more (1) trans-national corporations (large corporations commanding large amounts of capital and market influence with no national base), and (2) multi-national corporations (large corporations commanding large amounts of capital and market influence with a national base). These corporations command unprecedented market, political and social influence. Powell and Hewitt (2002, p 91) further highlight that globalisation involves global 'flows of capital, labour, finance and information' and is based on a more 'open international financial system' (although this 'openness' came somewhat under review following the financial credit crisis of 2008/09). Globalisation places pressure on national governments to attract global capital via more favourable tax regimes and lower production costs. More goods are imported from, and produced in, countries that offer lower production and labour costs. Technological change has furnished globalisation with IT systems facilitating 'action from a distance' (Giddens, 1998). Further, the post-industrial economy is 'highly differentiated' with a 'core workforce' with more secure employment, specialised skills, occupational promotion structures, performance-related pay and contracts; and a 'peripheral workforce' with lower wages, temporary contracts and low union activity (Hirst and Thompson, 1999). Giddens (1998) argued that social class solidarities are fragmenting as a result. In this context, human capital (ie economically valuable qualifications and skills) becomes critical to securing better employment. The Leitch Review (2006, p 3) highlighted the strong correlation between having no or low qualifications and unemployment, welfare reliance and long-term poverty.

A related trend is converging male and female employment rates. Between 1971 and 2008 men's employment rate fell from 92% to 79% and women's rose from 56% to 70% (ONS, 2010b). However, employment rates among married and cohabiting fathers remain high, standing at 86% in 1993 and rising to 92% in 2008 (ONS, 2010b). The rise in female employment rates includes increases in mothers' employment rates. Overall, 61% of mothers with children aged 16 and under were employed in 2008 (LFS, 2009). The employment rate among married and cohabiting mothers is higher and rose from 67% in 1997 to 72% in 2008 (ONS, 2010b). Although the majority of mothers continue to work part time, Klett-Davies and Skaliotis (2009) found the increase in couple mothers' employment reflected an increase in full-time working. Table 3.3 shows that in

1996, 25% of couple mothers worked full time, while in 2008 the figure had risen to 31%. In comparison, the proportion of couple mothers working part time had fallen slightly, from 42% to 41% (Klett-Davies and Skaliotis, 2009, p 48). The majority of couple-headed families are now 'dual earner' families, also known as 'work-rich' families when both adults work full time (ONS, 2010b). However, lone-parent employment rates fell in the 1980s and early 1990s and the numbers of lone-mother families reliant on welfare rose – subsequently causing alarm about welfare dependency and labour market exclusion among this group (Duncan and Edwards, 1999). Lone-parent employment opportunities became a priority for the Labour government and since 1997 their employment rate has increased by 11% – from 45% in 1997 to 56% in 2008 (ONS, 2010b). Table 3.3 shows that Klett-Davies and Skaliotis (2009, p 48) found this reflected more full-time and part-time working among lone mothers. Policies, though, have not raised employment rates among mothers with no qualifications – the employment rate among mothers (couple or lone) with no qualifications fell from 49% in 1989 to 33% in 2008 (Klett-Davies and Skaliotis, 2009, p 52). Under Labour, there was investment in promoting employment opportunities among disabled adults, but this group still suffer low employment rates. The employment rate for disabled adults stood at 46.3% in 2005.[2] This was lower than for the lowest qualified (49.6%); lone parents (56.6%); ethnic minorities (58.4%) and the over 50s (70.7%). It was well below the national employment rate, which stood at 74.6%. However, the employment rate for disabled people increased under Labour, from 38.1% in 1998, when it was first recorded.

Table 3.3: Employment rates, mothers and lone parents, UK, 1996–2008

	Full-time		Part-time	
	Married or cohabiting mothers	Lone mothers (and lone fathers 1996–2004)	Married or cohabiting mothers	Lone mothers (and lone fathers 1996–2004)
1996	25	22	42	22
2000	28	25	42	26
2004	28	28	42	26
2008	31	27	41	28

Source: Klett-Davies and Skaliotis (2009, p 59).

Poverty negatively affects 'most domains of personal and family well-being' (Bradshaw and Richardson, 2009, p 347). Long-term poverty during childhood has strong negative effects on children's 'well-becoming and well-being in the here and now':

> Poor children are deprived of material assets, they experience higher morbidity and mortality, their activities and opportunities are constrained, they are more likely to be mentally ill and are more likely to live in poor housing in poor neighbourhoods. (Bradshaw, 2005, p 36)

Lister (2004) conceptualised poverty within affluent countries as having a 'material core' (insufficient material resources for basic health and standards of living, and to furnish social inclusion) and 'psychological, relational and symbolic' disadvantages such as:

> a lack of voice, a lack of control over one's life and environment, disrespectful treatment, an assault on one's dignity and self-esteem, humiliation, shame, stigma, denial of rights and diminished citizenship. (Lister, 2004, p 7)

The official poverty line measures households living on incomes below 60% of median household income, adjusted to take account of the number of adults and children in a household and calculated on a 'before housing costs' and 'after housing costs' basis. To measure more severe poverty, household incomes below 50% and 40% of the median household income are monitored, as is material deprivation. The latter term refers to the extent to which families and children are going without goods and services that constitute a basic standard of living relative to social norms, due to lack of income (Alcock, 2006).

Figures 3.6 and 3.7 show that during the 1980s and early 1990s, income poverty rose substantially in the UK. In 1983, 8 million households, 14.4% of the population, were living in poverty (DWP, 2010). However, by 1992 these figures had risen to 14.2 million households and 25.1% of the population (DWP, 2010). There was a particular increase in households living on incomes below 50% and 40% of average incomes. In 1983, 6.9% of the population fell into the former group, but by 1992 this had risen to 16.7%. From 1985 to 1992, the number of people living in households with incomes below 40% of the average income rose from 1.6 million to 4.8 million (DWP, 2010). Even though the economy experienced several years of growth, between 1993 and 1997/98, poverty rates did not significantly fall, but remained at these relatively high levels (although there was some reduction in low-income households, using the 50% and 40% thresholds, 1993–95/96). From 1998/99 to 2004/05, however, the proportion of individuals in households living below the poverty line reduced by nearly 4% from 24.4% to 20.5%, as did the proportion of individuals living in households at below 50% of the median income. Since 2004/05, however, the number of individuals in low-income households at the 60% threshold rose again from 12.1 million in 2004/05 to 13.4 million in 2007/08, and at the 50% threshold rose from 7.9 million to 9.3 million. Moreover, the HBAI analysis found the number of individuals in the poorest households (those living on household incomes below 40% the median average household income) remained fairly level from 1998/99 to 2004/05 and then increased by 800,000 from 2004/05 to 2007/08.

The UK has higher rates of poverty than most EU countries and comparably wealthy OECD countries. Figure 3.8 compares the percentage of the population living in households with income levels at 60% of the median household income according to 2008 data, and shows that only Greece, Lithuania, Spain, Bulgaria, Romania and Latvia (countries with much lower levels of national wealth, see Table 3.2) have higher rates of poverty in the EU.

The majority of poor households (53% in 2007/08) contain children (MacInnes et al, 2009). There was an increase in child poverty during the 1980s and early 1990s, where relative child poverty rose three-fold. From 1998/99 to 2004/05 relative child poverty fell from 34% of children living in low-income households to 28% using the after housing costs measure. Using the before housing costs measure, 26% of children were living in poverty in 1998/99 and this fell to 21% in 2004/05 (MacInnes et al, 2009, p 25). Part Two examines the role of Labour's anti-poverty measures. However, relative child poverty has increased again in recent years. Measures of absolute poverty include household incomes falling below 40% and 50% of average household incomes in 1997 recorded in 1998/99 or household income falling 70% below the median average income in 2000/01. The HBAI series reported more significant reductions in absolute poverty compared to relative poverty during the 1990s. In 1996/97, 26% of children were living in absolute poverty (before housing costs measure); by 2005/06 this had more than halved, to stand at 12% of children (DWP, 2008a). On the after housing costs measure, absolute poverty rates are higher, but still fell considerably, with 17%

Figure 3.6: Number of people in low-income households, UK, 1979–2008/09

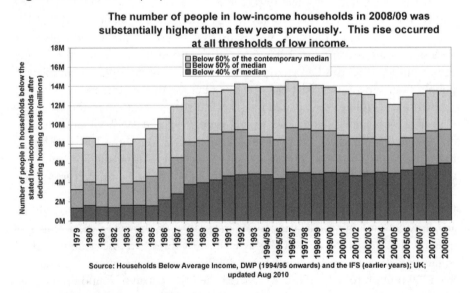

The number of people in low-income households in 2008/09 was substantially higher than a few years previously. This rise occurred at all thresholds of low income.

Source: Households Below Average Income, DWP (1994/95 onwards) and the IFS (earlier years); UK; updated Aug 2010

Source: Guy Palmer (2010), The Poverty Site, poverty.org.uk,

of children in absolute poverty by this measure (DWP, 2008a). The HBAI series (DWP, 2010) found that in 2007/08, 10% of children were living in persistent low income (in poverty for 3 out of 4 years, before housing costs), which reflected a

Figure 3.7: Proportion of people in low-income households, UK, 1979–2008/09

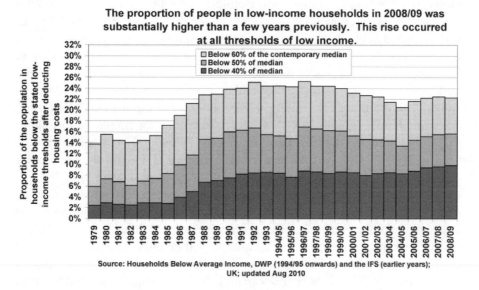

Source: Households Below Average Income, DWP (1994/95 onwards) and the IFS (earlier years);
UK; updated Aug 2010

Source: Guy Palmer (2010), The Poverty Site, poverty.org.uk,

Figure 3.8: Proportion of the population in low-income households, EU27 countries

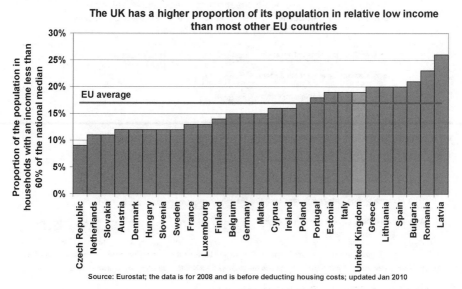

Source: Eurostat; the data is for 2008 and is before deducting housing costs; updated Jan 2010

Source: Guy Palmer (2010), The Poverty Site, poverty.org.uk,

reduction of 7%, compared to 1993 (although the figures for 2007/08 increased to 20% using the after housing costs measure).

Figure 3.9 details patterns of material deprivation for children. In general, children experience lower levels of material deprivation compared to adults, as low-income families often prioritise spending on children (Middleton et al, 1998). However, according to this data many children go without social opportunities and material goods, which promote physical, cognitive and social development and are valued by children as important to their well-being. According to the data from the Family Resources Survey 2008/09, around 57% of children living in low-income households were in families who could not afford to go on a week's holiday once a year; around 22% of children did not have their own bedroom; around 21% did not go swimming at least once a month and around 15% could not afford leisure equipment or having a friend round for tea once a fortnight.

Table 3.4 illustrates the risk of poverty among different social groups and family types in 2006/07 using HBAI data. It highlights that children had a greater risk of poverty when no adults in the household were in paid work; they lived in social housing or they lived in large families, lone-parent families or in families affected by disability; their parents were a lone parent or were of Bangladeshi and Pakistani ethnic origin. However, the majority of poor children were of White British backgrounds and lived in couple-headed families, families not affected by disability or families with one or more adults in paid work. Other figures additionally highlight the greater risk of poverty among family households where: parents have low educational attainment; parents only work part time; parents are of Black or Black British ethnicity; parents are under 25 years (Bradshaw, 2005);

Figure 3.9: Material deprivation among children, UK, 2005/06–2008/09

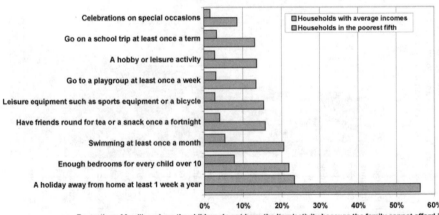

Regular holidays are by far the most common 'essential' item that children in low-income households lack because their parents say that they cannot afford them

Proportion of families where the children do not have the item/activity because the family cannot afford it

Source: Family Resources Survey, DWP; the data is the average for 2006/07 to 2008/09; UK; updated Aug 2010

Source: Guy Palmer (2010), The Poverty Site, poverty.org.uk,

Table 3.4: Risk of child poverty and proportion of poor child population across various social groups and family types, UK, 2006/07

	Risk of poverty	Proportion of children living in poverty
Lone parent	52	42
Couple with children	23	58
One or more parent in work	22	59
Workless household	81	41
Large families (3+ children)	42	40
Affected by disability of family member	38	28
Not affected by disability of family member	28	72
White children	27	79
Pakistani and Bangladeshi children	63	8
Home owners	17	37
Social-rented sector tenants	61	43

Note: Based on data from DWP (2008), *Households Below Average Incomes 1994–2006/07*
Poverty measure = household income 60% below median household income, after housing costs
Source: CPAG (2008, p 10).

and among children living in London, Wales and Northern Ireland and families with no or little savings (MacInnes et al, 2009).

These trends demonstrate that poverty is highly associated with unemployment, part-time working, low pay and inadequate social security benefits; and the relationship between age, social class, educational attainment, disability, caring responsibilities, family size, ethnicity and poverty. Earlier, mothers' higher rates of part-time working were noted. But part-time work is often lower paid. Using 2008/09 data, MacInnes et al (2009) found that children living in 'workless households' are at the greatest risk of poverty but an increasing proportion of poor children are in households where at least one parent works. Between 1997 and 2007 they found the proportion of poor children in families where at least one adult works full time had remained the same, while the proportion in workless households had fallen but the proportion in families where adults only work part time had increased (MacInnes et al, 2009). Other aspects of gendered labour market disadvantage include gender pay gaps and gendered occupational segregation. Women continue to be concentrated in lower-paid and lower-status service sector jobs (ONS, 2010b). There were more female managers in 2008, as compared to 1998, but women only made up 35% of managers (ONS, 2009). Table 3.5 finds that the largest gender pay gaps persist among full-time private sector employees and part-time public sector employees. According to the Annual Earnings Survey (which measures the gender pay gap in terms of the difference between men's and women's hourly pay), median average earnings were 20% higher among men who worked full time in the private sector compared to women in similar

Table 3.5: Gender pay comparisons for median hourly earnings excluding overtime by public and private sector, UK, 1999–2009

	Full-time	Part-time	All employees
Public sector			
1999	14	7	27
2009	10	21	19
Private sector			
1999	22	-2	32
2009	20	-2	29

Source: ONS (2010e)

full-time private sector employment (which represented a fall in the gender pay gap among full-time private sector employees by 2% since 1999). Median hourly earnings among men working part time in the public sector were 21% higher than among women working part time (a threefold increase in the gender pay gap among part-time public sector workers since 1999). The gender pay gap remains significant among full-time public sector employees, with men on hourly rates 10% higher than women. However, among part-time private sector employees men earn slightly less than women. The UK has above-average gender pay gaps, as compared to many EU countries (Women and Work Commission, 2009). These figures help to explain vulnerability to in-work poverty among part-time paid workers. With women with children most often working part time, these figures indicate one dimension of poverty among lone mothers and 'hidden' poverty or 'hidden economic dependency' among couple mothers who work part time. Young parents are vulnerable to poverty. The unemployment rate among young adults aged 16–24 years rose by 6% in 2004–09 to stand at 18.5% in 2009 – the highest rate since records began in the 1980s (ONS, 2010b). The Equalities Review calculated the 'employment penalty' for different social groups, which referred to a measure 'of the disadvantage individuals and groups face in the labour market' (Equalities Commission, 2007, p 62). The Review found that having younger children was associated with a higher employment penalty – both lone parents and partnered mothers with a child aged under 11 years were nearly twice as likely not to be in paid work, compared to partnered men with children (Equalities Commission, 2007, p 63). Other findings were:

• Compared to men, women were 23% less likely to be in paid work.
• Compared to White British women, Pakistani and Bangladeshi women were 30% less likely to be in paid work. Pakistani and Bangladeshi men were 12% less likely to be in paid work than White British men. Afro-Caribbean women were 7% more likely to be in paid work than White British women.

- Compared to partnered men, lone parents with children aged under 11 were 49% less likely to be in paid work; partnered mothers with children aged under 11 were 45% less likely to be in paid work and partnered mothers overall were 25% less likely to be in paid work.
- Compared to non-disabled adults, disabled adults were 30% less likely to be in paid work. (Equalities Commission, 2007, p 63)

Further important aspects of employment well-being are job satisfaction, work-related health risks, work–family conflict and satisfaction with one's working hours, pay or working conditions. Dame Carol Black was commissioned to review 'health and well-being among working age adults and in workplaces' for the Department of Work and Pensions (DWP) (Black, 2008). Her report found that workplace health and safety had improved overall, but the number of days employees were absent from work due to illness had increased during the 1990s and 2000s (Black, 2008, p 14). Mental health problems and musculoskeletal disorders were the most common reasons. Of new Incapacity Claimants (ICs), 55% had previously been off work due to sickness in 2006/07 (Black, 2008, p 13; see Part Two). Good working relationships with colleagues, anti-discriminatory workplaces, access to professional development and training opportunities, access to promotion, effective management, occupational health schemes, family-friendly working practices and good support and supervision were associated with promoting well-being among employees (Black, 2008).

In contrast to concerns about low income poverty, economic well-being debates attend to issues of excessive wealth, sustainable development and the dangers of materialism. The unsustainable nature of contemporary consumption in the UK raises issues about the negative personal and social effects from the commercialisation of childhood. The National Consumer Council conducted a survey and focus groups with young people aged between 11 and 14 years and found that British children were more materialistic than children in America (Mayo, 2005). The Good Childhood Inquiry raised concerns about the consumer market targeted at young people and their families and the messages in popular culture, marketing and advertising 'playing on emotional vulnerabilities' (Layard and Dunn, 2009, p 56). The Good Childhood Inquiry argued that children have 'unprecedented purchasing power' today; that 'the flow of information, consumer choice and advertising that children experience was previously more confined to adults' and criticised popular cultural messages that state 'to be happy and successful you have to be wealthy and beautiful' (Layard and Dunn, 2009, pp 56–8). Policy responses seek more parental responsibility and consumer rights, but the debate has not been informed by much research about how parents and children in practice negotiate commercialism (see Part Three). Chapter Seven details parental strategies which seek to promote children's 'critical autonomy' and resilience as consumers, but also highlights the significance of consumption to parents' and children's social belonging.

Education, skills and well-being

Formal education has become more significant in young people's lives and adults are more expected to be 'lifelong' learners. Between 1970 and 2002 there was a three-fold increase in full-time undergraduates at university in the UK. Furlong and Cartmel (2007) evaluated these changes with reference to education policies and wider socio-economic change. Within this context, the significant differences in higher education participation among social classes and the numbers of young people who do not complete or extend their compulsory education are of concern. Around 10% of 16- to 18-year-olds were not in education, training or employment during the 1990s to early 2000s (DfES, 2005b). Secondary and primary school exclusion rates have been a cause for concern during the 1990s and 2000s, although they have decreased. Exclusions are higher among children eligible for free school meals, boys, looked after children, children from ethnic minorities and children classed as having special educational needs (DfES, 2005b). Overall, though, if we consider educational attainment rates, there have been significant improvements in the last decade. In 1998, figures showed that 50% of children in their final year of primary school (Year 6) in schools with higher rates of children in receipt of free school meals did not gain the expected national standard in English, and 60% of children in these schools did not attain the expected national standard in Maths (MacInnes et al, 2009, p 56). By 2007/08 equivalent data found these figures had reduced to 30% of children, a significant reduction, although comparatively high levels of underachievement in comparison to many other EU countries (MacInnes et al, 2009, p 56). The proportion of 16-year-olds with no GCSEs has halved and there has been an increase in the percentage gaining 5 GCSEs at A–C grades. According to Fernstein et al's (2008) research, however, social class differences in cognitive and educational scores appear from when children reach 2 years old (Fernstein et al, 2008). Lower educational attainment rates also occur among Black and 'mixed' ethnicity children (Platt, 2007). Parental and family-level factors are related to these trends. Parental (and 'family') levels of income (economic capital which can enable families to live in neighbourhoods with higher-ranked schools and invest in private schooling, private tuition or educationally important recreational, social or leisure activities); parental levels of education; parental and family support networks (social capital); parental knowledge of the education system (cultural capital); parents' support for their children's educational progress (emotional and social capital); parental health and well-being, and the quality of the 'home learning environment' are key factors influencing children's educational achievements, progress at school and dispositions towards post-compulsory education (Barnfield and Brookes, 2006; Fernstein et al, 2008). Children's subjective well-being at school, however, appears to be linked to the quality of their whole school experience, support with their learning needs and the nature of peer and teacher relationships (Madge, 2006).

Although most parents in the UK continue primarily to use informal childcare, more children attend formal childcare and pre-school settings. In 1970/71, 21% of children under 5 attended day care or pre-school care or education, and this rose to 64% in 2007/08 (ONS, 2009). Quality early education is associated with beneficial developmental outcomes for children. However, the levels and range of childcare provision differ across localities in the UK; the cost of full-time day care and early education remains relatively high in EU terms and participation in early education is significantly lower among working-class families and some ethnic minorities (Daycare Trust, 2009; see Chapter Six).

Qualifications and skills gaps among the working population led the previous Labour government to commission Lord Leitch to undertake a 'Review of Skills' in the UK economy. The Leitch Review compared educational attainment and accredited skills rates across OECD countries (Leitch Review, 2006). This report found severe shortages in 'basic, intermediate and technical skills' (Leitch Review, 2006, p 1). It highlighted the strong correlation between having no or low qualifications and long-term welfare receipt (Leitch Review, 2006, p 3). The Leitch Review (2006, p 3), however, also identified gaps in vocational and specialist skills and training opportunities, and provided influential policy recommendations leading to new legislation such as the recent increase in the compulsory school leaving age to 18 years.

Physical and mental well-being

This section examines health indicators. Health inequalities between social classes remain significant in the UK. For example, premature mortality is higher among unskilled and manual occupational classes, as is the infant mortality rate (ONS, 2010a). Beresford et al (2005, p 75) noted that the UK 'was one of the OECD countries with the highest proportion of low birth weight live births in 2000,' with 7.6% of infants of low birth weight. Factors associated with low birth weight are: lower social class; 'mother-only' birth registrations and mother's age, with teenage mothers and mothers over 40 more likely to have low-weight babies (Beresford et al, 2005).

Breastfeeding has been on the increase in the last 10 years, with an estimated 73% of babies initially breastfed in England and Wales in 2002 (Beresford et al, 2005). England and Wales have relatively low levels of fruit and vegetable consumption, as compared to other OECD countries (Finch and Seale, 2005). Rates of obesity have increased, with official data finding that 31% of boys and 30% of girls were classified as 'obese' in 2007, and a corresponding increase in obesity among men and women over 16 years old during the 1990s and early 2000s (ONS, 2010a). Regular alcohol consumption among young people is associated with health problems and anti-social behaviour (Rutter et al, 1998). In a survey conducted in 2006–07 around a third of young people aged between 11 and 16 years reported drinking alcohol during the past week, a slight reduction from 2002 data (ONS,

2010a). Older teenagers, boys and young people in Scotland report higher levels of consumption (Finch and Seale, 2005). Among adults and young people smoking rates have declined, but in 2007, 65% of men over 16 years old and 49% of women reported drinking over the recommended daily number of alcohol units at least one day in the previous week (ONS, 2010a). There are, additionally, concerns about declining rates of physical activity and exercise. Finch and Seale (2005, p 124) referenced data from 2004 that estimated the proportion of children aged 11, 13 and 15 who were not undertaking the recommended amount of physical activity per day was 58% in England, 62% in Scotland and 64% in Wales. Factors associated with decreasing levels of physical activity among children include: increasing reliance on cars; parental reluctance to allow children to play outdoors, due to safety concerns; the increase in housebound sedentary entertainment activities, such as watching TV, using the internet or electronic gaming; and the costs associated with leisure and recreational services (MacInnes et al, 2009).

In terms of incidents of reported diseases and illnesses, incidence of diabetes and asthma among children has increased in the last 10 years, with chronic cases higher among lower social classes (Bradshaw and Mayhew, 2005). Emotional and behavioural problems affect around 10–20% of school-aged young people (Barlow and Stewart-Brown, 2000). Mental health problems in surveys have been found to be higher among older children, children from Black and Asian ethnic groups and refugee children (Quilgars et al, 2005). Across all age groups, the General Lifestyle Survey found that 29% of people reported suffering from a long-term illness and 17% reported that this restricted their activities (ONS, 2010d, p 4). This survey also reported a four-fold increase in prescriptions for anti-depressants, from 9 million prescriptions in 1991 to 34 million in 2007 (ONS, 2010d). Family and socio-economic factors have been associated with poor mental health among children and young people, including growing up with a parent who has poor mental health, coming from a lone-parent or step-family, having a poor relationship with parents and family members, experiencing multiple stressful life events and living in poverty (Finch and Searle, 2005). Likewise parental health, particularly maternal mental health, is found to highly correlate with poor outcomes for children (Holmes and Kiernan, 2010).

Child maltreatment and domestic violence

In recent years the UK has had a number of highly publicised child deaths and child abuse scandals (see Part Two). Overall, though, non-intentional injuries and accidents are the leading cause of death among young people (Bradshaw and Mayhew, 2005). However, statistics for rates of child maltreatment and abuse cause concern. Cawson et al (2000) conducted a survey of maltreatment experiences among a random sample of 2,689 young people aged between 18 and 24 years. They found that:

- 25% of respondents had experienced physical punishment or abuse, 78% of which had occurred within the home and 15% in school. Overall 21% of respondents had experienced physical punishment or abuse from their parents/carers.
- 18% of respondents could be said to have suffered neglect in terms of experiences of 'absence of care' and 20% of respondents felt they had inadequate adult or parental supervision.
- 16% (21% girls and 11% boys) of respondents had experienced some form of sexual abuse.
- 34% of respondents reported some experiences of emotional abuse.
- 43% of respondents reported experiences of bullying by other children.

There are well-known risk factors associated with children's poor safety and experiences of abuse. Poverty, financial insecurity, long-term unemployment and material deprivation are associated with an increased risk of child accidents, child neglect and physical abuse but are not so prominent in cases of child maltreatment where sexual or emotional forms of abuse are of primary concern (Cawson et al, 2000). Lonne et al (2008) argued that child neglect was highly correlated with family and parental poverty, isolation, poor mental health, substance abuse and domestic violence. More severely disabled children are at particular risk of all forms of abuse – within both families and institutions (DH, 1995). The figures above suggest that girls are more vulnerable to sexual abuse, while boys are more vulnerable to physical abuse (Cawson et al, 2000). Women are more vulnerable to domestic violence than men (Radford and Hester, 2006). Feminist research highlights the 'cultural supports for abuse' such as a poor social status for children and women; pathological views of children and behaviour; hegemonic masculinity (which constructs maleness in terms of authority and power over others); and women's and children's economic vulnerabilities (Radford and Hester, 2006). Children from Black ethnic groups are also disproportionately represented in child protection trends. Minority ethnic children report higher levels of bullying and racial discrimination (Bradshaw and Mayhew, 2005). Girls report higher levels of sexualised bullying, and looked after children, disabled children and lesbian, gay and bisexual young people further report higher levels of bullying (Bradshaw and Mayhew, 2005).

Other crime trends

Overall, recorded rates of violent crime and burglary have fallen since the early 1990s. In 1997 there were around 1.6 million recorded burglaries. By 2008/09 this had halved to around 0.8 million (MacInnes et al, 2009). There were around 2.1 million victims of violent crimes in 1999, and this fell to just below 1.2 million in 2008/09 (MacInnes et al, 2009). There was also a decline in 'fear of burglary and violent crimes', according to British Crime Survey data. Around 15% of respondents were fearful of violent crime, while 10% were fearful of burglary in the 2010 British Crime Survey (MacInnes et al, 2009).

Neale (2005, p 242) calculated that, according to recorded crime figures, 23% of all arrested individuals were under the age of 17 in 2002/03, and most of these were boys aged 14–17 years. Over one in three offences were for theft and handling stolen goods (Neale, 2005, p 242). Although there has been a fall in these types of crimes, around the same number of young people were found guilty or cautioned for an offence in 1999 as in 2008/09 (MacInnes et al, 2009, p 7). However, Newburn (2002) found a rise in juvenile drug-related offences between 1985 and 2001 and violent offences by young people between 1987 and 2001.

Public discourses tend to fuel alarmist responses to these trends – portraying young people as increasingly dangerous and anti-social, and parents as neglectful and inadequate (Duncan Smith, 2007). These explanations are limited. Informed by an ecological approach, Neale (2005, pp 258–9) reviewed the evidence base to identify known family, neighbourhood, school, individual and peer risk factors, and concluded:

> Family risks include: poor parental supervision and discipline; family conflict; a family history of criminal activity; parental attitudes that condone anti-social behaviour and criminal behaviour; low income; poor housing; and large family size. Community risks include: living in a disadvantaged neighbourhood; community disorganisation and neglect; availability of drugs; and lack of neighbourhood attachment. School factors include: low achievement beginning in primary school; aggressive behaviour (including bullying); lack of commitment to school (including truancy); and school disorganisation. Finally individual risks encompass: hyperactivity and impulsivity; low intelligence and cognitive impairment; alienation and lack of social commitment; attitudes that condone offending and drug misuse; early involvement in crime and drug misuse; and friendships with peers involved in crime and drug misuse.

Research has considered 'anti-social behaviour' from young people's own viewpoint. MacDonald and Marsh (2005) carried out an ethnographic study of youth experiences in multiply deprived neighbourhoods. They found youth anti-social behaviour related to boredom, anger and frustration; gender identities and cultures; peer and family relationships; educational disadvantage, truancy and school exclusion; and living in a deprived neighbourhood (MacDonald and Marsh, 2005).

Family relations

Earlier sections have alluded to the important role family, friends and supportive relationships play in personal and social well-being. As the majority of children are raised in family households, parents and other family members are influential in their upbringing. The range of resources and support functions families provide helps adults and children to get on and cope with life. Likewise, having children and being a parent/carer provides much life satisfaction and meaning, and children support and care for adults in a range of ways too (Edwards, 2004). Earlier discussions have noted the changes in family formations, average family size and partnering/living arrangements in recent decades. This section highlights change, anxieties and inequalities in family relations. The themes raised here are discussed further in Part Three.

According to the British Social Attitudes Survey (BSA), fewer adults hold traditional views about gender roles, but gender divisions of labour and responsibility remain. In 1989, 64% of respondents agreed that 'a woman should stay at home full-time to look after a pre-school age child', but by 2006 this had fallen to 40% – just over 20% of men and slightly less than 20% of women subscribed to this view (Crompton and Lyonette, 2007). However, the same survey found a slight reversal of these trends in recent years – reflecting the ambivalence about mothers with young children working full time in the UK. In 2006, 25% of women agreed with this statement (Crompton and Lyonette, 2007). These attitudes vary across social class groups, geographical areas and ethnic groups, leading sociologists to examine 'gender cultures' (norms and assumptions about gender identities and roles); gender norms across social groups and contexts; and the social construction of gender (ie via popular culture, the media, family practices, schools, peer groups and social policies) (Duncan and Edwards, 1999; Pfau-Effinger, 1999). Studies find that paternal identities remain strongly tied up with the status of primary breadwinner, and the image of the full-time, stay-at-home mother remains 'a normative reference point' for good motherhood in several European countries, North America and Australia (Warren, 2004; Maher and Saugeres, 2007). However, mothers and fathers are encouraged to fulfil their traditional responsibilities, as well as to conform to the 'universal adult worker, nurturing mother and involved father' ideals (Daly, 2004). This is thought to generate more work–family conflict. The OECD Family Database reported social survey data about men's and women's weekly hours in employment and preferred amount of weekly hours. Table 3.6 reports the findings for selected OECD countries and illustrates that the majority of men and women would prefer to work fewer hours.

Table 3.6 further shows aspects of the ongoing gender divisions of labour and the national differences in working and preferred hours across the genders. According to this data, men in the UK preferred to work slightly longer hours than most men in the other countries, while women in the UK preferred lower

Table 3.6: Parental labour market position, selected OECD countries, 2007

	Maternal employment rate (mothers with children aged 0–16 years)	Part-time employment (proportion of total employment)		Average current and preferred working times by gender and households with children (hours per week)			
		Men	Women	Men: Current hours	Men: Preferred hours	Women: Current hours	Women: Preferred hours
Austria	64.7	5.2	31.5	45.7	39.9	32.2	29.3
Belgium	59.9	6.3	32.9	40.7	35.9	32.9	29.8
Denmark	76.5	12.4	23.9	40.6	35.1	35.8	29.5
Finland	76.0	8.2	15.5	42.3	36.4	37.8	33
France	59.9	5	23.1	40.8	36.1	34	31.1
Germany	54.9	7.9	39.2	43.4	37.4	28.9	27.8
Ireland	57.5	7.6	35.6	42.7	37.1	31.6	26
Italy	48.1	5.4	29.9	39.9	36.9	34.2	29.6
Netherlands	69.2	16.2	60	43.2	37.6	21.2	21.3
Spain	52	3.8	20.9	40.8	36.2	34.4	33.1
Sweden	82.5	9.5	19.7	42.9	36.2	35	31.5
UK	61.7	9.9	38.6	46.9	38.3	28.3	25.8
OECD	61.6	7.2	25.6	42.4	36.8	32.5	29.3
EU27	59.5	6.3	24.1	42.5	36.9	32.5	29.3

Source: Adapted from Lohmann et al (2009, p 32). Based on OECD Family Policy Database and OECD Employment Outlook data, 2005–07.

levels of part-time work, as compared to the majority of women in the other countries. The UK Time Use survey asked about the gendered division of unpaid care and domestic labour. The survey found in 2000 that women on average spent 1.5 hours more a day on childcare and domestic labour than men (ONS, 2000). However, the UK Time Use survey uses a narrow definition of 'childcare and domestic labour' (Folbre and Yoon, 2007) which is likely to underestimate the demands on both mothers and fathers. Folbre and Yoon (2007) concluded that it provides an 'incomplete picture of the temporal demands that children impose on parents' (Folbre and Yoon, 2007, p 224).

These trends are related to the 'transformation of intimacy' and 'partial democratisation' of family, gender and generational relations (Giddens, 1992; Beck and Beck-Gernsheim, 2002). Alongside changing attitudes towards gender roles, family and parent–child relationships in the Western context have become less autocratic and hierarchical, and place more emphasis on 'investing in children', intimate family relationships, 'spending time with children and partners', 'doing things together' and parental availability to children (although historians question the accuracy of common-sense portrayals of the past) (Smart, 2007; Heath, 2009). Beck and Beck-Gernsheim (2002) argued that parenthood and parent–child relationships take on a new symbolic status as the more permanent relationship in the context of more contingent adult intimate relationships. Henwood and Procter (2003) argued that transformations in masculinities are critical to changing meanings of fatherhood. Many studies find that children themselves report that 'love, emotional security and support' are what matter most in parent–child and family relationships (Madge, 2006; Madge and Willmott, 2007).

These trends and others noted earlier are further associated with 'individualisation'. For Beck and Beck-Gernsheim (2002), individualisation in late modernity is associated with two social processes:

> On the one hand individualisation means the disintegration of previously existing social forms – for example, the increasing fragility of such categories as class and social status, gender roles, family, neighbourhood etc. [...] [T]he second aspect of individualisation [is] that in modern societies new demands, controls and constraints are being imposed on individuals. Through the job market, the welfare state and institutions, people are tied into a network of regulations, conditions, provisos. (Beck and Beck-Gernsheim, 2002, p 2)

Individualisation, for these theorists, relates to the contradictory effects of social and political change, leading to new 'social risks and citizen responsibilities' (in 'the risk society') and new opportunities due to 'de-traditionalisation' and 'democratisation' (Beck and Beck-Gernsheim, 2002). Citizens have more choices and opportunities but they are also expected to 'constitute themselves as individuals' from a young age: to 'plan, understand and act as individuals responsible for their own biographies' (Beck and Beck-Gernsheim, 2002). These processes produce contradictions and tensions in everyday personal lives, especially in the context of 'partial democratisation for women' and social class inequalities (Beck and Beck-Gernsheim, 2002) – two issues which are particularly pertinent to the UK. Individualisation highlights inequalities in households, marriage, families, the labour market and society more broadly, and can create conflicts and tensions in relationships and personal lives. Likewise, parents and carers negotiate the demands of 'institutionalised individualism' alongside caring responsibilities. However, individualisation theories have been criticised for overstating 'epochal social change' and understating the significance of relationships in people's lives (Williams, 2004a).

Part Three examines anxieties, challenges and dilemmas associated with contemporary parenting. The Fabergé Family Report (Edwards, 2004) interviewed around 1,000 parents in 2003 to find out about contemporary parenting anxieties and found 63% of mothers and 54% of fathers were worried about 'whether they are doing a good job as a parent', and 75% thought teenagers aged 13–15 years were the most challenging age group to raise (the sample was purposefully over-represented with parents with teenagers) (Edwards, 2004). The 2001 survey by the National Family and Parenting Institute found parents were most worried about children's safety, family economic well-being, peer influence, substance misuse and children's behaviour (NFPI, 2001).

Many family events and contexts raise concerns about family well-being, such as parental separation and divorce, poor parental mental health, young people with parental responsibilities, step-parenting and non-resident parenthood. Concerns are fuelled by the correlations between family structure, events such as divorce/parental separation/step-parenting and children's outcomes. For example, Holmes and Kiernan (2010) analysed child and adult well-being across family types using the Millennium Cohort Survey (MCS) data on 18,000 families with children born in 2000. They found that single mothers and their young children had lower levels of child and adult well-being, as compared to couple parents and their young children. However, they also found that families headed by cohabiting couples with young children tended to be more 'fragile, vulnerable and impoverished', as compared to married couples with young children (Holmes and Kiernan, 2010). Within these groups, though, there was much diversity and complexity. Kiernan (2006) previously examined non-resident fathers' involvement with young children using the MCS baseline survey data. Kiernan (2006, p 659) found that among the MCS sample of families, 2% of fathers lived part time or temporarily with the mother and their baby when the child was 9 months old, while 84% of fathers lived permanently with the mother and child, and 14% of fathers were non-resident. Fathers therefore do not neatly fit into the categories of resident and non-resident, and some fathers live part time or temporarily with their children even though they are not married to, or in a long-term relationship with, their child's mother. Of the 14% non-resident when their child was 9 months old, 60% were in regular contact with their child, 29% paid regular maintenance and 75% of mothers stated that they were on 'friendly terms' (Kiernan, 2006, p 660). According to this sample, non-resident fathers provided more contact, practical and emotional support and childcare than regular maintenance.

Much research has considered the effects of parental separation, divorce and lone parenthood on children. Golombok (2000, p 5) reviewed longitudinal studies conducted in the US and UK that examined children's 'psychological development' following divorce and parental separation. Golombok's (2000) analysis highlighted diverse experiences and outcomes among children and young people in respect of divorce, parental separation and lone motherhood. This is because the 'effects' are mediated by so many different factors and processes (hence Bradshaw and Richardson (2009) found 'family type' a poor predictor of national child well-being – see Chapter Two). Parental separation and divorce, which most often leads to fathers moving out of the family home and can also lead to siblings moving out, are likely to be traumatic experiences – but individual (ie the age of the child and gender), parental (ie parental health and well-being, 'parenting style'), family (ie the history and quality of family relationships and family size) and socio-economic (ie ethnicity, culture and poverty) factors mediate outcomes (Rodgers and Pryor, 1998; Golombok, 2000). Where there are few additional serious family problems, most children fare better after an adjustment period of around two years (Rodgers and Pryor, 1998; Golombok, 2000). Holmes and Kiernan (2010) found that, according to the MCS baseline data, parental economic resources, mother's mental health and family instability (ie parental separation, divorce, parental partnering patterns) correlated most strongly with children's outcomes. Child welfare experts argue that it is family processes, relationships and contexts which are most important to children's outcomes (Utting, 2009). The traumatic nature of parental separation and divorce depends on social norms, how much this 'event' makes family life relatively better or worse, how parents are coping, the effects on parenting and family relationships and the degree of social support for everyone involved (Rodgers and Pryor, 1998; Golombok, 2000; Smart et al, 2003). Similar conclusions are reached about lone, non-resident and young parenthood – children are more at risk of poor outcomes when individuals and families experience multiple problems and disadvantages and have little social support (Rodgers and Pryor, 1998). The higher risk of poverty among lone-mother families is a critical factor related to children's risk of poorer outcomes. Rowlingson and McKay (2005) examined the relationship between social class and lone parenthood using data from the MCS 2001–03, the British Household Panel Survey 2001–02 and the 1994/95 Family and Working Lives Survey; and qualitative analysis of 44 interviews conducted with women who had been or were lone mothers, collected as part of an ESRC study in 1996. Rowlingson and McKay concluded that (2005, p 31):

> women from working class backgrounds are more likely to become lone mothers (especially never-married lone mothers) than women from middle class backgrounds. Moreover, the experience of lone motherhood is very different for women from working class backgrounds compared with other women [...] Poor women become lone mothers, and remain poor or become poorer.

Economically based explanations for children's poor outcomes, however, are inadequate in themselves. For example, the quality of relationships, care and parenting have an independent effect on child well-being. This is recognised in the 'resilience' literature to explain children's resilience in disadvantaged families (Seaman et al, 2007) and taken forward by the feminist ethic of care viewpoint (Williams, 2004a).

Citizenship, civic involvement and neighbourhood well-being

This final section raises issues about citizenship and community well-being and participation. A report by the UK Children's Commissioners in 2008 argued that rates of child and family poverty; the treatment of asylum seekers and refugees; levels of racism; negative media discourses towards teenage boys and young people; the poor outcomes among children and young people in care; increasing educational pressures on young people; and the degree to which children and adults were affected by domestic violence, poor health and substance misuse were critical human rights issues in the UK (UK Children's Commissioners, 2008). Other research found that adults and children feel they have limited influence in local and political decision making, and young people feel increasingly subject to restrictions when using public spaces (MacInnes et al, 2009). Further, children fulfil 'adult roles' (ie as consumers or young carers) but receive very little recognition or support for these roles. Mayhew (2005, p 175) stated that young carers tend to care for family members 'who are ill, have a disability, are experiencing mental distress or are affected by substance misuse'. According to the 2001 Census, 114,000 children and young people aged between 5 and 15 years were carers (1.4% of the general population of children in this age range, 53,000 boys and 61,000 girls) (Mayhew, 2005, p 176). Of these, nearly one third provided 20 or more hours of care a week and just under one fifth provided at least 50 hours of care. Being a young carer was found to be associated with living in a deprived area, higher reports of 'poor health' and higher referrals to child protection agencies (Mayhew, 2005). However, Olsen and Clarke (2006) found that young carers for disabled parents constituted a diverse group in terms of the extent and nature of care responsibilities, and argued that the term 'young carer' obscures the two-way nature of care in family relationships.

Looking to the neighbourhood level, social survey research finds high levels of satisfaction with 'where one lives' (MacInnes et al, 2009). However, there is indication that many experience a lack of access to local amenities and shops, due to a lack of local services and facilities, or their poor quality; or due to mobility constraints, not having a car or being on a low income (MacInnes et al, 2009). Other surveys have asked questions about community spirit. The British Crime Survey found that from 1984 to 1996 an increasing number of respondents felt 'people go their own way' in their neighbourhood (40% of respondents took this view in 1984, compared to 46% in 1996) and the proportion of people who 'help each other' was in decline (40% of respondents felt neighbours routinely helped each other in 1984, compared to 31% in 1996). However, by 2000, 36% of respondents thought people helped each other (ONS, 2003). Overall, though, people living on low incomes and in deprived neighbourhoods are more dissatisfied with their neighbourhoods and report that 'drug dealing, rubbish and vandalism' are 'a bad problem' (MacInnes et al, 2009).

Studies have examined the concentration of social problems in deprived neighbourhoods. Ghate and Hazel (2002) drew on ecological theories to examine individual, family and neighbourhood factors that influence parenting in deprived neighbourhoods. Ghate and Hazel (2002) argued that the quality of parenting in poor neighbourhoods is influenced by:

- *Community or neighbourhood-level factors:* Whereby 'living in an impoverished environment characterised by high concentrations of poor families and high levels of social and environmental problems' increased risk factors in parents' and children's lives; or where better-quality housing and local infrastructure, accessible and quality childcare, education, health and public services and supportive 'but not oppressive' social networks promote resilience (Ghate and Hazel, 2002, pp 15–16).
- *Family and household-level factors:* with 'high levels of poverty and social and material disadvantage associated with lone mother headed families, low household income, "worklessness", poor quality rented housing and higher residential mobility'. Having a 'supportive relationship with a spouse or partner' and 'help from friends and relatives' were in contrast important protective factors (Ghate and Hazel, 2002, pp 15–16).
- *Individual characteristics of family members:* where individual resilience and coping strategies buffer some of the effects of poverty or 'a diminished capacity to cope with stress and the parenting task, coupled with a tendency to show extreme responses to stress' and 'factors such as parental social isolation and depression, child ill health or challenging behaviour and parental psychological immaturity' increase parenting difficulties (Ghate and Hazel, 2002, p 15).

Ghate and Hazel (2002, p 14) argued that persistently poor individuals and families living in deprived neighbourhoods face multiple sources of strain and disadvantage that undermine adult and child well-being, and 'undermine parenting skills and the ability to cope with the demands of childcare'. However, the data generated by the research was contrasted to national trends in child and adult well-being. Without a comparative study of parenting in other types of neighbourhoods, it is unclear how experiences differ between families and neighbourhoods. Further, gender, ethnicity and migrant status issues were not systematically analysed in this research. However, Reeve (2008) argued that the spatial dimension of recent migration trends led to a sharp increase in ethnic diversity in many deprived neighbourhoods. The neighbourhoods targeted by Labour's policy of 'dispersing asylum seekers' to areas outside London and the South East were overwhelming among those listed as the most deprived in England and Wales (Reeve, 2008). In the absence of an active role for local authorities in promoting community support and supporting communities through change, Reeve (2008, pp 191–2) argued that established communities could feel 'hostile towards newcomers and resent the additional demands on local services, housing and employment they represent, particularly in the context of poverty and many years of struggle for local facilities, resources, recognition and political voice'.

Conclusion

This chapter has examined many aspects of 'child, family and social well-being'. On some social indicators, the UK performs relatively well, on others not so well. Priorities for social policy are: the quality of family and social relationships; levels of informal and formal social support for young people and families; out-of-work and in-work poverty rates; educational, health and income inequalities; labour market disadvantages; gender inequalities in the private and public sphere; mental health trends; substance abuse trends; levels of child maltreatment and domestic violence; the commercialisation of childhood; discrimination and human rights; neighbourhood deprivation; the lack of community involvement in decision-making processes; and environmental degradation from unsustainable economic development. For many, these issues relate to 'a decline in parental, family and community responsibility', 'excessive individualism' and 'social breakdown'. However, many trends are not that recent and differ across similar capitalist economies. While individual, family and community factors play a part, there are multiple structural factors at work.

Notes

[1] The TFR is calculated from the average number of live births registered over the lifespan of individual women in the population (ONS, 2009).

[2] www.dwp.gov.uk/publications/policy-publications/opportunity-for-all/indicators/table-of-indicators/people-of-working-age/indicator-19/.

FOUR

Children, families and welfare state restructuring

Introduction

This chapter examines the 'politics of parental rights and responsibilities'. Social policies are rarely 'rational comprehensive' responses to social needs and problems (Hudson and Lowe, 2009). Rather, they promote social and political values about the respective social roles and responsibilities of parents, families, young people and the state. The analysis aims to: (1) provide the historical and policy background to post-1997 developments in parental rights and responsibilities; and (2) locate British developments within a broader Western and Northern European context. The chapter draws on typologies of policy regimes and debates about the internationalisation of social and family policy. It highlights the radical developments towards more state support and intervention in parenthood and families in the UK context under New Labour but critiques these developments against feminist and social democratic perspectives and in light of the social inequalities and welfare trends set out in Chapter Three. The discussion contests the 'individualisation' of social problems reflected in many UK social policies and the extent to which this remains a feature of early policies of the new Conservative–Liberal Democrat Coalition government.

Welfare regimes in the 1980s and early 1990s

Welfare states are often categorised according to the welfare contract between citizens and the state, that is, according to the nature and level of social entitlements to welfare state support and the institutionalised roles and responsibilities of citizens, families, the state and markets. In the work of Esping-Andersen (1990; 1999, p 73) 'welfare regimes' are the 'ways in which welfare production is allocated between the state, market and households'. Esping-Andersen (1990) contrasted the degree to which welfare states 'decommodified' citizens. 'Decommodification' 'occurs when a service is rendered as a matter of right and a person can maintain a livelihood without reliance on the market' (Esping-Andersen, 1990, pp 21–2), and refers to the degree to which social welfare entitlements and state regulation of the economy 'diminish citizens' status as commodities' (Esping-Andersen, 1990, p 3). Esping-Andersen (1990, p 21) examined the degree to which social rights 'emancipate citizens from market dependence', particularly in respect of welfare rights to financial support and income maintenance. The focus on welfare rights and income maintenance systems was later critiqued. Alongside redistribution and decommodification, Esping-Andersen's (1999) later work examined defamilialisation and public sector employment conditions across welfare regimes. Lister (1997) argued that defamilialisation was critical to women's economic independence. Defamilialisation here refers to the degree to which social rights afford all adult citizens a minimum income standard independent of family relationships and dependencies. Overall, welfare states in the early 1990s were described as broadly falling into one of four welfare regime types:

- **Liberal welfare regimes** were 'dominated by the logic of the market'. They encouraged reliance on the market via minimum and modest state welfare provisions; 'subsidised private welfare schemes'; and prioritised the interests of capital in labour market and macro-economic policies. Welfare provisions were based on 'means-tested assistance, modest universal transfers and modest social insurance schemes'. The benefits system provided a 'basic safety net' targeted at those most in need and designed to stigmatise 'welfare dependency' and promote the 'work-ethic' and family responsibility for welfare (Esping-Andersen, 1990, p 26).
- **Corporatist-conservative regimes** were not so dominated by the market logic but by corporatism and 'the preservation of status differentials'. Private provision of welfare was less developed and the state provided more generous welfare entitlements to class and social status groups, as compared to liberal welfare regimes. Welfare entitlements remained highly based on social insurance contributions via employment or 'the fabric of eligibility and benefit rules for different social class and status groups'. Corporatist regimes were found to be influenced by organised religious interests, particularly the Catholic church, and strongly supported the preservation of the traditional family unit. The principle of 'subsidiarity' operated, whereby the state 'will only interfere when the family's capacity to service its members is exhausted' (Esping-Andersen, 1990, p 27).
- **Social democratic regimes** had the highest levels of decommodification. These welfare states developed more generous income maintenance systems on the basis of 'equal benefit to all, irrespective of prior earnings or contributions' and more individualised notions of 'the adult citizen'. The welfare system was based on an alternative welfare and economic contract: 'all citizens should benefit, all citizens are dependent on the state and all citizens should pay via higher taxes and in-work contributions' (Esping-Andersen, 1990, pp 22–8).
- **Southern European welfare regimes**, where the welfare state was institutionally, politically and culturally underdeveloped, and provision was characterised as consisting of a mixture of state and market provision and insurance schemes, based on the commodification of citizens and limited state income protection schemes (Esping-Andersen, 1999).

The UK was classed a 'liberal regime' along with the US, Canada, Australia and New Zealand, while countries such as Austria, France, Germany and Italy were classed as 'conservative-corporatist' and Sweden, Denmark and Finland classed as 'social democratic' (Esping-Andersen, 1990). Britain was classified a liberal regime due to: (1) long-standing liberal tendencies in British social policies and the post-war welfare state, and (2) the neoliberal restructuring of the welfare state under the Conservative government which held office from 1979 to 1997. Before the post-war welfare reforms, British social policy in the 19th and early 20th centuries was dominated by 'social liberalism' with an emphasis on minimal state welfare provided to those in the greatest need; stigmatising and demeaning poor relief for the 'destitute' and 'moral correction for the poor' via education and health provisions (Fraser, 1997). The post-war welfare state, established between 1945 and 1951, marked a significant break from social liberalism, and by 1951 encompassed the following principles, entitlements, institutions and services:

- full employment for men;
- Keynesian economic management, where economic policy sought to invest in job creation during economic downturns to increase employment rates and raise taxes in times of economic growth to raise state revenue;
- a national minimum standard: 'the provision of a common safety net that central government would place under all members of society' which provided 'protection against loss of earnings through sickness and long-term disability, unemployment or old age or the death of a spouse', financed through the tax and national insurance contributions of husbands (Glennester, 2007, p 6);
- universal access to health and education services: available to all, regardless of income and financed out of taxation;
- a housing rebuilding scheme;
- centrally designed and provided services, based on a belief in the virtues of central planning, public bureaucracies, welfare professionals and nationalised public services, to fairly distribute resources, services and access to services across the country, and a central role for the state in responsibilities for social security, health, education and housing.
- children's departments at the local level, responsible for child protection (Williams, 1989; Fraser, 1997).

The post-war welfare state entailed a new capital–labour settlement: state command of the economy to boost job creation and promote full employment; corporatist wage agreements; state regulation of prices; and unemployment/ sickness and pension entitlements for working-class men and their dependents, based on social insurance and direct taxation contributions while in continuous full-time employment (Pierson, 2006). Marshall (1950), hence, argued that the working classes had gained full citizenship through universal social rights and more state regulation of the economy and employers in the interests of labour. However, much of the old 'liberal' tendencies remained: welfare benefits continued to be set at a lower level so as not to dampen the 'work ethic'; proposals such as a national minimum wage were rejected in the name of the national economic interest; housing reforms focused on house building rather than 'building communities and social facilities'; education and health reforms did not diminish the significant role of private sector provision (Fraser, 1997). Many argued that the post-war agenda benefited dominant economic interests as much as male labour interests: national economic and social revival was to be secured via full male employment and appeals to the re-establishment of 'the traditional family unit' – entailing a gendered welfare contract, and expectations (and state supports) for women to leave the labour market and return to their primary social duties as procreators, mothers, carers, family makers and wives (Williams, 1989; Fraser, 1997; Pierson, 2006).

Social democratic ideals, however, influenced developments in the 1960s and 1970s. The Labour governments of 1964–70 and 1974–76 promoted social equality and sought to redistribute wealth between the social classes (Fraser, 1997). Feminist, disability, anti-racist and social welfare movements gained ground and fought for policies to address discrimination and maltreatment within the welfare state, the family and the labour market (Williams, 1989). Immigration legislation passed in the early 1960s (which restricted the social rights of migrants) was not repealed, but the Race Relations Acts 1965 and 1968 were passed, which outlawed racial discrimination in 'certain public places'. The Equal Pay Act 1970, Sex Discrimination Act 1975 and Employment Protection Act 1975 were passed, introducing some reforms required as part of the requirements for EEC membership. The Equal Pay Act established the principle of equal pay for work of equal worth and a system of legal redress; the Sex Discrimination Act outlawed direct victimisation and discrimination on the grounds of sex and direct discrimination in employment; the Employment Protection Act introduced a new system of statutory maternity pay and leave. The Finer Report, published in 1974, catalogued the material disadvantage among lone-mother headed families. The mid 1970s saw the introduction of lone-parent welfare benefits; Child Benefit (a universal benefit paid to all families with dependent children); more state investment in childcare provision for families in need; more state investment in social housing; and the introduction of further and higher education grants (Williams, 1989; Fraser, 1997). Wage agreements sought to protect employees from low pay and public sector employees enjoyed more favourable work-related entitlements and benefits. More redistribution of wealth was secured via higher taxation rates for the better-off. Government taxation revenue substantially increased during this era, as did public spending and public sector borrowing. For example, the social security budget constituted 7.2% of GDP in 1964–65 and rose to 9.3% of GDP in 1969–70 (Glennester, 2007).

However, social democratic welfare states remain bound by the imperatives of economic growth and performance, and maintaining social order (Pierson, 2006).

The social democratic agenda relied on the logic of economic growth and full male employment. The fiscal crisis of the mid 1970s and subsequent recession and social unrest meant liberal critiques gained ground (Pierson, 2006). Margaret Thatcher became leader of the Conservative Party in 1975 on a neoliberal New Right mandate for welfare reform and went on to win the 1979 General Election. Thereafter, until Labour came to power in 1997, the Conservative governments sought to reinstate individual and family responsibility for welfare, 'roll back the state' and promote the role of the market. Williams (1989) summarised the New Right critique of the welfare state:

> [The New Right philosophy] presented state intervention and the welfare state as a *hindrance* to economic growth, first because the burden of taxation and interference with market forces acts as a disincentive to investment; secondly, because the provision of welfare encourages scroungers, saps individualism and initiative, and generally acts as a disincentive to work; thirdly, because the state is seen as inefficient, wasteful and bureaucratic, whereas the private market is a superior mode of organisation offering freedom of choice. (Williams, 1989, p 11)

This period saw the privatisation of national industries and legislation to reduce the powers of the trade unions. Monetarist economic policies sought to reduce public spending and borrowing. The Conservatives at this time introduced major reforms to local government and public services which sought to 'outsource' more services to cheaper, private providers who secured cost efficiencies via lower labour and production costs. Local authorities became 'enablers', 'purchasers' and 'contract regulators' rather than direct providers of services. Public sector reforms introduced more charges in public services; partially privatised public services with 'quasi-markets' and 'purchaser–provider splits'; promoted market mechanisms and competition within public services; and 'modernised' the management of public services based on business principles, New Public Management and consumerist notions of citizen rights (to choice and value for money) (Newman, 2001). For example, NHS reforms introduced 'internal markets' through the purchaser–provider split and a competitive system of outsourcing services on a cost-effectiveness basis. GPs were afforded more autonomy and options for devolved budgets. Social housing was transformed via the 'Right to Buy' initiative whereby social housing tenants could buy their council houses, thus promoting private home ownership. Housing associations and private landlords were able to bid for contracts to take over local authority housing stock. A number of policy developments sought to deregulate the labour market and corporate markets, withdraw state welfare and reinforce family and market provision of social welfare. Corporation and income taxes were reduced. Wage protection mechanisms were abolished. Housing Benefit was cut, Child Benefit was frozen, state pensions were no longer linked to earnings and young people aged between 16 and 25 years, particularly, saw reductions in their entitlements to higher education maintenance grants, unemployment benefit, Income Support and Housing Benefit. By the time of the Major government in the mid 1990s, social security reform was infused with disciplinary measures to encourage claimants to return to paid work as soon as possible. The 1996 Jobseeker's Allowance emphasised requirements for claimants to actively seek paid work or take up training. Chapter Two charted the rise in poverty rates during this era. Some outcomes were contrary to the stated aims of the reforms. For example, periods of relatively high unemployment pushed up social security budgets; privatisation and deregulation of the economy led to the demise of manufacturing employment opportunities and 'privatisation and marketisation' extended the role of the state as market regulator (Newman, 2001). However, national policies were not implemented to the same degree across local authorities, and social democratic principles in the welfare, health and education system were more prominent in Scotland. For example, charges in the social care system were not implemented to the same degree in Scotland, and higher education grants remained.

In contrast to the preference for market-based solutions to social problems, marketisation of public services and low levels of benefit entitlement in the British liberal welfare regime, Conservative and Social Democratic regimes, according to Esping-Andersen (1990), provided more generous welfare benefits and rights. Several countries, such as France and Sweden, developed their modern welfare states from the 1930s and provided more generous welfare benefits. Esping-Andersen (1990) went on to examine the political economy of welfare regimes and their social outcomes. Regime differences were explained with reference to: (1) the economic imperative of capitalism, the structural dependencies of the welfare state on economic growth and the social class conflicts generated by capitalism; (2) the historical development of the welfare state and history of 'welfare politics' within and beyond the welfare state and how these reflected the configuration of organised social class interests operating within and beyond the welfare state; (3) the role of broader cultural influences. Liberal welfare regimes were associated with a less powerful organised working class; an extensive role for the private sector in welfare provision (health, education, pension or insurance schemes), with strong traditions among the middle classes of using such provision and liberal cultural tendencies which prized beliefs in the work ethic, individual hard work, individual and family responsibility, individual freedoms and choice, competition, entrepreneurialism and self-help. 'Conservative-corporatist welfare regimes' were associated with the political-economic influences of conservatism and Catholicism, where capitalist development indicated continuities in feudal organised interests and organised religious interests. The broader socio-political-cultural conditions associated with social democratic regimes were a widespread acceptance of social democratic principles (such as beliefs in state intervention and paternalism; more widespread ideological support for the role of the state in combating the inequities of markets and providing basic universal social rights), centralised trade unions, corporatist policy processes and multi-party political systems. Esping-Andersen's (1990, p 23) research challenged assumptions that 'welfare states inevitably create more egalitarian societies' and examined the welfare state as 'an active force in the ordering of social relations, divisions and inequalities'. Liberal welfare regimes were associated with creating 'social dualisms' (ie notions of the deserving and undeserving poor which underpin entitlements to state welfare and the punitive, targeted and stigmatising approach to welfare benefits) (Esping-Andersen, 1990, p 24). Here, state welfare sustained the widest social class inequalities. The conservative-corporatist welfare state was aligned with social status groups and 'unique rights and privileges for different social class and status groups' (Esping-Andersen, 1990, p 24). State welfare reforms tended to respond to particular categorical and employment sector claims and the organised working class did not generally promote solidarity among all workers or citizens (Esping-Andersen, 1990, p 25). State welfare did not significantly redistribute wealth between social class and status groups, and family and children's services (such as formal childcare) were underdeveloped. The social democratic welfare state was associated with the promotion of 'equal status and entitlements among citizens', which in turn furnished social solidarity (Esping-Andersen, 1990, p 25). Higher investment in services and public sector wages and professionalism sought to raise standards for all in public services. Higher levels of welfare benefits sought to redistribute wealth more evenly. Economic and employment policies sought equal rights and opportunities within the labour market, leading to a greater emphasis on women's and men's equal rights to employment. The state took on more responsibility to provide services for childcare, 'the aged and the helpless' (Esping-Andersen, 1990, p 28). However, changes in class structure in the post-war era, with rising household incomes and growing labour market and income inequalities, led to increasing dualism within social democratic systems, as the 'poorest rely on the state, and the remainder on the market' (Esping-Andersen, 1990, p 25).

Welfare regime theory has been extensively critiqued, applied and extended (see Esping-Andersen, 1999; Pierson, 2001; Castles and Obinger, 2008). There were debates about the classification of specific countries and the neglect of many differences and similarities within and across regime types (Leira, 2002; Castles and Obinger, 2008). Others have raised concerns about the limited empirical foci of Esping-Andersen's research (the focus on income maintenance neglected the role of services: Pierson, 2006) and the narrow focus on social class and organised religious interests, as opposed to the 'patriarchal and nationalistic' alliances within welfare states (Orloff, 1993). Williams (1989) argued that the focus on labour–capital settlements in political economy analysis of the welfare state ignored the extent to which notions of social citizenship were informed by notions of 'family' and 'nationhood' (with full social rights afforded to men as breadwinners and to British citizens with full citizenship status, based on residence and nationality).

These debates as well as patterns of family and social change since the 1970s prompted more analysis of the relationship between social and family policy.

Alternative regime typologies

Other comparative research has examined the relationship between family policy and wider social and economic policies; and the relationship between welfare states and family, gender, socio-economic and generational relations. With a focus on gender, feminist policy analysts have analysed 'the norms and assumptions about gender roles embedded in welfare policy and provision' (Daly and Rake, 2003, p 12). The political economy literature on the welfare state was criticised for neglecting the gendered nature of social citizenship and the social contract between citizens and the state. Feminist analysis examined the way gender ideologies and assumptions are institutionalised in social policies, legislation and social welfare institutions, in ways which sustain or transform gender differences and inequalities and influence the everyday lives, decisions, resources, opportunities and constraints of individuals (Daly and Rake, 2003). In the early 1990s, Lewis (1992) conceptualised a typology of 'gender regimes' based on empirical research about Britain, Ireland, France and Sweden. Lewis's typology produced a classification of three ideal types in the early 1990s:

• The **strong breadwinner model**, exemplified by Britain, where social policy promoted a gendered division of labour. Women were encouraged to be in paid work but mothers' employment was viewed as a matter of personal choice and childcare provision as a private issue. Policies did not extensively seek to promote gender equality in the private and public sphere. Lone-mother households were extremely vulnerable to low income and labour market exclusion.
• The **modified male breadwinner model**, exemplified by France, where social policy was based on the traditional family unit and gendered division of labour, but where the traditional family unit is afforded more public support. Church groups, republicanism and state feminism secured more support for families and working mothers.
• The **weak male breadwinner model**, exemplified by Sweden, where social policy was more 'individualised' and less based on the traditional family. State feminism and social democratic ideals led to more support for families, children and working parents on the basis of need and rights. Women and children were less vulnerable to poverty in these gender regimes and women enjoyed more equality in the labour market.

In her subsequent work, Lewis (2002) set out the shift to the 'adult worker norm' model within many advanced European welfare states whereby the rights and responsibilities of mothers and fathers as paid workers are promoted. The shift to the adult worker norm represented state responses to increasing rates of women's employment and economic imperatives to raise productivity via higher employment rates among women as well as men (Lewis, 2002). During the 1990s this became a more universal normative perspective underpinning social policy and emerged as a key principle in the 'European' approach to family policy set out by the European Union – discussed further later on in this chapter (Hantrais, 2004). However, as we shall see, welfare regimes continue to differ in respect of notions of gender-equality agendas; the degree of state support for both mothers and fathers as 'workers' and 'carers'; and the degree of state support for full-time work among mothers and part-time work for all (Fraser, 2000). Fraser (2000, pp 13–18) found that welfare state 'modernisation' indicated two future gender regimes: (1) a universal breadwinner model, whereby gender equality was equated with converging rates of female and male employment and equal access for men and women to full-time paid work opportunities (and hence an independent income); and (2) the caregiver parity model, whereby the economic costs of caring for children and other family members were recognised by the state and carers were afforded more support financially and via services. However, the former model is based on a liberal feminist equality-of-opportunity perspective and does not adequately address gender stereotypes and cultures in society or gender inequalities in the private sphere. The latter model is equally insufficient for similar reasons. Here, women's identities, interests and roles as carers can be reinforced. Fraser's (2000) alternative was the 'universal caregiver' model, whereby care work and responsibilities and full-time and part-time paid work are equally valued and promoted for men and women. This was similar to Sainsbury's (2001) 'adult citizen model'. In the adult citizen model, social rights and responsibilities are not attached to a particular family form and men's and women's dual roles as parents and paid workers are recognised (for example, via parental leave and pay for both fathers and mothers; state support for childcare for working parents; and financial support for full-time care). The basis of entitlement becomes individual citizenship status based on residency rather than the marital status, maternal status or employment status. This 'neutralises the impact of marriage on social rights as marital status does not affect entitlement and paid and unpaid work are recognised as citizenship contributions' (Sainsbury, 2001, p 124). From a human rights perspective, however, a critical aspect of citizenship becomes the basis upon which individuals are afforded citizenship status and social rights.

Another approach to feminist comparative policy analysis is to pursue an integrated social policy and sociological analysis of 'institutions, culture and agency' as constituting gender relations (Duncan and Edwards, 1999; Pfau-Effinger, 1999; Daly and Rake, 2003; Pocock, 2005; Kremer, 2007). Drawing on Connell (1987), Pocock (2005, p 38) used the concept of the 'gender order' to analyse the relationship between welfare regimes and gender inequalities. The 'gender order' was defined as 'historically constructed patterns of gender relations' which are 'constructed by the division of labour (ie paid and unpaid work, paid and care work) and gendered social and power relations' (Pocock, 2005, p 38). The gender order and gender cultures (the norms and assumptions about gender identities and roles which are differentiated according to multiple social identities and locations such as ethnicity, social class and age) are 'institutionalised in gender, work and care regimes', such as within the labour market, social policies, families or schools (Pocock, 2005, p 38). Pocock (2005, p 39) argued that gender orders are 'always under construction' and 'the factors that make up the work/care regime may be mutually reinforcing or contradictory', which in turn sustains the prevailing order or creates instability and institutional change. These analyses point to the need to examine the political representation of women and relative influence of state feminism within the organised working class, policy communities and dominant political parties in relation to welfare regime characteristics. They highlight the transformative role of tensions and contradictions between institutions, culture and agency. The demographic and socio-economic challenges facing welfare states today and the gap between preferences and behaviour in contemporary family lives are two such pressure points.

With a more direct focus on family policy and based on an analysis of 22 advanced welfare states, Gauthier (1996; 2002) set out a typology of family policy regimes which consisted of four main approaches:

- The **pro-natalist and pro-family** approach, where concerns about fertility rates and population decline can lead to family support measures.
- The **pro-traditional** approach, where support for the traditional family could lead to investment in cash support for families and, to a lesser extent, family support and childcare services.
- The **egalitarian** approach, which sought to promote social democratic ideals, recognise family diversity and promote more equality, particularly in terms of gender and generational relations.
- The **pro-family and non-interventionist** approach, where the traditional family was ideologically supported but cash benefits and services for families were more limited.

This typology recognised the role of different ideas about children and childhood, and normative parent–child relations, in family policies. Some comparative policy analysts working in these policy fields, however, warn of the limitations of constructing national-level policy regime types. Hantrais (2004) examined responses to demographic and family change across the EU25 countries. Welfare states were categorised in terms of degrees of 'familialisation' and a range of policy and institutional characteristics (ie the explicit and coherent nature of family policy, rhetoric and enacted policy, systems of taxation, the role of the market in the mixed economy of welfare, processes of policy legitimation and social citizenship entitlements). Hantrais (2004) categorised the UK along with Ireland, Austria, the Netherlands and Germany as 'partially defamilialised', as the state had taken on new responsibilities in relation to supporting working parents, subsidising childcare and social care services, promoting child welfare and providing financial support to (deserving) low-income families – in response to social and family change. However, assumptions about gender roles and emphasis on family responsibility for children and welfare remained. Denmark, Finland, Sweden, France, Luxembourg and Belgium were categorised as 'defamilialised' welfare states with more extensive entitlements and services for families and individual adult citizens. Greece, Italy, Portugal, Spain, Cyprus and Malta were described as 'familialised' welfare states where citizens needed to rely heavily on private and informal forms of welfare. The new Eastern European EU members – Estonia, Latvia, Hungary, Lithuania, the Czech Republic, Slovenia, Slovakia and Poland were described as 'refamilialised' welfare states, as state restructuring after state socialism entailed the state withdrawing from forms of centralised state provision of welfare and moving towards more family and personal responsibility and reliance on the market.

Daly and Rake (2003) were critical of the typology approach. They argued that policy regime typologies were descriptive rather than explanatory and understated the contested, contradictory and fragmented nature of welfare settlements within national contexts. Daly and Rake (2003) took an alternative in-depth case study approach, empirically analysing the relationship between national similarities and differences in social rights entitlements, statutory social welfare and family services, and gendered patterns of behaviour, outcomes and attitudes across eight advanced welfare states. The welfare state was conceptualised as 'an active site of and source of adjudicating particular claims' and a site where 'competing claims are brought by different interests' (Daly and Rake, 2003, p 41). These researchers analysed the framework and politics of social citizenship, the prevailing conditions for and entitlements to benefits and services within welfare states, and considered the role of social citizenship and welfare states in gendering the 'resources, social roles and power relations' between men and women, and gendering 'care' and 'paid work' (Daly and Rake, 2003). Akin to the broader focus on institutions, culture and social relations considered earlier, Daly and Rake (2003) viewed the welfare state as influencing but not determining gender relations, as a structuring context that interacts with other structuring contexts and is changed through actions and tensions: 'what interests us is the layering of factors one upon another and the placement of social relations in their varied contexts' (Daly and Rake, 2003, p 43).

Bearing these perspectives in mind, it is worth detailing some of the major developments in child and family policies in the 1980s and 1990s before Labour first took office in 1997. Within the narrative it is important to be mindful of the contested nature of policy developments and long-standing historical tensions and ambivalences about state intervention in family life in the British context, and conflicting notions of social citizenships. Gauthier (1996) categorised UK family policy as 'pro-family and non-interventionist' label, due to ideological support for the traditional family unit, combined with low levels of state supports for families. In line with the liberal welfare regime, family policy was orientated towards targeted support for families and children in need and child protection concerns, with little state support for working mothers or universal support for families. However, the relationship between 'family support' and 'child protection' has long been contested and has varied over time (Featherstone, 2004). When it has been deemed politically, economically or socially necessary, the family has been afforded more support. Featherstone (2004, p 69) noted how the Children and Young Persons Act 1963 afforded local authorities funding to provide more practical, childcare and material support to mothers considered in need, as part of the development of a more preventative approach in social care and based on ideas of maternal care responsibilities and children's developmental needs. However, the child protection system tended to intervene sharply, intrusively and punitively in families thought to place children at risk (Featherstone, 2004). The 1960s and 1970s additionally led to developments in provisions for family support. In 1968 the Seebohm Committee advocated more extensive family support and community-based services to prevent child neglect and abuse. This led to the Local Authority Social Services Act 1970, which created social services departments. Child Protection Registers were introduced to enable social workers to place children 'at risk of harm' on the register and monitor their welfare. In relation to welfare and childcare issues, the rise in child poverty rates in the 1980s led to pressure on the Conservative government to extend social rights to financial support for families with children (and led to the introduction of Family Credit in the late 1980s, an in-work benefit for low-income working parents). Further tensions between women's employment aspirations and lack of childcare provision led to initial forms of state-subsidised childcare provision for working mothers. Once more, the requirements of EEC membership saw tax concessions introduced for employers providing childcare, and maternity leave provisions extended in 1994. In 1996 the Conservatives pledged to provide free part-time nursery education for 4-year-olds – a pledge taken forward by New Labour.

The label of 'pro-family but non-interventionist' did not adequately reflect the multiple forms of state intervention in family life. An emphasis on personal and family responsibility for child welfare and social problems can entail policies aimed at clarifying, regulating and enforcing citizen and family responsibilities. In essence, the Conservative governments of the 1980s and early 1990s promoted the traditional family unit based on heterosexual marriage, and vilified lone parenthood and same-sex couples. However, several policies reflected a discursive shift from 'marital to parental' responsibilities. Parton (1991) examined how the Children Act 1989 reflected major tensions and contradictions in the relationship between the state, families and children. To preserve family responsibility for children in the face of rising divorce, lone parenthood and cohabitation rates, the Children Act 1989 stressed parental responsibilities for children rather than spousal responsibilities. The 1989 Act stated that parents have primary responsibility for birth children and that parental responsibility is lifelong, irrespective of parents' relationship to one another. In the context of concerns about balancing child protection concerns with the privacy of families, the Children Act 1989 stated that the primary concern of the state and parents should be children's welfare and best interests, and stated that parental rights to support and autonomy derive from parental responsibilities for child welfare. To clarify the responsibilities of professionals and local authorities, the 1989 Act distinguished between 'children in need', where children's development, health or welfare were at risk in the longer term (Section 17(10)) and 'children at risk', where children were considered to be at risk of immediate significant harm (Section 47(1)). The Act placed a duty on local authorities to safeguard children and promote their welfare through the provision of family support services. It restated 'child welfare as paramount' and stated that children's own views should be sought in social care decision making, reflecting a stronger commitment to intervene in parent–child relations to promote children's rights. Another important piece of legislation, introduced in the early 1990s, sought to clarify parental responsibilities. This was the Child Support Act 1991, which presented another definition of parental responsibility as providing financially for birth children, irrespective of marital or partnership status. Parental responsibility for child maintenance stretched to the state recouping the costs of welfare benefits, and penalties for non-compliance. The Child Support Act 1991 stated that all resident parents who received Income Support, Family Credit or Disabled Workers Allowance had to inform the state of the child's father. The emphasis on the responsibilities of non-resident parents in this context therefore did not entail an accompanying focus on children's rights or the rights of resident parents to financial support, but an additional focus on the responsibilities of resident parents to inform the state about the non-resident parent and the rights of the state to recoup the costs of welfare benefits for lone parents. The Criminal Justice Act 1996 emphasised parental responsibility for youth offending and child and youth behaviour. The Family Law Act 1996 represented similar concerns about parental responsibility and protecting children from harmful outcomes when parents divorce. Akin to the other legislative developments, the Act courted much controversy and accommodated multiple perspectives, but required parents to put in place adequate post-divorce financial and child contact arrangements before receiving a divorce.

Under similar political and socio-economic challenges, though, other welfare states pursued alternative family policies. Family policy has traditionally been more explicit in France, with a role for the state, alongside the third sector and communities, in protecting and supporting the family. The relationship between the state and the family was explicitly set out in the 1939 Family Code and 1990 Plan for the Family. Women were more overtly supported as paid workers. The state subsidised higher levels of childcare provision, mainly in partnership with church or voluntary sector agencies. Gauthier (1996; 2002) argued that the support afforded to families in France in the 1990s had much to do with the pro-natalist stance of governments. Gauthier (1996) categorised the Scandinavian countries of Norway, Finland, Sweden and Denmark as developing 'egalitarian family policies', as these countries provided more universal rights to state welfare. Women's rights as paid workers were more recognised. The state provided and subsidised more childcare. Formal childcare tended to be more professionalised and viewed as beneficial for children's social, personal and intellectual development. Women's interests and children's interests were not so overtly placed against one another – working motherhood and professional childcare were both viewed as in children's best interests. In Sweden, access to childcare, benefits and services was more extensively based on universal rights. Social policies in the other Scandinavian countries, such as Finland and Denmark, had similarly moved away from male breadwinner assumptions. For example, from the 1940s the women's movement in Denmark had called for universal childcare provision to enable women to take up paid work. The system of childcare that developed was informed by pedagogic perspectives about childcare and became highly professionalised, with well-trained, respected and paid staff (Kremer, 2007). The Labour Market Reform of 1994 established childcare as a universal right. Kremer (2007) points to the significance of the role of the women's movement and state feminism in challenging the traditional familial ideology in more egalitarian welfare states. For Gauthier (1996; 2002), the egalitarianism of the Nordic models went beyond a focus on gender equality and encompassed children's rights. For example, in 1977 Norway established a Children's Commissioner and in the 1980s Denmark promoted anti-discrimination, community facilities, family support, childcare and educational reforms which sought to improve the family, neighbourhoods, day care and school environments children were raised in (Gauthier, 1996). At times the Scandinavian model incorporated an explicit statement of parental rights and responsibilities which was informed by principles of child welfare and children's rights. In Finland, the Child Custody and Right of Access Act 1984 set out parental responsibilities in relation to children's upbringing and parental rights to family privacy and family support from the state. Important differences within these categories have been noted, though, as have similarities across regime types. For example, the Scandinavian countries differed in respect of the extent to which the gendered division of labour in the family was viewed as a public issue and the extent to which men were 'encouraged' to take on a greater role in the domestic sphere (Kremer, 2007). Kremer (2007) also noted how social class differences between women were important, with poorer families and communities having less access to better-quality childcare. Further, as noted by Williams (1989) in the British context, welfare and gender regimes were underpinned by immigration regimes which restricted the social rights of migrant families and often demonised the child-rearing practices of ethnic minorities.

The ascendancy of Third Way social policies and more interventionist family policies

The 1990s and early 2000s have witnessed the ascendancy of 'Third Way' social and economic policies. 'Third Way' politics are varied and highly contested (Giddens, 1998). Bonoli and Powell (2004) argued that 'Third Way' politics expresses a 'rhetoric of reconciliation' between liberal and social democratic viewpoints and is particularly relevant to US and UK politics dominated by two major political parties. The term was employed by Bill Clinton in the US to broaden the electoral appeal of the Democratic Party and was adopted by New Labour to gain electoral appeal in the 1990s (Bonoli and Powell, 2004). The term is used here to account for a variety of political standpoints that attempt to reconcile 'market friendly economics' with 'social democratic concerns'. Initially this section will chart the ascendancy of Third Way social policies within the British context and then debate the 'convergence' towards Third Way policies across many EU and OECD countries. Alongside a focus on welfare, childcare and parental employment rights policies, this section charts the development of more interventionist family policies in the UK and European contexts.

New Labour and parental rights and responsibilities

On its own terms, on coming to office in 1997, New Labour claimed to pursue traditional Labour Party social justice concerns through 'market means' (Blair, 1998). New Labour claimed a coherent economic and social policy agenda whereby economic policy 'embraced the market and globalisation', seeking to attract investment via favourable corporation tax regimes and raising productivity via full employment. Social policies under Labour were also orientated towards promoting social equality of opportunity via education and employment, and public sector modernisation sought partnerships and better coordination between state, market and third sector provision (Blair, 1998). Promoting equality of educational and employment opportunity promoted 'social inclusion' and enabled people to 'work their way out of poverty', as well as contributed to economic productivity and growth. Social policy became orientated towards 'social investment' as much as towards income protection (Brown, 1999). This led policy analysts to describe Labour's welfare reform project as a shift from the 'welfare state to social investment state', whereby social policy is orientated towards investing in human capital and equality of employment opportunity (Featherstone, 2010). Part Two of this book charts the evolution of New Labour's social investment approach in five key areas: welfare to work, financial support measures to families and children, childcare, family-friendly employment and family and parenting support services. Across all of these, parental rights and responsibilities were revised.

Labour's first term in government, from 1997 to 2001, involved the establishment of the New Labour political project, the introduction of a programme of public sector 'modernisation', major developments in social security policies, anti-poverty reforms, the introduction of a national childcare strategy and the setting out of a new approach to family policy. More areas of social policy were devolved to Scotland, Wales and Northern Ireland. These countries have since diverted somewhat from English social policies, with a stronger emphasis on children's rights and social democratic ideals. Initially, social security reform reflected much continuity with the previous administration, with benefit cuts and the introduction of the welfare to work programmes. By 1998, however, a stronger focus on tackling social exclusion, reducing child poverty and supporting families emerged. Labour set out a new 'welfare contract' based on 'work for those who can, security for those who cannot' (DSS, 1998). Labour subsequently introduced a new system of tax credits, a National Minimum Wage (NMW), targeted financial support for low-income families, a minimum income guarantee for disabled people and the first 'National Childcare Strategy' (DSS, 1998). 'Work for those who can' was promoted via compulsory welfare to work schemes and measures which made benefits more conditional on preparing for or taking up paid work.

Social policy agendas sought to reduce social exclusion. The Social Exclusion Unit was established in 1997 and came to define social exclusion as follows:

> Social exclusion is a short-hand term for what can happen when people or areas have a combination of problems, such as unemployment, discrimination, poor skills, low incomes, poor housing, high crime and family breakdown. These problems are linked and mutually reinforcing [...] This pattern of disadvantage can be transmitted from one generation to the next. (Social Exclusion Task Force webpage, available at www.cabinetoffice.gov.uk/social_exclusion_task_force/context.aspx, accessed 27 January 2010)

The 'causes' of social exclusion were defined as: 'individual and social' (SEU, 1999). The 'individual' factors included inappropriate individual dispositions, values and beliefs (such as irrational 'fears and anxieties about losing benefits' or 'the fear of not being able to find employment'); a lack of 'individual aspiration, motivation and hope', and a lack of 'work habits', low employability and poor skills such as 'basic literacy skills and job search skills' (SEU, 1999). The social factors included exposure to 'risk factors'; 'a culture of joblessness in some families and neighbourhoods' (SEU, 1999) and a number of 'barriers to employment opportunity' (SEU, 1999). The discourse of social exclusion could encompass recognition of multiple disadvantage and denoted concerns about the way unequal life chances led to social divisions and threatened social cohesion. The dual emphasis on citizen rights and responsibilities, and the individual and social causes of social exclusion, evoked what Levitas (2005) called the 'moral underclass' discourse of social exclusion, informed by long-standing social distinctions between the 'deserving and undeserving poor'. In moral underclass theories, individuals and groups are positioned as excluding themselves from mainstream society, being a burden on society and placing economic and social stability at risk. However, policy discourses were also informed by the 'social integrationist and redistribution' discourses which link social exclusion with labour market exclusion and vulnerability to poverty (Levitas, 2005). However, these discourses did not adequately reflect social inequalities. The construction of the citizen in terms of the gender-neutral and individualistic 'adult-worker citizen' does not recognise unpaid care and child-rearing responsibilities as economically and socially productive work (Lewis, 2002). A focus on redistribution does not address aspects of well-being and inclusion which go beyond economic well-being, such as discrimination. During Labour's second term in office, from 2001 to 2005, the social inclusion agenda expanded in some respects and narrowed in others. The preventative agenda was expanded, seeking to prevent poverty, social exclusion and 'serious family problems'. The inquiry into the death of Victoria Climbié led to the 2003 *Every Child Matters* Green Paper, which set out a new agenda to promote child well-being. Following two terms of reforms and declining unemployment rates, Labour's third term in office saw a greater emphasis on raising employability and basic skills among groups vulnerable to long-term welfare reliance. However, the social inclusion agenda also narrowed from 2005 towards a focus more on 'the most socially excluded individuals, groups and families' (Freud, 2007). Policy makers more prominently evoked the moral underclass view and the Conservatives, in opposition, began their 'Broken Britain' campaign. Chapter Two found these perspectives empirically and theoretically limited. They provide an inadequate basis from which to address child welfare concerns. The increasing significance of the moral underclass perspective was at odds with other developments in recent years, such as the commitment to addressing 'multiple disadvantage', eradicating child poverty, the Human Rights Act 1998, the new Equalities Duties and the commitment to implement the 1989 UNCRC.

Part Two will detail how parental rights and responsibilities were reformulated under Labour. In line with the shift from spousal to parental responsibility in the early 1990s, a number of policies were introduced which sought to formalise and enforce parental responsibilities for children's education, health and behaviour. The interventionist nature of family policy under Labour, however, took a step further in prescribing 'effective parenting practices' (Home Office, 2006). These policies sought to promote parenting norms and were informed by communitarian perspectives about a 'parenting deficit' in contemporary families. Labour invested in parenting support and education initiatives, and in 'family level interventions' for families in need. However, Chapter Seven will review research which has demonstrated that these policies reflect middle-class parenting norms and do not fully recognise the conflicts, dilemmas and challenges many parents face.

The Conservative–Liberal Democrat Coalition and parental rights and responsibilities

In the context of economic recession and a relatively high public deficit, the current political era is dominated by public spending cuts and seems set to reel in the 'social investment state'. However, 'protecting children', 'investing in the early years', 'supporting families' and addressing 'family and social breakdown' continue to be major themes. Chapter One highlighted cross-party support for the following child and family policies during the 2010 General Election:

- child poverty reduction targets
- sustained investment in early years services
- further welfare-to-work measures
- flexible parental leave
- 'intensive' interventions for families with 'multiple and serious problems'
- reforms to child protection
- reforms to address the commercialisation of children
- investment in couple relationships and mediation services
- family law reform aimed at promoting child welfare and fathers' involvement in children's lives (Conservative Party, 2010; Labour Party, 2010; Liberal Democrat Party, 2010; Plaid Cymru, 2010; Scottish National Party, 2010).

However, alternative discourses of 'parental rights and responsibilities' are emerging. In their 2010 General Election manifesto, the Conservatives emphasised 'personal, family and community responsibility' for social well-being. The 'Broken Britain' campaign referred to 'the breakdown of responsibility, the breakdown of morality, the breakdown of the family and the breakdown of community' in British society (Cameron, 2009). Responsibilisation and active citizenship are at the heart of the new Coalition government's talk of 'the Big Society'. To promote more personal and social responsibility, there is an associated need to reduce 'big government' (the latter being a reference to excessive public spending, harmful state interventions, wasteful bureaucracy, mismanagement of the economy and threats to civil liberties which occurred under Labour) (Conservative Party, 2010). A new programme for public service reform was set out which would re-assert 'the role of the private sector' in welfare provision and promote more third sector and citizen involvement in public services (Cameron, 2009). The Conservative Party sought a return to less state interference in families and a withdrawal of some of the support measures developed under New Labour.

Active citizenship was an additional theme to the Liberal Democrats' social policies, but there were alternative directions in rights recognition. The Liberal Democrat members of the new Coalition talk of 'contemporary risks to children', men's involvement in childcare and children's rights. The emphasis on fathers' rights might be translated into policy as more equal rights for mothers and fathers in several areas. For example, the Liberal Democrat Party manifesto for the 2010 General Election made commitments to extend parental leave and flexible working rights (Liberal Democrat Party, 2010). More universal pre-school provision was on the cards – with proposals to provide 20 hours of free nursery childcare to all children over 18 months old. The Liberal Democrat Party claimed that it would take forward Labour's 2009 Children Bill, which sought to make the UNCRC part of domestic law. There was a stronger emphasis on addressing risks to children, particularly poverty and abuse, and the risks associated with internet safety and the commercialisation of childhood (Liberal Democrat Party, 2010).

Chapter One stated that points of more distinction between the three main parties were: (1) a pro-active support for marriage versus recognition of family diversity, and (2) preference for highly targeted versus more comprehensive family support and child welfare services. Parts Two and Four of the book return to the issue of how far the Coalition government by the end of 2010 had integrated or compromised Conservative and Liberal Democrat agendas.

An emerging European model?

Similar reformulations of parental rights and responsibilities have occurred elsewhere in Europe since the late 1990s (Gauthier, 2002; Bonoli and Powell, 2004; Daly, 2004). At the level of policy rhetoric, an overt Third Way discourse is highly associated with neoliberal welfare regimes and has not enthusiastically been adopted by European social democrat parties (Bonoli and Powell, 2004). However, there are increasing similarities to policy foci, reflecting the common socio-economic and political challenges Western welfare states face and the 'internationalisation' of social and family policy (Gauthier, 2002). In contrast to these similarities, though, this section will illustrate ongoing differences in levels of public expenditure on family support measures across welfare regimes, and major differences in social policy agendas, goals and designs.

Many policy analysts highlight increasing policy similarities. Daly (2004) argued that a new model for family policy was emerging across EU member states. This was based on five key features:

- the re-ordering of family responsibilities as 'parental responsibilities', as opposed to spousal responsibilities
- the promotion of women's and men's roles, rights and responsibilities as paid workers
- the promotion of women's and men's active role as carers and parents
- the promotion of children's rights
- more prescriptive, instructive and regulatory 'parenting' policies (Daly, 2004).

Bonoli and Powell (2004) identified three common 'Third Way' policy goals and related these to 'the variety of constituencies and agendas that can be associated with the Third Way approach': raising employment rates; containing public expenditure; and strengthening the social investment state. Gauthier (2002) concluded that many OECD and EU countries were pursuing policies which sought to: increase support for working parents, promote a better work–life balance, promote child well-being and, at times, boost fertility rates. These common objectives are in turn associated with similar demographic and socio-economic challenges, globalisation and increasing European and OECD coordination of social and family policies. The European level of policy action, for example, has become increasingly significant. Part Two will show how European Union Directives for part-time workers, maternity and paternity entitlements, parental leave and family-friendly employment led to changes in UK legislation. The 2000 Lisbon Treaty set a target to increase women's employment rates across EU member states to 60% by 2010. This objective was linked to gender equality, anti-poverty and economic growth objectives. The Lisbon Treaty further led to the 'Open Method of Coordination', whereby EU member states established collective policy objectives via the development of national plans and targets. There have been national plans on social inclusion, child poverty, parenting policies and family policies. The 2002 European Council Agreement sought formal childcare provision for 90% of 3–6-year-olds in member states by 2010 and 33% of children aged 0–3 years in each member state. The 2006 European Council set further targets for reducing child poverty and promoting children's educational outcomes. The 2007 European Council Agreement promoted work–family reconciliation policies as key to addressing economic and demographic challenges (Guo and Gilbert, 2007). The 2007 Council further stated that family and parenting support services were central to promoting social cohesion, better parenting and better outcomes for children; and that young people should have access to recreational and leisure services, irrespective of family income. The EU in particular promotes support for working parents and rights to lifelong learning. The OECD recently established a 'family database' which monitors aspects of socio-economic and policy trends, while also promoting coordinated policy objectives and plans.

These changes and similarities, however, on the one hand reflect the re-ordering of citizen–state and gender, generational and social relations; but also reflect continuities in the social and economic imperatives informing the political economy of welfare states. Hudson and Lowe (2009) argued that the social policy priorities of the EU and British versions of the 'Third Way' reflect continuities in the economic imperatives of the welfare state to promote the standing of nation-states in the competitive global economy. From this perspective, policy priorities are essentially about restricting welfare expenditure, on the one hand, and investing in human capital deficits and 'high cost, low productivity' groups, on the other (Esping-Andersen et al, 2002). In contrast to cutting public spending, the social investment approach justifies increases in spending on specific programmes and areas which enhance human capital and social cohesion (OECD, 2005). The UK, under Labour, developed a 'child-centred' approach, while other European countries have been found to have a more 'adult-centred' focus. Jensen (2008) argued that a more child-centred approach can sideline issues of gender inequality. Bonoli and Powell (2004) found that social democrats were increasingly 'accepting fiscal discipline as an unavoidable constraint over policy making'. Entitlements and provisions subject to retrenchment, spending cutbacks and privatisation include: higher education, healthcare, social care, pensions, unemployment and disability benefits (Bonoli and Powell, 2004; Hantrais, 2004). However, on the other hand, expenditure in some areas has increased. Gornick and Meyers (2001) and Guo and Gilbert (2007) undertook a longitudinal analysis of public spending on families. Gornick and Meyers (2001) found that during the 1980s and 1990s some countries, such as Ireland, Finland and Norway, more than doubled their spending on families. However, in Sweden public expenditure on the family as a percentage of GDP reached a peak of 4–5% in 1992 and since then has declined to 3%, although it remains relatively high in OECD terms (Guo and Gilbert, 2007). These findings were associated with 'the combined impact of demographic and market forces' (that is, 'the combined social and fiscal demands' from ageing populations and changing family structures, and 'pressure to scale back social benefits which are seen as hindering a country's capacity to keep production costs low and attract foreign investment') and 'developments at the supranational level of the European Union' (Guo and Gilbert, 2007, p 312). Jensen (2006, p 31) set out some of the contradictory implications of these pressures and approaches:

> The market and family sectors are assigned greater responsibility for programmes designed to address 'old' social risks, such as pensions, health care, post-secondary education and the other classic service areas of the welfare state. At the same time, the family sector is relieved of some responsibility for caring, as public support for early education and care increases and new benefits to pay for the care of elderly and disabled persons are added to the social policy mix. In addition, wage supplements make the state and the market sectors jointly responsible for the earnings package of a significant proportion of the employed, a role that the state rarely assumed in the 'golden age' of the welfare state.

The social investment approach can further be linked to an agenda to combat moral decline and to the re-education of citizens towards responsible active citizenship, such as through parent training and citizenship education programmes. This relates to the moralistic and behavioural rather than structural and market-based explanations for social exclusion that are more consistent with Third Way thinking. Jensen (2006) found that concern about youth anti-social behaviour is more prominent in Britain, reflecting the long-standing concerns about delinquency, social threats and poverty in the British context. Rodgers (2003, p 47) notes similar stigmatising discourses in Scandinavian countries: 'in the Scandinavian countries there is a "moral agenda" shaping debate about the distribution of responsibility for social welfare between the state, the individual and the family'. Commentators have noted an increasing tendency for European welfare states to adopt conditional welfare rights and punitive welfare policies towards 'irresponsible parents' (Bennett, 2006).

Alongside convergence, however, there are major national differences in levels of public expenditure, the institutional nature of social and family policies, policy processes and influences, and policy objectives. Hantrais (2004) demonstrated the very different starting points and trajectories across the new EU member states, many of which are former communist Eastern European countries which have 'refamilialised' parents and children under major economic and social restructuring. The differences across welfare states fundamentally include alternative framings of parental and citizen rights and responsibilities.

To start with, as mentioned earlier, significant differences in levels of public expenditure on benefits and services for families and children remain. Chapter Two linked higher public spending on families and children with higher levels of child and family well-being. Table 4.1 illustrates differences in levels of public expenditure as a percentage of GDP, while Figures 4.1 and 4.2 break these figures down into spending on family benefits and services overall, and childcare subsidies and services. Table 4.1 shows that, as a proportion of GDP, public expenditure remained stable, decreased slightly or increased slightly in many countries. Countries such as the Netherlands, Sweden and Norway saw reductions in the proportion of GDP devoted to public expenditure. However, the UK, as well as other countries such as France, Ireland and Italy, have increased their proportion of GDP on public expenditure. Overall, though, the welfare states often classed as 'conservative-corporatist' or 'social democratic' devoted higher proportions of GDP to public expenditure.

According to the OECD data used for Figure 4.1, the UK in 2005 had the third largest expenditure on family benefits and services, devoting around 3.5% of GDP to this spending, while France devoted 3.8% and Luxembourg 3.6%. However, in the UK this proportion of GDP expenditure was mainly made up of cash benefits and tax credits, two policy areas up for review by the new Coalition government. The UK allocated a smaller proportion of expenditure to services, and countries such as France, Denmark, Sweden, Hungary, Finland and Iceland devoted a much higher proportion of spending to services. Figure 4.2 details these spending allocations further. When we look at expenditure on childcare and pre-school services, UK levels of public expenditure were slightly below the OECD average.

Major differences are further found in policy goals and designs. For example, active labour market policies and welfare to work programmes vary considerably across the EU. These policies aim to reduce unemployment and 'activate' groups previously assumed to be 'economically inactive' (ie mothers, lone mothers, older people and those in receipt of disability benefits). Carpenter et al (2007) argued that programmes and policy regimes differ in terms of:

- a 'work-first' approach versus the human capital approach: the former approach is associated with more conditionality in the welfare system; more compulsory participation in welfare to work schemes and harsher work-related requirements, while the latter involves more extensive investment in raising skills, lifelong learning and providing targeted back-to-work and in-work support;

Table 4.1: Total public expenditure as a percentage of GDP, OECD countries, 1998–2005

	1998	2000	2002	2004	2005
Australia	17.1	17.8	17.5	17.7	17.1
Austria	26.6	26.4	27	27.3	27.2
Belgium	26.1	25.3	26.2	26.6	26.4
Canada	17.8	16.5	17.1	16.6	16.5
Czech Republic	19.1	19.8	20.6	19.7	19.5
Denmark	26.6	25.8	26.8	27.7	27.1
Finland	26.3	24.3	25	26	26.1
France	28.9	27.9	28.6	29.1	29.2
Germany	26.3	26.2	27	26.7	26.7
Greece	18.6	19.2	20.0	19.9	20.5
Hungary	-	20	21.4	21.7	22.5
Iceland	14.8	15.3	16.9	17.9	16.9
Ireland	13.0	13.6	15.3	16.2	16.7
Italy	22.9	23.3	24	24.7	25
Japan	15.5	16.5	17.8	18.2	18.6
Korea	5.2	5	5.3	5.3	5.8
Luxembourg	20.9	19.7	22.0	23.9	23.2
Mexico	5.0	5.8	6.8	7.2	7.4
Netherlands	21.4	19.8	20.5	21.1	20.9
New Zealand	20.3	19.4	18.7	18.0	18.5
Norway	23.6	21.3	23.6	23.2	21.6
Poland	21.4	20.5	22.3	21.4	21
Portugal	17.9	19.6	21.3	23.1	-
Slovak Republic	18.0	17.9	17.7	16.5	16.6
Spain	20.6	20.3	20.4	21.2	21.2
Sweden	30.4	28.5	29.5	29.9	29.4
Switzerland	18.8	17.9	19.2	20.3	20.3
Turkey	11.1	-	-	-	13.7
United Kingdom	19.4	19.2	20	21.3	21.3
United States	14.7	14.5	15.9	16.1	15.9
OECD	19.8	19.3	20.3	20.6	20.6

Source: OECD Social Expenditure database, updated 9 August 2009.

Figure 4.1: Public spending on family benefits in cash, services and tax breaks for families, selected OECD countries, 2007 (% of GDP)

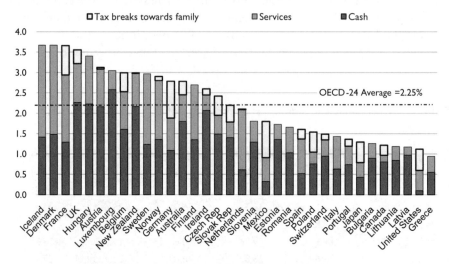

Notes: This data was generated by the OECD based on submissions from national governments for OECD social expenditure survey. Data refers to public spending for public support that is exclusively for families (e.g. child payments and allowances, parental leave benefits and childcare support). Spending recorded in other social policy areas such as healthcare costs support and housing costs support which assists families, but not exclusively, is not included as data. Data on tax breaks towards families was not available for Greece, Italy, Estonia, Slovenia, Finland, Luxembourg, Hungary, Denmark and Iceland.

Source: OECD Social Expenditure Survey, updated August 2010.

Figure 4.2: Public expenditure on childcare in 2005, selected OECD countries (as % of GDP)

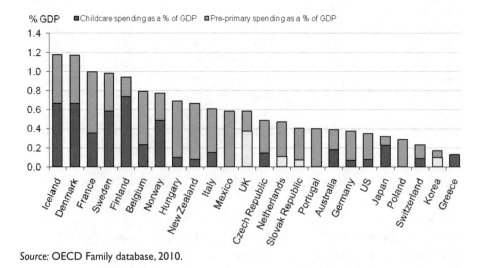

Source: OECD Family database, 2010.

- the range and extent of childcare and employment support policies aimed at promoting equality of opportunity and addressing the 'barriers to employment' experienced by different social groups;
- the degree of complementary 'demand-side' policies, such as those aimed at tackling the gender pay gap or discrimination in the labour market.

Bonoli and Powell (2004) found more extensive moves towards making welfare receipt more conditional on paid work in the Nordic countries, the Netherlands and the UK.

Another difference is in relation to gender inequality issues and the degree to which welfare state restructuring dismantles gender regimes which sustain gender inequalities (Lewis, 2002). Welfare regimes differ extensively in terms of the nature and degree of support afforded to working mothers and fathers; assumptions about gender norms in families and society; gender equality programmes; gendering of family responsibilities and gendering of 'the alternative ideal of care' promoted in contrast to 'full-time maternal care for children' (Fraser, 2000; Kremer, 2007). While many European states seek to increase women's labour market participation, some, including the UK, promote a 'one and a half earner model' whereby mothers' greater use of part-time working is viewed as a matter of personal preference and the means by which women can sustain their family responsibilities while participating in paid work. The greater investment in childcare services and the 'alternative ideals of care' promoted by social policies (such as more support for grandmothers to take on childcare responsibilities for working mothers) reinforce gender roles in caring work, when policies do not seek to actively recruit men into the childcare professions and promote a more equitable division of labour in the domestic sphere (Kremer, 2007). Further quality childcare provision, whether provided by men or women childcare workers, requires much investment in training, working conditions and professionalisation so as to combat the low status, female and low-paid nature of childcare in the UK. There is also generally limited state intervention in the domestic division of labour and to curtail men's longer working hours – which further sustains gender responsibilities for care and domestic labour. According to Fraser (2000), many states fall short of the 'universal caregiver' model which would promote models of 'good motherhood and fatherhood' as involving shared responsibilities and contributions to work and care, an ethic of care towards others, unpaid care work valued equally with paid work, equal treatment for part-time and full-time workers and equal care leave for mothers, fathers and carers. Figures 4.3 and 4.4 show data from the OECD family database on the length and remuneration of maternity and paternity leave across OECD countries. According to this data, the UK provides a relatively long period of maternity leave but much of it is unpaid, and offers very limited unpaid paternity leave for fathers.

Countries also differ in their approach to childcare. Kremer (2007) illustrated how Denmark, for example, has actively promoted and extensively invested in

Figure 4.3: Maternity leave in weeks of entitlement and duration of the full rate equivalent period where leave is with 100% previous pay rate (where available), OECD countries, 2006/07

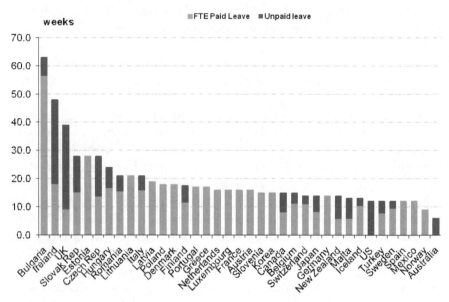

Source: OECD Family database.

Figure 4.4: Paternity leave in weeks of entitlement and duration of the full rate equivalent period where leave is with 100% previous pay rate (where available), OECD countries, 2006/07

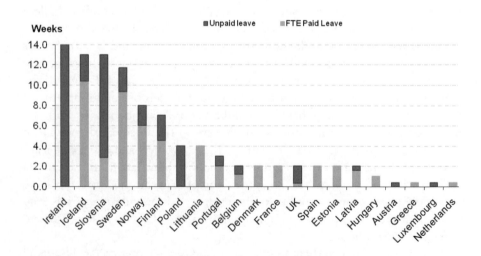

Source: OECD Family database.

social pedagogic day care for pre-school children. However, the UK has taken a mixed approach to childcare, promoting part-time early education for 3–5-year-olds, more extensive educare for poor children, after-school care for school-age children and parental/grandparental care for the under-3s. Likewise, social policy in Germany and the Netherlands represents an ongoing ambiguity towards professional childcare for younger children. These differences in policies have been systematically linked with different national rates of children's participation in formal childcare services and the beneficial impacts of pre-school care and education on children's outcomes (Penn, 2009). Penn (2009, p 3) undertook a review of early education interventions across EU countries and concluded that 'investing in quality childcare and early education provision contributes to children's well-being and helps to breakdown the inter-generational cycle of disadvantage'.

Further differences can be found across other areas of service provision and in the degree of investment in universal versus targeted family and parenting support services (Schulruf et al, 2009). An additional difference across the 'emerging model of family policy' is the extent to which the state explicitly sets out parental rights and responsibilities in respect of children. Earlier, the Finnish example of a national statement of parental rights and responsibilities was identified. The Scottish government has also adopted this approach to some extent. Family policy campaigners have called for a national statement about parental rights and responsibilities for England and Wales (Henricson, 2003).

Conclusion

This chapter charted the historical development of social and family policies in the British context and considered the ways in which welfare state restructuring in recent years has been conceptualised as the shift to the 'social investment state' and more interventionist family policies. In contrast to the 'emerging European models of family and social policy', however, there remain significant differences across welfare regimes, and national differences in policy goals, designs and path dependencies. Part Two takes a more in-depth look at policy change and the reformulation of parental rights and responsibilities in five areas of British policy since 1997.

Part Two
Social policy developments 1997–2010

FIVE

Welfare to work measures and financial support for families

Introduction

Part Two of the book turns to an analysis of social policy developments under Labour from 1997 to early 2010 in the areas of welfare to work, financial support for families with children, childcare services, family-friendly employment and parenting and family support. Each chapter in Part Two identifies: (1) the overarching policy approach, objectives, programmes, target groups and impacts; (2) the evolution of policy developments in response to criticism and change; and (3) revisions of social citizenship and parental rights and responsibilities.

This chapter examines key aspects of welfare reform. Macro-economic and social security policies are highly centralised in the UK, with the devolved Scottish, Northern Ireland and Welsh administrations constrained in respect of independent policy directions. Chapter Four set out the three overarching policy objectives informing Labour's welfare reform agenda: (1) to reduce welfare dependency; (2) to promote equality of employment opportunity; and (3) to reduce child poverty. Welfare to work, tax and benefit reforms were introduced to compel or encourage welfare recipients to take up paid work or back-to-work training, and to provide back-to-work and in-work financial incentives. The agenda to reduce child poverty and 'invest in children' emerged from 1998. This agenda led to more comprehensive welfare rights for (deserving) low-income families with children and redistribution within the benefit and tax system towards families with children. However, this agenda was informed by the 'responsibilisation agenda', and anti-poverty measures included extending back-to-work requirements for welfare-reliant lone mothers, couple mothers and disabled parents in receipt of disability benefits; and maintenance responsibilities among non-resident parents. Overall, this chapter demonstrates that Labour's reforms contributed to significant increases in employment rates among some groups and a reduction in child poverty. However, in relation to the scale of the problems of poverty, labour market exclusion, employment disadvantage and social inequalities, Labour's approach was limited. Crucially, limited welfare and equal rights in the UK continue to place families, adults and children at risk of poverty and employment disadvantage. This chapter charts the evolution of Labour's welfare to work, tax and benefit reforms and critically assesses the emergent welfare contract and degree of policy effectiveness. The conclusion deliberates the new policy context in the early days of the Conservative-Liberal Democrat Coalition government.

Policy developments

Benefit cuts and the New Deals

The 1997 Labour Party manifesto stated that a New Labour government would be 'the welfare to work government' (Labour Party, 1997). In line with the previous era of social security reform, Labour sought to address the problem of 'welfare dependency'. The Social Security Act 1998 took forward reforms drafted by the previous Conservative government: to abolish the Lone Parent Premium on Income Support and One Parent Benefit (an additional element to Child Benefit for lone parents worth around £6 a week in the late 1990s) and make eligibility for Incapacity Benefit (IB)[1] conditional on sufficient NI contributions. The former were thought to act as a disincentive to take up paid work while the latter aimed to 're-instate the original contribution-based intention to entitlement' (Brown, 1997). The Labour government suffered a major backbench rebellion and promised increases in Child Benefit[2] (CB) to compensate lone parents.

In 1997, Labour began to introduce the New Deal welfare to work schemes. A more compulsory and 'work-first' approach was evident in the New Deal scheme for long-term unemployed adults, while a more combined 'work-first and human capital' approach informed the New Deal scheme for young people. Gordon Brown, as Chancellor, described the New Deal for Young People (NDYP) scheme as 'replacing welfare with work' by providing 'new opportunities' alongside 'new responsibilities' (Brown, 1997). Concerns about welfare dependency and poverty among lone-parent families led to the New Deal for Lone Parents (NDLP). This was a voluntary programme aimed at providing advice and support for 'those who want to train or work' and to promote lone parents' 'right to work' (Brown, 1997). The scheme offered 'personalised and individually tailored support' for lone parents in receipt of Income Support (IS).[3] Participants would work with a New Deal Lone Parent Personal Adviser who could offer advice and information about employment opportunities, childcare, in-work income calculations, in-work financial support, job search strategies and training opportunities (Brown, 1997). In 1998, the New Deal for Disabled People (NDDP) was piloted as a voluntary programme aimed at providing employment support and advice for disabled people in receipt of disability benefits. Likewise, this scheme included working with a personal adviser and in addition provided access to 'specialist' support advisers. However, while the other New Deal schemes were rapidly rolled out nationally, it was not until 2008 that the NDDP went national (Wright, 2009). The New Deal schemes included area-based initiatives such as: the New Deal for Communities (a neighbourhood regeneration initiative with a strong focus on improving local employment opportunities) and Employment Zones (welfare to work programmes in areas with high rates of out-of-work benefit receipt) (Wright, 2009).

A new welfare contract

From 1998, Labour set out a 'new welfare contract': 'work for those who can work, security for those who cannot work' (DSS, 1998, p 1). This rhetoric symbolically differentiated New Labour's welfare reform agenda from the previous Conservative administration (where welfare rights were restricted) and from 'old Labour' (which promoted unconditional welfare rights). The new welfare agenda was 'rights with responsibilities': rights to a minimum income and back-to-work support with responsibilities 'to be in paid work, to be economically self-sufficient, to save for your retirement and to provide for your family' (DSS, 1998, p 11). In terms of specific policy proposals, to promote 'rights to a minimum income' and 'provide security for those who cannot work', Labour would 'make work pay', 'support families' and provide an adequate safety net entitlement for economically inactive groups (DSS, 1998). Labour would introduce a new system of tax credits, a National Minimum Wage (NMW), targeted financial support for (deserving) low-income families, a minimum income guarantee for disabled people and small increases in the amount of child maintenance and income disregards that lone parents on IS could receive (DSS, 1998). 'Work for those who can' would be promoted via making benefits more conditional on preparing or taking up paid work and via Labour's employment support policies – such as the NMW, the new system of tax credits and the 1998 National Childcare Strategy (see Chapter Six). Specific reforms to the welfare to work and social security system included the creation of a 'single work-focused gateway' to benefits whereby new claimants for Jobseeker's Allowance (JSA)[4] were required to participate in Work Focused Interviews (WFIs); new welfare to work measures for cohabiting partners of JSA claimants; area-based employment programmes and tougher measures to tackle benefit fraud (DSS, 1998). WFIs promoted 'a return to work among claimants', while joint claims meant that cohabiting couples on JSA were treated as a household unit, both subject to welfare to work schemes (DSS, 1998). The latter was justified on the grounds of promoting women's employment opportunities (Brown, 1998). Claimants could receive benefit-loss penalties for non-attendance at a WFI or for submitting a fraudulent single claim for JSA. By the end of New Labour's first term in office, compulsory WFIs were introduced for most new claimants of IB and IS as well as JSA. In 2001, WFIs were introduced for lone parents who made a new claim for IS (with children aged 5 years and 3 months) and lone parents in receipt of IS (with children aged over 13 years). These measures extended work conditionalities in the benefit system, even among groups not individually claiming welfare benefits – ie cohabiting partners of JSA claimants.

Better financial support for families and the pledge to eradicate child poverty

From late 1998 Labour's welfare reforms became more 'family and child centred'. This was because the government increasingly took the view that child poverty led to 'persistent life-long poverty' and poor outcomes in adult life (including a higher risk of welfare reliance), contributing to the intergenerational cycle of social exclusion (Home Office, 1998). In his second Budget, Gordon Brown, stated that 'investing in children' and 'reducing child poverty' would become major welfare reform objectives and would benefit the economy in the long run. The review of child and family benefits was informed by three principles: (1) to move away from benefit status tied to family structure (ie the abolition of lone parent-specific benefit entitlements); (2) to provide additional financial support for families with the youngest children and (3) to provide more support for 'hard working' low-income families (Brown, 1999). Towards these ends, Brown announced increases in CB and IS and 'a fundamental reform of the tax system' (Brown, 1998). From 1999, CB was raised by £2.50 for the first child in a family. Parents in receipt of IS gained an additional £2.50 a week in CB for their first child. Tax reform involved a more favourable tax regime for businesses (ie reductions in corporation tax) and 'a new working families tax credit', described as 'a tax cut for hard working low income families' (Brown, 1998). To 'make work pay' the latter measure was supplemented by the new NMW; 'benefit run-ons', whereby some claimants continued to receive IS and Housing Benefit[5] in the first two weeks of starting employment; help with childcare costs and a Disabled Person's Tax Credit. However, 'making work pay' was defined in narrow terms as 'ensuring work pays more than benefits'. Tax credits would mean 'claimants have no excuse not to take up work', but to escape benefit traps and enable claimants to sufficiently cover the costs of taking up paid work (such as childcare costs) tax credits would need to be set at rates which enable individuals and families to secure significantly higher levels of household income than those secured via benefits and associated support (Paull et al, 2002).

From October 1999 the Working Families Tax Credit (WFTC) replaced Family Credit, and the NMW was introduced. To qualify for WFTC a parent had to: (a) be the main carer for their child; (b) work more than 16 hours a week and (c) have a household annual income below £50,000. A principle of progressive universalism applied whereby family households with above-average household incomes remained eligible for an award but higher awards went to low-income family households. The WFTC included awards for an adult tax credit, a childcare tax credit and a 30 hour tax credit – the latter an incentive to work longer hours. The childcare tax credit paid up to 70% of childcare costs, with a maximum award of £100 a week for the childcare costs for one child and £150 a week for the childcare costs of two or more children. Child maintenance payments were not to be included in the assessment of an award. Tax credits were to be administered through the Inland Revenue rather than the Benefits Agency. The WFTC award was set by the Inland Revenue for a 6-month period and then reviewed. The Disabled Person's Tax Credit replaced Disability Working Allowance and was a more generous benefit with a couple's tax credit and disabled child's tax credit element. The award also ran for six months.

In the past, an NMW had been rejected by British governments on the grounds that it could lead to wages being both increased and reduced to the minimum level, was too costly for the state and employers, and could increase unemployment (Deacon, 2002). However, although Labour introduced the measure, there was severe neglect of low pay among young people. Initially only employees aged over 22 years were protected and the rate was set at £3.60 per hour. According to Sefton et al (2009), 1.5 million jobs (6.5% of jobs) had hourly rates below this level in April 1999, while a year later this was reduced to 300,000. Following this, the Low Pay Unit advised significant annual increases to the NMW. Labour adopted the recommendations of the Low Pay Unit until 2004, at which point the NMW was only increased in line with average increases in earnings. Gradually, young people were afforded more protection. By October 2010 a new 'apprentice rate' was introduced for young people under 19 in apprentice schemes set at £2.50 an hour and the NMW stood at:

- £5.93 per hour for workers aged 21 years and over
- £4.92 per hour for workers aged 18–20 years
- £3.64 per hour for workers aged 16–17 years.

In March 1999 Prime Minister Tony Blair famously pledged to 'eradicate child poverty in 20 years' and 'halve it by 2010'. Soon after the 1999 pledge the government set ambitious targets to reduce child poverty by a quarter by 2004–05; by 50% by 2010; and to eradicate it by 2020. Further measures were announced:

- from April 2001 the Child Tax Credit (CTC) would be paid to families 'irrespective of family status in recognition of the extra costs of bringing up children', with higher awards given to families with disabled children, couple families and families on lower incomes (although families with household incomes of up to £50,000 a year were also eligible);
- a further increase in CB, raising it to weekly rates of £15 for the first child in a family and £10 for the second and further children from April 2000;
- lowered income tax rates for low-income families, with no income tax paid until earnings reached £235 a week and a new 10p lower rate of income tax on the first £1,500 of earnings from May 1999;
- a guaranteed minimum income for working families of £200 a week;
- a new Sure Start Maternity Grant for the lowest-income families and mothers not eligible for Statutory Maternity Pay (SMP), worth £200 on the birth of a child, introduced from April 2000.

These financial support measures sought behavioural as well as financial objectives, namely, to increase labour market participation and, in the case of the Sure Start Maternity Grant, to require mothers to 'keep appointments for child health advice and child health check-ups' in return for the grant (Brown, 1999). These initiatives reflected the increasing commitment within the government to improving outcomes among poor children. However, New Labour's anti-poverty measures were firmly based on the dualism of the deserving and undeserving poor. Labour was increasingly prepared to place children at risk of poverty when parents were deemed the undeserving poor, or not fulfilling their duties in return for rights. The Crime and Disorder Act 1998 introduced new powers to withdraw welfare and housing benefits among 'anti-social' social housing tenants (Dwyer, 2004). The Immigration and Asylum Act 1999 and the Nationality, Immigration and Asylum Act 2002 withdrew and restricted welfare benefits from undeserving migrants, refugees and asylum seekers (Dwyer, 2004).

In Labour's second term in office, anti-poverty measures came in for criticism. The Institute for Fiscal Studies examined take-up of tax credits. It found only 3% of families were in receipt of the childcare tax credit, lower than expected take-up rates (Paull et al, 2002, p 6). The study surveyed parents and found take-up was limited by the eligibility criteria rather than lack of awareness about entitlements. The majority of low-income working parents relied on informal childcare – whereas the tax credit system only provided help towards the cost of formal childcare. Many mothers worked less than 16 hours a week or irregular part-time hours. Moreover, employment and childcare arrangements had to be in place prior to a claim for childcare tax credit, which created periods of financial uncertainty for families and could cause anxiety over making commitments to major childcare and employment decisions before financial issues were fully dealt with. Tax credits were also based on household income for the previous tax year. Many families subsequently received demands for 'overpayments' once more recent changes in income were taken into account. In addition, researchers argued that the emphasis on household income and parental work requirements provided incentives for lone parents to take up paid work but could provide disincentives for couple mothers to take up paid work, as any increase to the household income from a second wage earner was likely to lead to reductions in tax credits (Lewis, 2002). According to the HBAI series (DWP, 2004), in 2000–01, 90% of family households in receipt of WFTC were lone-parent households. Further, although it was recognised that large families accounted for 50% of children in poverty, the childcare tax credit provided higher payments for one child in childcare (Land, 2002). Paull et al (2002) recommended:

- expanding the eligibility criteria to recognise more home-based childcare provision and informal childcare providers
- providing 100% of childcare costs via the childcare tax credit system for working parents on the lowest household incomes

- reducing the work requirement to include those working less than 16 hours a week.

Reforms did follow. Labour introduced a new system from 2003, based on the CTC and Working Tax Credit (WTC), which expanded eligibility beyond families with children and separated out support for adults and support for families with children. The CTC included a family element, a baby element, a child element, a disability element and a severe disability element. The CTC was awarded on the basis of family status, child's age and disability – irrespective of employment status. The WTC provided support for low-income workers working more than 16 hours a week who could claim for a basic element, a couple or lone-parent element, a 30-hour element (a higher award for those working more than 30 hours a week), a disability element, a 50+ rate (for those over 50 years old), a disability element and a childcare element. The reforms introduced a more generous childcare tax credit – which paid up to 80% of weekly childcare costs for working parents, with a maximum award of £175 for the eldest child and £300 for two or more children in childcare. Labour additionally introduced more direct financial support for young people. For example, young people aged between 16 and 19 years from low-income families who decided to stay in full-time education post-16 could apply for an Education Maintenance Allowance, worth up to £30 a week and conditional on course attendance.

In 2003 the Green Paper *Every Child Matters* set out a radical reform of children's services, reflecting a major development in Labour's 'child-focused' social investment policies (Chief Secretary to the Treasury, 2003). The next two chapters detail the background, development and aims of the 2003 Green Paper. The 2003 Green Paper and subsequent Children Act 2004 stated that services should work together to promote child well-being, defined as: being safe, enjoying and achieving in childhood, being healthy, making a positive contribution to society and economic well-being (Chief Secretary to the Treasury, 2003, pp 6–7; see Chapter Two). However, although 'economic well-being' was one of the five outcomes for children set out in *Every Child Matters*, the Green Paper was based on an assumption that Labour's welfare reforms already adequately addressed the problem of child poverty. However, policies here were not sufficiently 'joined up'. A stronger anti-poverty programme would have incorporated a welfare rights agenda within the children's services reform agenda, and more extensive investment in raising incomes among out-of-work and in-work low-income families.

Concern over meeting the 2004/05 child poverty reduction targets led to the Child Poverty Review announced in the 2003 Budget. In 2004, the Review set out the next aims of reform:

- to subject lone parents in receipt of out-of-work benefits and non-working partners of JSA claimants to stricter WFI requirements and increase 'work premiums' (additional financial support for claimants when they started work) for lone parents;

- to reduce the proportion of children in workless households by 0.5% during 2005/06–2007/08;
- to increase the proportion of parents on benefits who receive maintenance;
- to improve financial support to larger families;
- to reform children's services and invest in targeted interventions to 'break cycles of deprivation' (HM Treasury, 2004).

In 2004/05 further increases in CB, IS, CTC and WTC occurred (Stewart, 2009). The Child Trust Fund was introduced in 2005. This initiative involved the government investing £250 into a Child Trust Fund for every child born after September 2002. Families on the lowest incomes received an additional £250 per child. When a child reached 7 years old the government placed another £250 endowment into their CTF (with the lowest-income families again in receipt of a further £250). The central idea of the CTF was that, as a savings and trust fund, young people could access their savings when reaching 18 years old and it was presumed that parents would add to the government's investments. This policy was dependent on favourable investment and financial market conditions. The Child Poverty Action Group (CPAG) criticised the policy for neglecting poverty in the short term and for optimistic projections about the saving capabilities of families on very low or insecure incomes (CPAG, 2009).

Institutional reform

The 2001 Labour Party manifesto reinstated Labour's primary policy objectives: to reduce welfare reliance, promote employment opportunities and reduce child poverty. 'Promoting employment opportunities' had now come to encompass 'reaching full employment', defined as an 80% national employment rate, which in turn was key to Labour's macro-economic policies as well as its social inclusion policies (Labour Party, 2001). To reflect the belief that the welfare system should be a 'springboard back into work', the Department of Social Security was renamed the Department for Work and Pensions in 2002. The aims of the DWP were more 'work-focused': 'to maximise employment and opportunity for all, reduce poverty and promote independence and well-being in later life', and the governance of these objectives was organised around accountability to targets for reductions in claimant counts and moving claimants from welfare into paid work. Alongside departmental reform, between 2002 and 2006 the Benefit Agency and Employment Service were 'merged' through the creation of Jobcentre Plus. Several functions of the benefit system were transferred to the Inland Revenue. The aims and objectives of Jobcentre Plus were to provide a 'single gateway to welfare to work schemes and benefit entitlements' so that claimants 'signed up for return to work schemes when they signed up for out of work benefits' (Labour Party, 2001, p 10). The creation of Jobcentre Plus extended work conditionalities in the benefit system by subjecting claimants and their partners to welfare to work measures.

Extending welfare to work measures

As indicated by the 2004 Child Poverty Review, Labour sought more conditional welfare rights. Early evaluations for the NDLP scheme found that the majority of eligible lone parents did not participate in the scheme (Millar and Rowlingson, 2001). However, those who did highly valued the 'personalised support' from the NDLP personal adviser (Lewis et al, 2000). It was suggested that the voluntary nature of the NDLP and the limited 'back-to-work' support available via the scheme meant that the scheme engaged lone parents who were the 'most willing and ready to take up paid work' (Millar and Rowlingson, 2001). Knight and Lissenburg (2004) found that, overall, by 2003/04 the NDLP and WFI schemes had contributed to an increase in the lone-parent employment rate, with 53% of lone parents employed in spring 2003, as compared with 47% the last quarter of 1997 (ONS, 2009). However, they found that rates of 'persistent long-term employment' were lower among lone parents, as compared to couple mothers. Using benefit data, they found that only 49% of employed lone parents were 'persistently employed'. Those 'persistently employed' tended to be lone fathers, parents with higher qualifications and those with fewer children (Knight and Lissenburg, 2004). Knight and Lissenburg (2004) claimed that around 30% of lone parents were vulnerable to low pay–no pay cycles of employment and associated this with insecure employment conditions, childcare difficulties, relatively low earning capabilities and financial problems. In addition to the introduction of mandatory WFIs in 2001, the DWP invested in a number of lone-parent pilot schemes offering additional in-work support for lone parents in receipt of IS for over 12 months, such as an In-Work Credit (an in-work payment), the Work Search Premium (an additional payment paid for an intensive job search period), childcare tasters (fully subsidised childcare for a limited period) and quarterly WFIs. Reform to the NDLPs in Labour's second term in office increased support to lone parents in the initial weeks of moving from welfare into paid work; established the 'New Deal Plus' scheme and increased requirements to attend WFIs. In 2004, WFIs became compulsory for all lone parents in receipt of IS, irrespective of the age of their youngest child. The Employment Retention and Advancement schemes were introduced for out-of-work lone parents entering the NDLP; lone parents working 16–29 hours a week and receiving WTC; and long-term unemployed people participating in the New Deals. Participants received more support from an in-work Advancement Support Adviser, in-work financial bonuses and help to access training. It was during Labour's second term in office that more welfare to work initiatives for people with disabilities and long-term health problems were developed. In 2002, the DWP announced the 'Pathways to Work' pilot schemes for people with long-term health problems and disabled people. These schemes involved mandatory WFIs for out-of-work claimants of disability benefits and a programme of employment support working with specialist advisers (who also worked with employers to 'broker' additional support for disabled claimants moving into work).

Refocusing on economically inactive groups

Chapter Three charted the fall in unemployment rates from the mid 1990s to 2003/04. The government associated these trends with macro-economic policies and welfare to work reforms. Labour's priority then became rates of economic inactivity, which were rising in the early 2000s. A few months before the 2005 General Election, the DWP published *Opportunity and security throughout life: A five year plan* (DWP, 2005). This document restated the government's goal to achieve 'full employment in every region'. As well as producing economic growth and raising incomes, full employment would maintain an adequate 'economic-dependency ratio' in relation to 'our greatest challenge' – the ageing population (DWP, 2005, p 4). The DWP asserted that Labour's welfare to work and macro-economic policies had 'resigned the problem of high unemployment to a past memory' (DWP, 2005, p 5). The next objective was to reassess the 'rights and responsibilities' of economically inactive groups, as these now constituted 'the majority of people who are not in employment' (DWP, 2005, p 7). The DWP argued that 'many of these inactive people can work' and the economy was 'losing out on their skills and contributions' (DWP, 2005, p 7). Priority groups were: lone parents, older people and individuals from ethnic minorities (with Pakistani and Bangladeshi women especially identified); and those in receipt of incapacity and disability benefits (DWP, 2005). The DWP continued to construct these groups as distinct groups that required targeted policies. Ethnic minorities had now become a priority group but there were no new reforms for this group. Subsequently, the DWP website aligned this objective with 'help for people with a poor knowledge of English to compete and retain employment' (dwp.gov.uk, 26 February 2010). To reduce welfare reliance among lone parents, however, the plan proposed: (1) extending employment support measures across welfare to work schemes; (2) investing in 'tailored' employability schemes; and (3) more conditional welfare rights (DWP, 2005, p 8). Reforms aimed at those on disability and incapacity benefits included: (1) extending the 'individually tailored employment advice and support' offered through the Pathways to Work schemes; and (2) major reform of IB and disability benefits. The latter agenda was framed as one of revising 'rights and responsibilities': 'it is right to expect those in receipt of incapacity benefits to look for work and take up opportunities to train for work where they can' in return for safeguarding 'their rights to financial security' when they cannot work and offering 'more help to take up work' (DWP, 2005, p 9). However, the proposals involved benefit cuts. The proposals were to replace IB with a new benefit (which became the Employment Support Allowance). On making a claim for the new benefit, claimants would enter an initial period of assessment and receive 'a holding benefit' set at the weekly level for JSA. Claimants would undergo a Personal Capacity Assessment which sought to establish what 'people can do' rather than what they 'cannot do' in terms of physical and mental capabilities, skills and suitable paid work/hours of work (DWP, 2005). Following this assessment, claimants with less severe disabilities would receive a form of in-work disability benefit, while those with more severe disabilities would receive a new disability allowance 'set at a higher rate than current disability benefits' (DWP, 2005). Receipt of the in-work benefit would be conditional on attending work-related interviews and activities, as well as taking up paid work if it was deemed appropriate. 'Those refusing to comply' would move onto JSA, leading in effect to benefit cuts for this group (DWP, 2005). Disability campaigners criticised the further entrenchment of the medical model of disability within these reforms; the demeaning portrayal of disabled people as an economic burden and work shy, and the resulting heightened risk of poverty from benefit cuts (Disability Alliance, 2007). Campaigners shared a concern about the extremely low employment rates and high risk of poverty among disabled people[6] but called for stronger anti-discrimination measures and more investment in personalised employment support, particularly for those with mental health problems and learning difficulties (Disability Alliance, 2007).

Welfare reform increasingly focused on 'economic inactive' groups. The Green Paper *Empowering people into work* (DWP, 2006a) went further in constructing claimants as work shy and welfare dependent. Lone parents were to make more 'serious efforts to return to work, especially once their youngest child goes to secondary school' (DWP, 2006a, p 8). The DWP sought to move 300,000 more lone parents from welfare into paid work by 2010. This would be achieved by increasing the financial incentives for lone parents to move into work and work conditions. These reforms were in line with the OECD recommendation that the UK increase work expectations on lone parents (OECD, 2005). The DWP further set a target to 'reduce by 1 million those on incapacity benefits by 2015', mainly via major reform of incapacity benefits and more investment in Pathways to Work schemes (DWP, 2006a). The 2006 Green Paper also proposed major benefit reform, moving towards a 'single system of benefits for all people of working age, with appropriate additions for those who have caring responsibilities and those with a long-term illness or disability' (DWP, 2006a, p 92).

Child maintenance reforms

Before the 2004 Child Poverty Review, Labour had not pursued many child support reforms, apart from allowing lone parents in receipt of IS to receive £10 of any child maintenance and lone parents working under 16 hours a week, £20 a week. Child poverty concerns, however, led to legislation that extended state powers to penalise non-resident and resident parents for misleading or not cooperating with the Child Support Agency (CSA) and to seek medical proof of paternity. Since its conception, though, the CSA (the agency responsible for assessing, collecting and administering child maintenance payments) had courted controversy. Under pressure to reform the system and take forward the aims of the 2004 Child Poverty Review, Sir David Henshaw was commissioned to review the child maintenance system (Henshaw, 2006, p 1). Henshaw (2006) concluded that the system was unfair, ineffective and inefficient. Based on a comparison of child support systems abroad, mainly the Australian system, Henshaw (2006) proposed an alternative approach. He believed that the child maintenance system should be more supportive, encouraging parents to make their own private maintenance arrangements and helping them to 'fulfil their financial responsibilities for their children' (Henshaw, 2006). It was proposed that the CSA be replaced by a new Commission which would facilitate private child maintenance agreements by offering support, information and legal advice to any parents who wanted it and, possibly, charging parents for the service. Henshaw (2006) was mindful of the role of the state in respect of child welfare and poverty. Hence, the state, according to Henshaw (2006), should intervene where necessary as an enforcement agency and assess, police and administer child maintenance payments in cases where 'parents cannot agree' or 'where one party tries to evade their responsibilities' (Henshaw, 2006, p 5). This agency could be a specialist arm of the new Commission and given new powers to penalise non-resident parents who refused to pay maintenance by, for example, withdrawing driving licences or passports (Henshaw, 2006). These measures could lead to higher rates of maintenance payments, which, it was claimed, could help lift 120,000 children out of poverty and lead to a 10% reduction in child poverty rates by 2010 (Henshaw, 2006, p 5).

This review informed the 2006 White Paper *A new system of child maintenance* (DWP, 2006b). The CSA was abolished and a new Child Maintenance Enforcement Commission (C-MEC) established. The aims of reform were framed as tackling child poverty and promoting a clearer framework of parental rights and responsibilities. Parental rights in this case were informed by notions of the consumer-citizen, as the role of the state had become one of providing a service which was purchased. The C-MEC would provide information and guidance to parents in making private maintenance arrangements. The White Paper proposed the phasing out of state retention of child maintenance payments for lone parents on benefits – although this would not commence until 2010/11. A 'tougher enforcement regime' was to be introduced to 'force payment where necessary' (DWP, 2006b, p 5). The government went so far as proposing to provide C-MEC with powers to suspend passports, impose curfews, withhold wages and take payments directly from bank accounts in respect of prosecution action against non-resident parents (DWP, 2006b, p 8). The Child Maintenance and Other Payments Act 2008 enacted many of these changes to the child maintenance system. The Welfare Reform Act 2009 introduced the requirement for the joint registration of births and extended state powers for enforcing child maintenance payments.

Towards a revised welfare contract

In the initial years of Labour's third term in office, a number of influential policy reviews were published (ie Harker, 2006; Leitch Review, 2006; Freud, 2007). Commissioned back in 2004, the final report of the Leitch Review identified severe shortages in 'basic, intermediate and technical skills' in the UK economy – as detailed in Chapter Three (Leitch Review, 2006, p 1). The Leitch Review highlighted the strong correlation between having no or low qualifications and welfare reliance. It called for investment in adult basic skills and vocational training; the establishment of a new 'integrated employment and skills service'; and legislation to make it law that young people remain in full-time education until they are 18 years old. The Leitch Review argued that if the UK were in the top 25% of OECD countries for educational attainment and skills by 2020, GDP could rise by 10%.

In 2004/05 the government narrowly missed the child poverty reduction target. The DWP commissioned Lisa Harker to undertake a policy review. Alongside reforms to increase family incomes, Harker (2006) criticised the lack of 'a family focus' in welfare to work initiatives. Beyond the NDLP, parents were not identified, targeted or supported as parents. Harker (2006) proposed that the NDLP scheme become a 'New Deal for Parents' and called for more in-work support for parents. Further, the welfare system focused on the child maintenance responsibilities of non-resident parents, but did not promote their social rights. Harker (2006) pressed the government to deliver on its National Childcare Strategy before increasing mandatory work requirements for lone parents. The government responded with further childcare reforms (see Chapter Six).

A few months later, Freud's (2007, p 3) review of welfare to work policies argued for more conditional welfare rights; employability schemes for those 'furthest away from the labour market' and major benefit reform. Freud evoked images of an underclass 'permanently cut off from the labour market' who were 'the most socially excluded', 'the lowest skilled', suffering from 'multiple disadvantage' and 'complex and demanding problems' (Freud, 2007). According to Freud (2007), the next steps in welfare reform were to: (1) reduce the numbers of claims for inactive benefits via stricter work conditionalities and benefit reform, and (2) invest in 'intensive' and 'personalised' welfare to work programmes for 'the lowest skilled' and long-term welfare reliant. Freud (2007, pp 8–9) recommended 'introducing stronger conditionality in line with Jobseeker's Allowance for lone parents with children aged 12 years and over ... as soon as is practicable', followed by the gradual extension of higher work conditions for lone parents with children aged between 10 and 12 years; and to 'move to deliver conditionality for other groups (including people already on incapacity benefits) along the lines of *Pathways to Work* and the *Employment and Support Allowance*'. Freud (2007) claimed that a 40% reduction in economic inactivity rates could lead to savings of £4,000–£9,000 per claimant.

Informed by these recommendations, welfare to work reforms took a decidedly 'human capital turn' as well as an increased 'work-first' emphasis. The 2007 Green Paper *In work, better off: Next steps to employment* (DWP, 2007b, p 4) announced 'a new social contract with lone parents' and proposed that from October 2008 lone parents in receipt of IS and whose child was 12 years or over would be transferred to JSA. The Green Paper proposed that from October 2010 lone parents in receipt of IS with a child 7 years or older would not be eligible for IS but, rather, eligible for JSA. In 2007, the DWP announced an intermediate stage, with out-of-work lone parents with children aged 10 and over no longer eligible for IS from October 2009. The 'new social contract' became a three-way contract between employers, citizens and the state. Employers were encouraged to 'pledge to employ welfare to work claimants' via participation in Local Employment Partnerships and the 'jobs pledge' (where major employers pledge 'to offer a quarter of a million job opportunities to people who are at a disadvantage in the labour market – such as lone parents and those on incapacity benefits', DWP, 2007a, p 6). Through a new 'right to request time off to train', employers were encouraged to allow employees time off for training. The role of the state was set to 'guarantee employers ... that job applicants will have the right attitude to work as well as the right aptitude' (DWP, 2007a, p 9). In return, apart from the severely disabled and parents responsible for children under 1 year old, citizens were assumed to be 'capable of work' and expected to 'undertake the training necessary' to find work and 'take up the job opportunities that are available' (DWP and DIUS, 2007, p 6).

Perhaps informed by Harker's criticisms of the overwhelming focus on lone parents, the Green Paper *In work, better off* (DWP, 2007b) included a section about 'parents' as opposed to just 'lone parents'. The Green Paper set out further childcare reforms (ie piloting upfront and full payments for childcare for working parents in London); and more financial incentives to move from welfare into work (DWP, 2007b). A 'New Deal Plus for Parents' was piloted in several areas and in London; mandatory work-focused interviews every six months for partners of JSA claimants with children were introduced; work trials for lone parents via the NDLP scheme were introduced and mandatory 'skills checks' for lone parents in receipt of JSA and IS were proposed. Increasingly, Sure Start Children's Centres were expected to work in partnership with Jobcentre Plus, providing back-to-work advice and support to parents (DWP, 2007b; see Chapter Six).

Investing in skills gaps

From 2007, a 'human capital' approach increasingly informed welfare to work initiatives. The Leitch Review (2006) set out three foci for reform. Firstly, it called for reform of the adult skills and training sector. The government announced the establishment of employer-led Employment and Skills Boards to identify sector-specific skills gaps and coordinate local developments; free basic numeracy and literacy courses for adults without basic qualifications; increases in funding for Level 2 and 3 training; more apprenticeships for young people; increased investment in workplace training via the Train to Gain and a new online Skills Account service. Secondly, Leitch (2006) called for an integrated adult careers and employment service within the welfare system. A joint report was then published by the new Department for Innovation, Universities and Skills (DIUS) and the DWP, stating that:

> welfare to work is no longer just about placing people in jobs but more and more about education and training to make Britain's workforce benefit from the challenges and opportunities of a globalised world. (DWP and DIUS, 2007, p 8)

From 2009, Jobcentre Plus started to undertake 'skills checks' and operate a new 'adult careers service'. Lastly, Leitch (2006, p 2) emphasised the need for a change in attitudes – both employees' and employers'. Alongside public awareness campaigns promoting further education and training, and the new online Skills Account service, the government introduced a 'right to request time off for training' in 2009. The Education and Skills Act 2008 required young people to remain in full-time education or training until the age of 18 and placed a duty on Learning and Skills Councils to grant adults free basic skills and first full Level 2 qualifications courses and to ensure that young people aged 19–25 years did not pay tuition fees for their first Level 3 course.

Disability benefits reform

Benefit reform had focused on the abolition of lone parent-specific entitlements and changes to disability benefits. From 2005 the DWP reviewed changes to IB. The Welfare Reform Act 2007 introduced, from 2008, a new regime for incapacity and disability benefits whereby new claimants were assessed in terms of what 'they can do' using the new Work Capability Assessments and received JSA benefit rates until their assessments were complete. Following these assessments, claimants could either remain on JSA; be awarded a lower rate of the new Employment and Support Allowance (ESA) (and be expected to participate in back-to-work schemes) or a higher rate of the ESA (for those with more severe disabilities or health problems who could voluntarily participate in back-to-work schemes).

A flexible New Deal offering 'progression into work' for all

The White Paper *Raising expectations and increasing support: Reforming welfare for the future* reorganised welfare to work schemes around 'a system of progression into work for all' (DWP, 2008b). The new welfare to work system was based on three categories: (1) those not subject to work conditionalities (a shrinking group reduced to lone parents in receipt of out-of-work benefits; JSA claimant partners whose youngest child was under 1 year old; and severely disabled people); (2) those expected to be 'progressing into paid work' (including lone parents and JSA claimant partners with children aged between 1 and 7 years; claimants receiving the new ESA; and new JSA claimants) and (3) a 'ready for work' group (including lone parents and JSA claimant partners with children aged 7 years and over; ESA claimants and JSA claimants). A new Flexible New Deal would be introduced from 2009 to serve these groups and would replace the NDYP, New Deal 25+ and Employment Zones schemes. The Flexible New Deal system was based on a system of 'increasing responsibilities and support for employment the longer someone is on JSA or ESA benefits' (DWP, 2008b, p 13). JSA and ESA claimants would initially enter a three-month period on benefit whereby they would experience gradual reductions in choice over whether to work and which job they had: 'job search requirements would be widened, based on travel to work, wage and working hours rather than by preferred employment or occupation' (DWP, 2008b, p 13). This would be followed by a 'further three months' whereby claimants would 'enter the Gateway stage with a formal review with a personal adviser to revisit the needs identified in the earlier Jobseeker's Agreement and to draw up a back-to-work action plan'. The 'agreed activities' would be mandatory and subject to benefit-loss sanctions for non-compliance. If a claimant then remained on JSA or ESA after 12 months they 'would be referred to a specialist return to work provider from the public, private, or voluntary sectors who would provide the most appropriate intensive, outcome-focused service, funded on the basis of results' (DWP, 2008b, p 14). After two years on out-of-work benefits, claimants would be compelled to undertake full-time work experience 'to develop their work habits and employability' (DWP, 2008b). While these reforms in 2007/08 were legitimated in terms of 'promoting the right to employment among economically inactive groups', after economic recession hit in 2008 they were framed in terms of 'containing unemployment' (HM Government, 2009a). Work conditions in the benefit system would be increased through this regime, and welfare to work schemes were incorporating a notion of mandatory and prescribed employment options rather than employment based on claimant choice or preference.

Gregg (2008), however, set out a different direction for further reform, based on an independent international evaluation of welfare to work schemes. Gregg (2008) was in favour of conditional welfare rights and reported evidence that welfare to work schemes were effective in moving people from welfare into paid work. However, Gregg (2008) warned that workfare schemes can be stigmatising and, presenting evidence from the US workfare schemes, suggested that social exclusion may be increased if individuals and families are 'disconnected' from social security, the labour market and social services. Gregg (2008) argued that effective welfare to work schemes combine: (1) personalised flexible support appropriate to claimants' support needs; (2) regular contact with personal advisers, and (3) appropriate, clear and effective sanctions. In respect of the UK schemes, Gregg (2008) highlighted the key role of the personal adviser and their expertise in working with claimant groups. Gregg (2008) argued that the UK system suffered from low take-up in respect of voluntary schemes; a complex and incoherent benefit system; a misunderstood system of sanctions; and inadequate support (such as for those affected by issues of poor health, disability, drugs/alcohol addictions, low skills and childcare needs). The latter issues required a more responsive system of support and comprehensive assessment of service-users' needs. Organising the system around claimant groups or length of claim was limited in this respect.

Towards a single working age benefit?

In their report about the introduction of a single working-age benefit in the UK, Sainsbury and Stanley (2007) stated that 'benefit reform' had been 'the missing jigsaw piece' in Labour's welfare reforms. While a range of policies sought to 'reform welfare around paid work', they argued that the benefit system continued to restrict opportunity and trap people on benefit while being inefficient and costly to administer (Sainsbury and Stanley, 2007). The new ESA system was criticised for not simplifying the system and for sustaining disincentives to work. Other influential policy actors promoted the introduction of a single working-age benefit (Freud, 2007; *Official Journal of the Council of Europe*, 2007). A step towards a single benefit system was taken via the Welfare Reform Act 2009, which legislated to replace IS with a system based simply on JSA or ESA. This piece of legislation extended work conditionalities with new requirements for ESA claimants and partners of JSA claimants to undertake job search activities as a condition of benefit receipt, and increased the benefit sanctions for non-compliance. Gregg (2008) supported the introduction of a single working-age benefit if this was combined with a more comprehensive and effective assessment of new benefit claims in terms of work aspirations and support needs, and backed up by an effective, flexible and responsive set of support services and training options.

Policy impacts and critique

Labour's welfare reforms were extensively evaluated (Hills et al, 2009). Official statistics show significant increases in employment rates and reductions in unemployment and child poverty – trends that were noted in Part One of this book (Hills et al, 2009; ONS, 2010a). However, child poverty returned to an upward trend from 2004/05, and economic recession from 2008 reversed employment/unemployment trends (although there is an argument that Labour's welfare reforms helped to reduce the amount and length of unemployment since 2008 (Gregg, 2008)). Levels of economic inactivity rose slightly, from 20% to 22%, between 1997 and 2009 (ONS, 2010a). When analysed in terms of maternal and paternal employment patterns and family/household income trends, there were significant increases in parental employment and reductions in family/child poverty under Labour (see Chapter Three). Brewer et al (2007) showed that the reduced number of children in workless families was a major contributor to the fall in child poverty between 1998 and 2004. Stewart (2009) found that the largest reductions in child poverty rates coincided with increases in CB, IS, tax credits and the NMW. Sefton et al (2009, p 29) found that there had been some redistribution of income towards families with children: 'the risk of poverty for children and their parents has fallen most among lone-parent families (in or out of work) with smaller reductions among workless couples and couples where one parent is not working or both are working part-time'. Millar and Gardiner (2004) also found that low-income, lone-parent family households had benefited the most from Labour's financial support measures for families. However, relative child poverty has increased again since 2004/05. Stewart (2009) associated the slowdown in child poverty reductions with a lack of sustained increase in public expenditure on financial support for families since 2004/05. Moreover, systematic patterns of labour market inequalities and disadvantage remain significant (see Chapter Three). There remain significant regional and local variations in average employment, unemployment and economic inactive rates (ONS, 2010a). Disabled people, people with long-term health problems, those with the lowest qualifications and young people, in particular, have seen their employment prospects change little or even get worse (see Chapter Three).

Another policy impact is the revised welfare contract. Labour reformulated the rights and responsibilities of parent-citizens in the following ways:

- rights and responsibilities have become more aligned with participation in the labour market and employability schemes;
- welfare rights have become more conditional on regular engagement with state, medical assessment of health and disability, and employability measures;
- partners of out-of-work claimants have responsibilities to engage in welfare to work measures;
- deserving low-income paid workers have gained new rights to in-work financial support;
- deserving low-income families and children have gained new rights to financial support;
- welfare rights have become more conditional on behavioural change and withdrawn for undeserving citizens;
- welfare rights for non-resident fathers could become more conditional on providing maintenance for birth children;
- the child support system attends more to the rights of the consumer-citizen, with the state providing a support and enforcement service purchased by parent-consumers.

Overall, welfare rights have become more conditional and those considered legitimately 'economically inactive' are an ever smaller group – lone parents with children under 1 year old and the severely disabled. In the JSA regime conditional work responsibilities now encompass responsibility to take up available paid work rather than preferred paid work. These developments aim to promote active citizenship. For parents, active citizenship refers to their rights and responsibilities as adult citizens and their rights and responsibilities as parents (to raise 'future active citizens') (Lister, 2002). Labour's approach, however, risked elevating paid work and economic responsibilities above parental responsibilities for caring for children, and meant the welfare system did not support parents as parents or promote key aspects of child and family well-being – such as via reducing poverty, 'being there' for children or addressing family and child welfare problems (via comprehensive welfare needs assessments within welfare to work schemes). On coming into office the new Conservative-Liberal Democrat Coalition government indicated alternative directions in welfare rights recognition combined with further extensions to the responsibilities agenda. In the new policy context of severe public spending cuts, welfare rights to financial support for families with children are under review. The commitment to progressive universalism within state-provided financial support for families with children is under threat. Proposals for welfare to work reform suggest policy priorities remain benefit system simplification and enhancing the outsourced nature of employability schemes (HM Government, 2010). There are proposals to integrate welfare to work schemes into one unified system (HM Government, 2010). These priorities are justified on the grounds of public spending cuts and improving cost-effectiveness but also entail commodification and responsibilisation, emphasising citizen responsibilities for economic self-sufficiency and labour market participation.

Conclusion

This chapter has reviewed Labour's welfare to work and financial support for families policies. Policy developments were driven by an agenda to revise citizen rights and responsibilities, raise employment rates and reduce child poverty. The focus on children led to revisions in parental responsibilities for children and parental rights to financial support and targeted services. However, families, adults and children require better welfare rights in order to escape poverty, and employment rights need to be more effectively implemented so as to address labour market disadvantage. Welfare to work reform has not effectively developed a 'needs-led' system to enabling employment opportunity and has not taken account of gender and social inequalities in and beyond the labour market.

Notes

[1] Incapacity Benefit is a contribution-based weekly payment for people who become unable to work due to poor health or a disability. From October 2008 this was replaced by the ESA but IB can still be claimed by people who became ill or disabled before October 2008 (www.direct.gov.uk/en/DisabledPeople/FinancialSupport/DG_10016082?, accessed 13 March 2010).

[2] Child Benefit is a universal cash benefit paid to families with children aged 16 and under, and unmarried children aged 16–19 years in full-time education. The benefit is set at a higher rate for the first child.

[3] Income Support is a means-tested income benefit for people who do have to sign on as unemployed. To qualify for IS you need to be of working age (over 16 years old and under pension age), work less than 16 hours a week, have a low income, have low savings and not receive Employment Support Allowance. Refugees, lone parents and parents on parental/paternity leave may be eligible for IS (although Labour reduced entitlements for lone parents).

[4] Jobseeker's Allowance is the main unemployment benefit for people of working age. To claim, you need to be actively seeking work and aged over 18 years.

[5] Housing Benefit is a means-tested benefit for help with rent payments, available to those working and not working.

[6] The employment rate for working-age (registered) disabled people stood at 46.3% in 2005. This was a lower rate than for the lowest qualified (49.6%); lone parents (56.6%); ethnic minorities (58.4%) and the over 50s (70.7%) (www.dwp.gov.uk/publications/policy-publications/opportunity-for-all/indicators/table-of-indicators/people-of-working-age/indicator-19/).

SIX

Childcare and family-friendly employment policies

Introduction

This chapter reviews developments in childcare and family-friendly employment policies. Policy discourses distinguish between parental, informal and formal childcare; different types of formal services and different sectors (ie private or statutory provision). Chapter Four considered how childcare policies in the UK prior to 1997 were shaped by the division between 'care' and 'education', and state provision was restricted to families in need (Randall, 2000). Local childcare services, however, varied somewhat, as local authorities (LAs) have much say over local services and because education, health and social services are devolved areas of policy. 'Family-friendly employment' relates to employment rights, policies and practices targeted at parents, carers and families with children. The British Workplace Employment Relations Survey (WERS) collects data on the following measures: maternity leave and pay, paternity leave and pay, parental leave, job sharing, flexible working hours, home working, support for carers, time off for emergencies and childcare provision. The focus of this chapter is national family-friendly employment policies and changes in statutory rights and entitlements. The broader term of 'work–life balance' policies is often used interchangeably with family-friendly employment, and encompasses a broader perspective about work–life balance entitlements (potentially for all citizens). For the purposes of this chapter, however, the focus is changes to parental rights. In contrast to childcare policy, employment is not a devolved area of policy, placing constraints on alternative policy directions in Scotland, Northern Ireland and Wales.

Chapter Three highlighted the radical departures in policy since 1997. This chapter details the priority given to childcare, early education and family-friendly employment reforms under Labour. These issues were central to Labour's macro-economic policies (to raise productivity via full employment and investing in human capital) and became increasingly important to Labour's social policy objectives: 'investing in children', reducing and preventing social exclusion and reducing 'anti-social behaviour'. Between 1997 and 2010, the state took on new responsibilities for childcare provision and pre-school education. Parents gained rights to access childcare to enable them to take up paid work and training. Parental employment rights to maternity, paternity, parental and adoption leave and pay were strengthened. Working parents gained new rights to request flexible working options. These developments championed the rights of working parents and the educational needs of disadvantaged children, and were supported by human rights and anti-discrimination legislation (although these developments are not reviewed in this book). However, policy targets for improving the 'cost, accessibility and affordability' of formal childcare were not met and the policy approach in both areas was limited in respect of changing the gendered division of labour in the private and public spheres. Labour was critiqued for a 'consumerist' approach to childcare, for too much reliance on targeted, area-based provision, and for putting 'business rather than families and children first' in employment policies (Lewis, 2009). The childcare and family-friendly employment policies of the new Conservative-Liberal Democrat Coalition government appear to represent considerable cross-party consensus on these issues. This chapter reviews the key policy developments and their impact in terms of overarching policy objectives and reformulations of parental rights and responsibilities.

Policy developments

Implementing EU Directives

Chapter Four discussed the limited paternity and parental leave rights in the UK in the late 1990s. On coming to office, Labour implemented several EU Directives and stated that policy in this area 'support[s] family life' while 'protecting business from undue burdens' (Labour Party, 1997, p 25). In 1998 the European Time Directive came into force, introducing a maximum working week of 48 hours; rights to annual leave of at least 21 days; and rights to minimum weekly rest periods. However, the Labour government amended the Directive to allow individual employees to opt out under certain conditions and was subsequently found guilty of inadequate implementation. The EU Directive on Part-time Workers was agreed in December 1997 and came into force in July 2000. This granted part-time workers the same employment rights as full-time workers and made it unlawful to treat part-time workers 'less favourably'. The EU Directive on Time Off for Emergencies was implemented, granting employees reasonable time off for emergencies involving dependants. These were progressive developments but Labour's approach could be described as one of minimal compliance – indicating continuity in British employment laws.

Towards the 1998 National Childcare Strategy

Chapter Four highlighted developments in formal childcare provision prior to 1997 such as the introduction of Family Credit (an in-work benefit for low-income working parents); the nursery voucher scheme (a demand-side subsidy to enable parents to purchase pre-school nursery provision, thus stimulating supply); and investment in out-of-school clubs (Randall, 2000).

Childcare policy became a high priority under Labour. On coming to office, New Labour promised the first peacetime 'national childcare strategy', the aims of which were to:

(1) 'increase the provision of formal childcare to match the requirements of the modern labour market and help parents, especially women, to balance family and working life';
(2) reduce gaps in educational attainment between poorer and better-off children – 'Labour's number one priority' – by expanding pre-school opportunities for young children and out-of-school clubs for young people;
(3) reduce youth anti-social behaviour and crime by improving educational opportunities and investing in more supervised recreational opportunities for young people (Labour Party, 1997, p 24).

Childcare therefore was aligned with Labour's welfare to work and employment opportunity agendas as well as with the objectives of education and criminal justice policies. Labour took forward ideas proposed by childcare experts and developed elsewhere, particular in the US. Labour piloted Early Excellence Centres (EECs) from December 1997. Drawing on models of integrated early years services and 'educare', EECs sought to 'give a practical reality to joined-up thinking, offering one-stop-shops where families and children can have access to high quality integrated care and education services delivered by multi-agency partners within one centre or a network of centres' (Bertram et al, 2002, p 1). The EEC pilots were funded to provide integrated early education and day care provision with additional family services and to promote good practice locally. Labour's commitment to pre-school educational opportunities led to free (fully state subsidised) part-time nursery provision for all 4-year-olds.

Chapter Five charted the development of Labour's child poverty reduction and family support agendas from 1997 to 1999. The National Childcare Strategy (NCS) was published in 1998 and, echoing the slogan of the 1980s childcare campaign by the Daycare Trust, sought to improve the 'affordability, availability and quality' of formal childcare services and 'support parents and informal carers' (DfEE, 1998). The first three aims dominated reform. Central–local responsibilities for childcare were revised. The DfEE became the lead department for childcare policy and local Early Years Partnerships (EYPs) were introduced (formalised networks, usually dominated by statutory agencies, representing the main local stakeholders and sectors in the childcare and early years field). From 1998, local authorities (LAs) were asked to develop EYPs into Early Years Development and Childcare Partnerships (EYDCPs), responsible for 'all forms of formal provision for children up to the age of 14' (DfEE, 1998, p 8) and including a wider range of local stakeholders and providers, including parents, private sector providers, the voluntary sector and childcare training bodies. In the first instance, EYDCPs were to review provision and demand and produce a 'local childcare plan' by April 1999 (DfEE, 1998, p 16). The NCS aimed to 'fill the gaps in formal services' by stimulating market provision via supply–side subsidies for providers and demand–side subsidies for parents. The bulk of supply–side investment was

Table 6.1: Types of formal childcare in England

Service	Overview of service	Age range	Type of provider
Day nursery	Full- or part-time day care, education and play for children below compulsory school age.	0–5 years	Public, private or voluntary
Nursery school	Education of pre-school age children. Staffed with a high ratio of qualified teachers.	3–4 years	Public or private
Nursery class	Can be attended either full or part time one year before a child starts compulsory education. Term-time only.	3–4 years	Public
Pre-school playgroup	Part-time playgroup sessions for 2–3 hours each week day.	2.5–5 years	Private or voluntary
Childminder	Self-employed person who provides day care for more than two hours a day. Care is usually provided in the childminder's home. Hours can be flexible.	Up to 8 years, sometimes older	Private
Reception class in a primary or infant school	Children attend a reception class in a school setting before starting compulsory education. Reception classes have the highest child: staff ratios.	4–5 years	Public or private
After-school, out-of-school care, breakfast clubs or holiday schemes	Cater for children of school age before or after school or in the school holiday. Provision can supply a range of play, recreational or educational activities.	Mainly 5–14 years	Public, private or voluntary
Creches	Short-term childcare for young children. Can operate all week or on a session basis.	0–5 years	Private or voluntary
Nannies/au pairs	Qualified or unqualified nannies and au pairs can be employed to care for one or more children in their own home.	0–14 years	Private

Source: NAO (2004, p 5).

for the creation of new out-of-school childcare places and the provision of free part-time nursery places (amounting to 12.5 hours a week) during term time for all 4-year-olds by September 1998. This expansion required workforce expansion. The DfEE proposed a national recruitment campaign and targeted recruitment via the New Deal schemes – especially the New Deal for Lone Parents. To boost demand, the NCS pointed to the role of Labour's financial support measures – the increases in CB; help with childcare costs via the New Deal schemes; and introduction of the WFTC (see Chapter Five). To improve the 'accessibility of formal childcare', the DfEE announced £300 million for subsidising providers and a childcare information service for parents and carers. To improve 'quality', the government had already announced a review in systems of registration and quality assurance across the formal childcare sector; had transferred responsibility for day care from the Department of Health to the DfEE (in an attempt to bridge the divides between care and education, and in response to new discourse about 'integrated care and education' provision); and had invested in the EEC pilots. The 1998 NCS announced a doubling of investment in EECs. Standards in childcare and early education were to be raised via the introduction of a new early years curriculum and 'early learning goals' which all providers registered to provide early education would be required to implement. The quality of out-of-school provision was a major priority. Local education authorities (LEAs) became responsible for the registration and regulation of out-of-school activities and this provision was linked to national curriculum objectives. It was announced that £15 million from the New Opportunities Fund would be invested between 1999 and 2003 in the 'development of integrated out-of-school childcare and study support schemes in England' (DfEE, 1998, p 20). Investment was targeted at economically deprived areas, with £2 million for the development of early years provision in Education Action Zones.[1] The NCS also aimed to 'support parenting in the early years' and support 'informal arrangements' (DfEE, 1998). This reflected a new 'parenting' agenda and could have led to investment in universal community facilities and services for families with young children. However, in practice, proposals in these areas were limited, reflecting the 'private' nature of these issues and clear focus on early education for children aged 3–5 and childcare provision for working mothers.

Following the turn to 'early intervention' in Labour's social inclusion agenda, interest grew in integrated services for families with young children living in deprived areas. In 1998 the Sure Start programme was announced, backed up with £540 million of investment. By 2001 the government sought to establish 250 Sure Start Local Programmes (SSLPs) in the 20% most deprived wards in England. This programme is discussed in Chapter Seven. Here it is important to note that Sure Start aimed to provide 'a seamless' range of early years and family services to all families with children under 4 years old living in designated Sure Start areas (deprived neighbourhoods). In comparison to EECs, SSLPs reflected a stronger focus on health and family support services. Initially, SSLPs were given flexibility on whether to deliver full-day childcare and early education.

The NCS established more state responsibility for childcare services for poor children and working parents. However, the substance was not sufficient to meet the vision (Lewis, 2003). Neglected issues included: the rising and relatively high cost of day care; the gendered division of labour in respect of informal childcare and the childcare workforce; children's rights; the low status and pay of the childcare workforce; the inequity of the mixed economy of childcare and state provision of childcare for children in need or in the care system. Funding appeared to be limited in comparison to the investment needed. Harker (1998, p 462) commented that 'kids clubs are the big winners of the national childcare strategy', receiving 90% of the funding announced. Harker (1998, p 462) stated that 'the sums going towards developing services for children under school age were paltry by comparison: in 1998/99 only £7.5 million of a total of £57 million was specifically earmarked for this age group'. The main demand-side initiative was the childcare tax credit, but this was only available to parents working more than 16 hours a week and covered 70% of childcare costs. Further, in the context of inadequate funding, trade-offs arose between the aims of the NCS. Measures to improve the quality of childcare push up the costs of providing, regulating and paying for childcare and are likely to drive out some childcare providers – which occurred in respect of childminders or playgroups – thereby reducing local choice (Lewis, 2003). Another uncertainty was whether the NCS could deliver the promise of meeting 'the full range of children's and families' needs' (DfEE, 1998, pp 4–5). From an employment perspective, few jobs would fit around the part-time term-time provision for parents of 4-year-olds. There was only a passing reference made to children with special educational needs and no mention of culturally sensitive childcare services. Other overarching issues were, arguably, inconsistent views about the needs of young children, and parental rights and responsibilities as carers versus paid workers. 'Quality childcare' was defined, on the one hand, as caring adult–child attachments, primarily provided in the context of the family. But, on the other hand, quality childcare was provided by professional childcarers and led to early educational outcomes. Ultimately, 'care and education' were at the heart of 'educare'. Quality 'educare' requires good staff training and a lower staff:children ratio. However, in school nursery and reception classes staff:children ratios in the early 2000s could reach 1:18 and 1:30 respectively (Lewis, 2003). Both care and education were stressed as key to children's emotional, social and intellectual development. Mothers and fathers, however, were encouraged to take up paid work and use formal childcare services – in order to raise family incomes and prevent poverty, as well as to promote children's early development. But mothers, and some fathers, may prefer to care for and educate young children themselves and there is inconsistent evidence about whether full-time formal childcare provision is detrimental to children under 3 (Lewis, 2003). The construction of children's needs and parental (mainly maternal) responsibilities within the NCS differed from that in other areas of policy (the Children Act 1989 promoted 'putting children's needs first'). On the other hand, the Green Paper attempted to bridge 'parental choice versus responsibility' discourses, recognising mothers' choice to take up paid work when children were young. Moreover, the Green Paper had very little to say about the role of fathers (fathers were mentioned only four times) and downplayed the overwhelming focus on mothers with the gender-neutral discourse of 'parent'.

Extending parental employment rights

The Employment Relations Act 1999 (ERA) followed the Green Paper *Fairness at work* (DTI, 1998). Labour claimed to seek 'a new industrial relations settlement' between employers, trade unions and employees. The ERA 1999 strengthened statutory rights to form trade unions, maternity leave and pay rights and set out plans to introduce the EU Directive on Parental Leave. Working parents with one year's continuous employment and whose child was born after 15 December 1999 gained entitlements to 13 weeks' unpaid leave before their child's fifth birthday. However, the EU Directive promoted entitlements to take leave up to a child's eighth birthday. Chapter Five described the increase in SMP at this time and the introduction of the maternity allowance for low-income mothers. From April 1999 all mothers earning over £30 a week gained rights to 18 weeks of maternity pay. The rate of maternity pay was also increased from £60 a week to £75 a week from 2000, with a planned increase to £100 a week in 2001. Employees with one year's continuous service were eligible for an extended period of a further 17 weeks of unpaid maternity leave.

The 2000 Green Paper *Work and parents: Competitiveness and choice* (DTI, 2000) set out more ambitious reforms. The proposals related to changes in maternity rights, developments in parental and paternity leave and the introduction of rights to request flexible working options. The Green Paper proposed simplifying maternity rights; increasing the length and pay attached to Statutory Maternity Leave (SML); new rights to 'share' maternity leave with fathers; better maternity rights for employees on casual and temporary contracts; and better rights for parents of adopted children. The Women's Budget Group (2000) criticised the reforms, though, for not adequately raising levels of maternity pay and leaving the majority of the extended leave period unpaid. The 2000 Green Paper further proposed changes to paternity and parental leave. The Green Paper set out plans to introduce two weeks' paid paternity leave for fathers (to be paid at the SMP flat rate). These were limited rights compared to those granted to mothers, sustaining the traditional gender regime. The proposals for parental leave did not respond to some of the criticisms of the current system – such as the limited eligibility criteria or unpaid nature of the leave – but did propose longer leave for parents of disabled children, beyond their entitlement to 18 weeks' leave. The Green Paper announced consultation on granting parental rights to flexible working. In 2000 the work–life balance campaign was launched to promote the business case for family-friendly employment.

Improving access and quality in early education

By 1998 free nursery provision was available to all 4-year-olds. In 1999 the government announced similar provision for all 3-year-olds by 2004. The first Parental Demand for Childcare survey confirmed that lower-income families purchased less formal childcare – trends contrary to policy objectives to increase uptake and employment in these families (La Velle et al, 2000). These concerns prompted the introduction of the Neighbourhood Nurseries Initiative (NNI), whereby highly subsidised 'neighbourhood nurseries' were established in the 20% most deprived areas in England, with funding of £346 million for 2001–04. The aim was to create 45,000 new nursery childcare places for children from birth to school age (aged 0 to 4 years) by 2004 (Smith et al, 2005). Neighbourhood nurseries were encouraged to provide family support, family learning and health services alongside nursery provision (Smith et al, 2005). Following three years of 'pump-priming', NNIs were expected to become sustainable via parental demand and childcare tax credit (Smith et al, 2005). From the outset, though, the area-based approach which underpinned the NNI, akin to Sure Start, was limited, given that the majority of poor families lived outside these areas (Land, 2002).

By the end of Labour's first term in office, 'childcare and education' were better integrated via the Ofsted inspection role and the introduction of the 'Foundation Stage' curriculum and 'Early Learning Goals' for 3- to 5-year-olds.

An extended role for schools

The 2001 Labour Party manifesto stated that 'education remains Labour's top priority' and 'the early years of a child's life are vital' (Labour Party, 2001). Labour intended to increase investment in early education, to better meet the needs of families with disabled children and to promote 'wraparound care' (Labour Party, 2001). Wraparound pilots involved schools providing (directly or in partnership with childcare providers) pre-school childcare. Schools appeared to offer a cost-effective way of increasing the availability and accessibility of childcare. The new Department for Education and Skills (DfES, 2002) then set out a more extensive vision of 'Extended Schools', whereby primary and secondary schools operated as 'the hub of the community' to deliver a range of services to children, young people and families (including day care, pre-school provision, breakfast and after-school clubs, holiday provision, family learning and advice for parents). Following this, the Education Act 2002 encouraged schools to develop 'extended services'. Policy success, however, depended on the willingness and capacity of schools to engage with the vision. By 2002/03, 25 LAs were developing Extended Schools (Sylva and Pugh, 2005).

Extending parental employment rights

In 2001 the Work and Parents Taskforce was established. Key proposals led to the Employment Act 2002. From 2003, SML increased from 18 weeks to 26 weeks and would be paid at a higher rate, increasing from £60.20 per week to £100 per week. From April 2003, fathers were granted rights to two weeks' paid paternity leave (paid at the SMP rate of £100). Basic rights to adoptive leave and pay were set out so that, from 2003, parents adopting a child were eligible for adoption leave and pay equivalent to SML and SMP. Eligibility for adoption leave was dependent on length of employment service and was earnings related. The Employment Act 2002 further set out a new right for employees to request flexible working, and employers had a duty to consider the requests. Employers do not have to accept the request and can refuse it with a viable business case, but employees have the right to receive a formal explanation and to appeal the employer's decision. Parents with children under 6 years old or disabled children under 18 were a priority group.

The 2002 inter-departmental childcare review

At the beginning of Labour's second term in office it established an inter-departmental review of the NCS. At least two factors prompted the review: positive evaluation research findings and evidence of slow progress towards making childcare 'more affordable, accessible and of a better quality'. An extensive national evaluation examined the development and impact of the 29 EEC pilots established by December 1999 (Bertram et al, 2002). The first two reports from the national evaluation of the EEC pilots found beneficial outcomes for children, families and practitioners (Bertram and Pascal, 2001; Bertram et al, 2002). The evaluations found that the early EEC pilots were appropriately developed in areas with higher numbers of families in need and lone parents (Bertram and Pascal, 2001); and that EECs provided the expected range of services for children and families, breaking down the silos between education, social care, childcare and health services, and improving access to services (Bertram and Pascal, 2001, p 35). EECs were found to provide high-quality early education and childcare services, with year-round and extended opening hours and better than average numbers of qualified early years practitioners. The evaluation found that children accessing services over time had improved scores for cognitive development, attitudes and dispositions towards learning, social skills and emotional well-being (Bertram and Pascal, 2001; Bertram et al, 2002). EEC areas also witnessed a decline in the number of children placed on the 'child at risk' register and an increase in the number of children identified as having special educational needs (Bertram and Pascal, 2001, p 32). The national evaluation team found evidence of a range of beneficial outcomes for parents, carers and families, including enhanced confidence, reduced isolation and better access to childcare provision, to enable the take-up of paid work or training opportunities, better access to services and educational opportunities, and improvements in family relationships (Bertram and Pascal, 2000, p 35; Bertram et al, 2002). EECs were highly valued by those families engaging with their services and this was associated with an empowering and inclusive ethos towards working with families. EECs were also found to have better-paid and qualified staff and more staff development opportunities, as compared to other early years settings (Bertram and Pascal, 2000, pp 42–6). However, Bertram et al (2002) found that EECs were mainly providing childcare for 3- to 5-year-olds and called for more research into integrated educare for children under 3 years. Further, the evaluation identified the challenges in developing an integrated ethos, delivering joined-up services, retaining staff and generating funding post the pump-priming period (Bertram et al, 2002).

However, in other respects, progress was patchy. While the National Audit Office (NAO, 2004) found government expenditure[2] on the early years rose from just over £2 billion in 1997/98 to £2.75 billion in 2000/01, the OECD categorised the UK a low investor in pre-school services (OECD social expenditure database: oecd.org/els/social/expenditure). The OECD (2001) argued that low investment threatened policy success, especially for meeting child reduction and lone-parent employment targets for 2010. Further while there was evidence of 'dramatic changes to the landscape of childcare services', the growth in provision was slower than expected; the availability of childcare remained highly variable across localities; improvements in standards and quality were hampered by sustainability and workforce problems; and access to formal services was based on three key factors: where families live, their income and their employment status (NAO, 2004). Although local data on childcare places is not fully reliable, the National Audit Office (NAO, 2004) found that between 1998 and 2003, 626,000 new childcare places had been created for children aged 0–14 years in England, but 301,000 places had closed. Further, the increases in childcare places had not been evenly spread across sectors or geographical areas. The largest growth was in out-of-school places, followed by private day nurseries. There was a decline in the number of childminders – a popular, lower-cost form of childcare which tended to offer more flexible hours of care for parents – and playgroups – also a popular form of provision, particularly for stay-at-home mothers (Lewis, 2003; Sylva and Pugh, 2005). The affordability of childcare remained another critical issue. Alongside the limitations of the eligibility criteria for tax credits (see Chapter Five), the childcare tax credit did not serve the needs of larger families. Beyond those families fortunate enough to be eligible for the childcare tax credit (and who claimed their entitlement) – and those served by Labour's highly subsidised Sure Start, EEC and NNI provision – childcare costs were rising. The Daycare Trust's survey of childcare costs found that the costs rose above the rate of inflation between 1997 and 2001 (Daycare Trust, 2002). This survey found the typical cost for a full-time nursery place for a child under 2 years old was £120 a week, or

£6,200 a year in 2001 (Daycare Trust, 2002). But costs rose to £150–£200 a week in the South East.

In response, the government established a cross-departmental review. This set out 'a vision for 2010 for childcare in England': that 'every parent should be able to access affordable and quality childcare' (Cabinet Office, 2002, p 4). The 2002 Review prioritised:

(1) investment to boost the supply and use of formal childcare in deprived areas and among low-income families via short-term pump-priming to providers in deprived areas and more generous tax credits;
(2) the development of Children's Centres and Extended Schools;
(3) local childcare places targets;
(4) targeted funding and support to address sustainability problems for childminders and out-of-school clubs;
(5) the need to address 'initiative confusion' and the 'patchwork of provision' for parents via mainstreaming initiatives into a single 'brand' (ie EECs, NNIs and SSLPs to become Sure Start Children's Centres), and better information for parents;
(6) better-clarified central–local–EYDCP responsibilities and simplified funding streams.

The 2002 Comprehensive Spending Review (CSR) announced an additional combined budget for childcare, early years services and Sure Start of £1.5 billion between 2002/03 and 2005/06 to create 250,000 new childcare places by 2005/06. This funding would also provide: 'time-limited support' to new childcare providers; a sustainability grant for providers in the 20% most deprived areas; childminder start-up grants; and funds to support local childcare providers (ie to provide 'business support' for out-of-school clubs). Changes to the tax credit system introduced in 2003 increased the financial support for parents (see Chapter Five). All SSLPs, EECs and NNIs were to become Sure Start Children's Centres, mainstreaming these initiatives into one combined model, with some areas receiving capital funds for new centres. However, compared to the SSLPs, childcare and early education was central to the 'core offer'. Children's Centres would provide integrated early education and childcare for at least 5 days a week, 48 weeks a year and 10 hours a day. Children's Centres would employ at least one qualified early years teacher. Alongside childcare, Children's Centres would provide child and family health services, family support services, outreach services, and make links with Jobcentre Plus, adult education providers or welfare benefit services – demonstrating a vision of more joined-up policy making across social security, education and health. The 2002 Review sought to clarify policy and delivery responsibilities. The Sure Start Unit was established to integrate central responsibility for early years, childcare and Sure Start policy and operated as a cross-departmental unit informed by DfES and DWP policy. EYDCPs became subject to new childcare places targets.

While these developments were widely welcomed, they remained limited. In relation to child poverty reduction, campaigners called for Children's Centres to be provided in more local areas, ideally universally across communities (Land, 2002). Universal coverage was necessary to capture the wider population of children in need, as only a third of poor children lived in the 20% most deprived areas (Land, 2002). Further, the reforms continued to rely on two assumptions: (1) that an increase in the supply of formal childcare and the tax credit reforms would enable parents to secure sustainable employment opportunities; and (2) that reliance on 'stimulating the market' via short-term subsidies to providers and demand-side subsidies to parents would deliver 'greater choice to parents' and more 'affordable and higher quality' childcare services. The first of these assumptions was questioned by the vigorous debate about whether factors such as the availability and cost of childcare were the primary factors preventing low-income mothers from taking up paid work or whether mothers' childcare preferences were primary (see Chapter Nine; Duncan et al, 2004). The second was heavily criticised. Land (2002, p. 1) felt that the 'Government was not wise to rely on the private for profit sector to deliver affordable, high quality and sustainable childcare'. Drawing on trends in private sector provision for social and residential care services for older people, Land (2002) argued that: (1) access to private sector services was based on ability to pay; (2) the private sector had a poor record of investing in its workforce (and relied on poorly qualified, young female childcare workers), (3) the private sector charged the highest fees. Land (2002) warned that, as private-for-profit social care agencies were subject to higher quality standards during the 1990s, the number of residential care places fell, small providers went out of business and the private sector lobbied the government to relax the standards or protect providers via guaranteed subsidies to cope with fluctuations in demand and profit. As a result, both of these measures were introduced. Despite this, a postcode lottery remained in social and residential care for older people and the UK workforce was among the 'least qualified and lowest paid' in the EU (Land, 2002).

Supporting and regulating childminders

One development from the 2002 Review was the targeting of investment into childminding. This was in recognition that reform so far had neglected this sector. Research also argued that many childminders were not operating under 'full capacity' and could care for more children (NAO, 2004). Alongside additional funding, Children's Centres were expected to engage with home-based carers and set up initiatives such as childminder groups. The DfES consulted on how to improve standards in childminding. Controversial proposals included stricter bans with respect to childminders smoking while taking care of children and on the use of smacking. Such issues were traditionally thought of as matters of parental choice. Nevertheless, the bans were introduced to bring childminding in line with other sectors and promote child welfare.

Childcare and the 2003 Green Paper Every child matters

In 2003 Labour set out a radical reform of children's services in the Green Paper *Every child matters* (Chief Secretary to the Treasury, 2003; see Chapter Seven). To promote the five key outcomes among children, *Every child matters* proposed child protection reforms, the merger of local social services departments with education departments and other institutional/service delivery reforms which aimed to 'integrate services around children's needs' (Chief Secretary to the Treasury, 2003). A key emphasis was on early intervention and prevention (see Chapter Seven). Alongside 'early intervention' as early years services, it referred to 'intervening [in families] at the earliest stage of a problem' (Chief Secretary to the Treasury, 2003, pp 20–1). Within this preventative agenda, childcare and early education services were described as critical to the 'first tier of services for parents and carers', defined as those services providing universal support and services. In addition, Level 2 services provided 'targeted and specialist services for parents who need additional support' (which included childcare and education for families in need and disabled children) and Level 3 interventions: statutory child protection procedures and compulsory interventions in families to safeguard children (Chief Secretary to the Treasury, 2003). The 2003 Green Paper restated the aim to establish Sure Start Children's Centres in the 20% most deprived wards; to 'promote full service Extended Schools' and to increase out-of-school activities for children and young people.

Towards universal early years and childcare provision

With policy agendas refocused on the *Every child matters* five outcomes for children and reforms under scrutiny against the 2004/05 targets to reduce child poverty and for the lone-parent employment rate, the 2003 Budget announced a Child Poverty Review. Chapter Five detailed the subsequent welfare reforms and Chapter Seven will consider the parent education proposals. However, in relation to childcare, the Child Poverty Review announced investment for another 100,000 childcare places. The Sure Start Unit became subject to new targets and measures: to increase the stock of Ofsted-registered childcare by 10% by 2008; to increase the take-up of formal childcare by lower-income working families by 50% by 2008 and to introduce a 'light touch' childcare approval scheme (HM Treasury et al, 2004). Funding included funds to pilot free part-time nursery provision for 6,000 2-year-olds in disadvantaged areas (HM Treasury et al, 2004, p 105). A further review was announced to examine the childcare needs of parents with disabled children.

Critical to policy developments at this time were the findings of the DfES-sponsored 'effective provision of pre-school education' (EPPE) research project (Sylva et al, 2004). The EPPE study was 'the first major European longitudinal study of young children's development' and examined the effects of pre-school education for 3- and 4-year-olds (Sylva and Pugh, 2005, p 14). The UK study collected data on 3,000 children who had attended 141 early years providers (representing LA day nurseries; integrated centres; playgroups; private day nurseries; nursery schools and nursery classes) and a 'comparison group' of 'home children who had no or minimal' pre-school provision (Sylva and Pugh, 2005). Data was collected on parent–child relationships, parenting, the home environment and characteristics of the pre-school setting. Twelve intensive case studies examined effective practice in settings found to have good outcomes for children. The key findings of the EPPE study were that:

- children attending pre-school provision had enhanced intellectual, social and emotional development compared to children with no pre-school experience;
- these developmental differences persisted when children were assessed at age 7, although 'behavioural outcomes were longer lasting than cognitive ones';
- children from low-income families in particular benefited from quality pre-school provision. Pre-school provision was thought to 'reduce the negative effect of family background and a poor home learning environment' via effective practice with children and engaging parents more in their child's learning;
- disadvantaged children do well in settings where there is a 'mixture of children from different social backgrounds';
- the duration, quality and approach of pre-school provision matters: full-time attendance did not lead to better outcomes for children compared to part-time attendance; commencing pre-school attendance earlier (from a child's third birthday) was positively correlated with stronger effects; and good quality was found in all settings but services based on 'educare' models and integrated early years services performed best. This was related to lower staff:children ratios and better-trained staff;
- 'for all children the quality of the home learning environment promotes more intellectual and social development than parental occupation or qualification';
- the findings were replicated in a study in Northern Ireland (Sylva and Pugh, 2005, p 15).

The EPPE findings provided further evidence that high-quality pre-school provision promoted children's development and raised educational attainment in the first two years of school, particularly among poor children. They led to more investment in early education provision and greater attention towards parental involvement in children's learning and improving 'the home learning environment' (see Chapter Seven).

The *Ten year childcare action plan* (DfES, 2004b) followed, which pledged there would be 2,500 Children's Centres in the 30% most deprived wards by 2008. Parental entitlements to a free part-time pre-school place for all 3- and 4-year-olds were to be extended so that, from 2006, parents would be entitled to 36 weeks as opposed to 33 weeks of provision and, from 2007, parents would be entitled to 15 hours a week of nursery provision rather than 12.5 hours, with more opportunity to make up these hours in flexible ways. The strategy set out a longer-term vision of 20 hours of weekly pre-school provision over 38 weeks of the year. The long-term vision was also to create 3,500 Children's Centres and Extended Schools so that every community would be served by these two key services (DfES, 2004b). Affordability for parents was to be addressed through further increases in tax credits (see Chapter Four). The new Childcare Approval Scheme meant that parents could claim tax credit support for 'home-based care' (ie au pairs and nannies). Sustainability and quality issues for providers were recognised with the announcement of a Transformation Fund worth £125 million to support subsidies to providers and quality-raising initiatives. The strategy further proposed a 'new statutory duty' whereby LAs would be required to ensure there was available childcare for working parents and that provision better met the needs of disabled children and families from ethnic minorities (DfES, 2004b).

In many respects several critical issues were recognised: the need for accessible, high-quality, integrated early education and childcare services; affordability issues; sustainability issues; and the decline in numbers of childminders (Lewis, 2003). Childcare policy had adopted a more pro-universal discourse, prompted by a range of concerns: to increase employment rates, reduce child poverty, improve educational opportunities to children and develop 'early intervention' and preventative services. However, would more universal services mean compromises in quality and funding per centre? The House of Commons Children, Schools and Families Committee (2010) found funding levels per centre were substantially reduced.

Increases in maternity pay and consultation on changes to paternity leave

The previous chapter and the discussion above highlighted the concerted efforts during 2002–04 to review financial support policies for families in an attempt to meet the 2004/05 child poverty reduction targets. From April 2004, SMP was increased to a weekly rate of £102.80 and Statutory Paternity Pay and Statutory Adoption Pay were set at the same level. The 2004 *Ten year childcare strategy* proposed, from 2007, to extend SML to 9 months (rather than 6 months) and to extend SMP from 26 weeks to 39 weeks and, from 2010, to extend SML to 12 months (DfES, 2004b). The government announced a consultation about giving mothers the right to transfer a proportion of their maternity pay to fathers and for fathers to be entitled to better paternity leave. These developments were justified in terms of children's needs in the first year of life for full-time parental care; the benefits of better father involvement in parenting and childcare; and meeting parental preferences for a better work–family balance (DfES, 2004b). However, campaigners emphasised the need for adequate paternity pay to be on the agenda and for a pro-active government campaign to promote these new entitlements among employees and employers (Lewis, 2009). Further, in 2005 the government proposed extending rights to request flexible working options to parents of older children and carers. This subsequently led to the Work and Families Act 2006 whereby, from April 2007, SMP, maternity allowance and adoption pay were paid for 52 weeks rather than 26, and parents and carers of older children gained rights to request flexible working hours.

Rights to childcare for working parents

In May 2005 Labour was elected to a third term. A new Childcare Bill was drafted which proposed: (1) a duty on LAs to manage local childcare markets and ensure there was sufficient childcare to meet the needs of working mothers and fathers; and (2) a requirement that all registered early years childcare settings deliver the Early Years Foundation Stage – a revised early education curriculum for 0–5s. This subsequently led to the Childcare Act 2006 which, from April 2008, placed a 'sufficiency duty' on LAs. The Childcare Act 2006 stated that LAs were not to provide childcare directly unless no other provision was possible, but rather were to assess demand and ensure market supply. The social justice implications have been debated. To effectively exercise this right and have access to quality services, legislation needs to be backed up with sufficient investment in the workforce and with standards (including investment in specialist training for working with children with special educational needs) and more financial support to low-income parents (Lewis, 2003). Ball and Vincent (2005, p 558) argued that the Childcare Act 2006 extended parental rights as consumer-citizens. From a social democratic perspective this expressed limited notions of social justice, as access to provision remained based on ability to pay. This perspective, for Ball and Vincent, is also problematic due to the 'particularities of childcare markets' (ie the lack of parental choice in most areas and the lack of information about day-to-day childcare provision provided to parents) and promoted the commodification of childcare. These researchers sought more commitment to parental and children's rights to information about the quality of care in a childcare setting and a greater voice in the development of childcare policies; more debate about the desirability of the market-based approach; and more debate about what constitutes a quality childcare experience for young children (Ball and Vincent, 2005).

Childcare and the Children's Plan 2007

Following the Childcare Act 2006, the DfES developed a stronger focus on 'workforce reform'. A host of childcare workforce issues needed to be addressed: 'how it is gendered, how it is organised, its pay and other employment conditions, how it is trained and how the work is understood' (Moss, 2003, p 1). Attention was refocused on some of these issues following the UK's poor performance in the UNICEF report on child well-being (UNICEF, 2007; see Chapter Two). In 2007 the DfES became the DCSF and subsequently published the Children's Plan (DCSF, 2007b) (see Chapter Seven). In respect of childcare policy, the Children's Plan on the whole sustained the same policy directions and priorities: seeking to close the gap in educational achievement between advantaged and disadvantaged children, improve children's health, safeguard children and young people, reduce child poverty and promote pro-social behaviour and social inclusion. However, the 2007 Children's Plan reflected a more explicit emphasis on 'children's health' and 'recreational and play services for children and young people' alongside the focus on educational attainment rates. To improve children's outcomes in line with the five *Every child matters* outcomes, the Children's Plan set out the following priorities:

- to invest more in early education provision
- to provide more outreach services via Children's Centres
- to place Children's Centres on a statutory footing so that LAs could sustain them as part of their mandatory duties for children's services
- to invest more in support for families and parents 'so that they can support their child's development'
- to better meet the childcare needs of disabled children
- to develop a child health strategy
- to develop a play strategy, invest more in recreational opportunities and outdoor play facilities for children and young people, and encourage childcare providers to improve outdoor and indoor play facilities where needed
- to develop a 'world class workforce' (DCSF, 2007b).

The early years sector received additional funding for 2008–11: (1) for investment in graduate qualifications for managers of childcare settings (the Graduate Leader Fund); (2) to support staff to train up to NVQ Level 3 (and provide funding for 'cover' while staff attended training); (3) to support providers to deliver the expansion in pre-school nursery provision for 3- and 4-year-olds; and (4) to promote the development of local 'good practice' networks and joint training across sectors. Overall, the government announced that £4 billion would be invested between 2008 and 2011 on Children's Centres, early years education and childcare.

Improving access to childcare

Next steps for early learning and childcare responded to some concerns about slow progress in childcare reform and pressure to improve childcare provision in order to meet lone parents' employment targets (HM Government, 2009a). This review of childcare policy was influenced by the greater emphasis placed on the role of parent–child relationships and parenting in a child's early years (see Chapter Seven). *Next steps* reaffirmed the government's commitment to the NCS in a time of economic recession (HM Government, 2009a). It stated that parents with 2-year-old children living in disadvantaged areas would become entitled to a free nursery place for 10 hours a week over 38 weeks of the year (HM Government, 2009a). LAs were required to produce 'sufficiency action plans' setting out how they would sustain the supply of childcare during the recession (ie through crisis funds to local providers and help for childcare workers to find new jobs) and continue to ensure increases in supply according to local demand. More financial help for parents was on the agenda via promises of free childcare for out-of-work parents taking up training or work and increases in tax credit payments for low-income parents living in London or those who suffered higher childcare costs due to having a child with a registered disability. Campaigners had further taken up the issue of providing better support to grandparents who provided childcare. The 2009 Budget announced the development of a new scheme for grandparents who gave up work to provide such childcare, whereby they could receive National Insurance credits towards their basic state pension.

Extending rights to flexible working

The *Next steps* proposals led to extensions in parents' rights to request flexible working (HM Government, 2009a). From April 2009 all mothers and fathers with children under the age of 16 were entitled to request flexible working arrangements. This right remained dependent on at least 26 weeks of continuous contracted employment with an employer. In late 2009 Labour set up the 'Family Friendly Working Hours Taskforce'. The remit of the Taskforce demonstrated the wide range of policy objectives that had become aligned with promoting flexible working hours. The Taskforce stated that its aim was to identify the challenges for employers in providing flexible working hours and patterns in ways that ensured part-time and flexible working did not mean lower work prospects and status. Providing more opportunities for employees to work flexibly was associated with benefits for employers, employees and society more broadly. That is, for employers, providing flexible working opportunities can reduce absenteeism, increase staff retention and loyalty, increase productivity and provide a wider 'talent' pool from which to recruit. In terms of employees, flexible working patterns were thought of as beneficial for women, carers and older people. Further, providing these groups with better employment opportunities would, it was believed, lead to reductions in family and pensioner poverty and welfare reliance. Many of the recommendations of the Taskforce are in line with the policies of the new Conservative–Liberal Democrat Coalition administration.

Policy impacts and critique

There were major developments in English childcare policy between 1997 and 2009, many of which echoed or prompted developments in Wales, Scotland and Northern Ireland (Foley and Rixon, 2008). A review of childcare policy by the Daycare Trust (2008) highlighted policy cost-effectiveness in terms of stated policy aims and programme targets, including:

• virtually full take-up of the free nursery places for 4-year-olds and over 80% take-up among 3-year-olds by 2007
• significant increases in day care and out-of-school services
• increases in mothers' employment rates
• improved quality of early years settings (although quality tended to be most variable in the private sector)
• increases in the number of qualified childcare practitioners
• more financial support for parents.

Policy agendas and developments have sought to promote maternal employment opportunities, invest in children and promote out-of-school activities for young people. Policy change has led to revisions in parental rights and responsibilities. The state has taken on more responsibility for regulating standards in childcare provision, subsidising suppliers and providing pre-school provision for 3- to 4-year-olds. Parents have gained new rights to access childcare services. In 2009, the role of grandparents as informal childcare providers was getting recognition. The early days of the new Conservative–Liberal Democrat Coalition government suggest considerable continuity in policy priorities. Both parties declared a commitment to extend state-subsidised nursery provision for pre-school children and maintain the expansion in early years services. However, the proposed spending cuts are aligned with a return to more targeted financial support and early years services aimed at 'disadvantaged and dysfunctional families' (Conservative Party, 2010). Moreover, the new Coalition government is moving away from notions of 'neighbourhood deprivation' and seeks a greater role for private sector provision. These proposals do not address the limitations of, and tensions surrounding, the previous government's approach. A critical issue is that there is little recognition of the need for more effective implementation and regulation (ie around quality and workforce issues, information to parents) so that the policy 'vision' and framework is effectively implemented across LAs and settings. Moreover, Chapter Nine will show that childcare policies are at odds with parental preferences in some respect and could do more to meet the support needs of all parents with young children, whether in paid work or not. Grandparents are more recognised as informal childcare providers but support for them continues to be limited and there is a lack of recognition of other informal carers who support resident parents. For example, the Families and Children Survey (FACS) in 2008 found that non-resident fathers provided childcare for 14% of the lone mothers interviewed who were in paid work (Conolly and Kew, 2008). The cost, quality and availability of childcare services remain critical issues for many parents, with prices rising in the recession as well as family incomes falling (Caluori, 2009). Related to these issues are a number of ongoing challenges:

- gaps in the evidence base
- pay levels, the status of the childcare profession and training for all childcare staff
- the limited supply of childcare for parents working atypical hours
- improving provision for disabled children
- improving school holiday provision
- uncertainty over whether early years settings can extend their nursery provision in line with the expansion of free places for 3- and 4-year-olds
- sustainability issues for providers, especially in the context of economic recession
- mistrust of formal childcare provision among many parents and families
- the above-inflation increases in childcare costs for parents (Caluori, 2009).

Turning to developments in family-friendly employment, a stronger commitment to more radical reform developed from 2001. There were extensive increases in statutory maternity, paternity and adoption leave and pay, and in parental leave. Business lobby groups such as the CBI were often critical of the 'regulatory and financial' demands on employers associated with these but the Labour government pursued reform, requiring employers to balance their business needs with the needs of employees with children. By May 2010, SMP was payable for 39 weeks at 90% of weekly earnings for the first 6 weeks and at a rate of £123.06 a week for 33 weeks (with proposals to extend it to 52 weeks if Labour won the 2010 General Election); employees with children had the right to request flexible working options; fathers or same-sex partners had the right to two weeks' paternity leave and pay. Labour attempted to address the disparity between mothers' and fathers'/ partners' entitlements via new regulations that allowed mothers to 'share' the second six months of their maternity leave and pay with fathers. The WERS found significant increases in the range of family-friendly employment rights and options available to employees since 2003 and the number of employees taking up these rights (Hooker et al, 2007). The new Conservative-Liberal Democrat Coalition government has suggested extending rather than repealing these rights – either in terms of more rights to flexible working for parents with older children or for all employees, and in terms of more extensive paternity leave and pay rights. As discussed in Chapter Four, however, UK developments lag behind developments in more progressive EU nations, particularly with respect to SMP and paternity leave and pay. For some, the flexible working rights brought in since 2003 offer too much of a compromise in the favour of business (Lewis, 2009). There is no right to return to work on part-time hours for new mothers, for example. In terms of developments among individual employers, Hooker et al (2007) found that employers are likely to meet the British legislative standards and indeed go beyond them, offering good working conditions and prospects even for part-time workers, if: family-friendly employment practices are highly related to issues of organisational performance and productivity; there is high involvement in developing policies on the part of senior management and an effective human resources team; and the workforce is predominately female. However, mothers, fathers and carers often report an unsatisfactory 'work–family' balance. Their concerns include but also go beyond issues of working hours, and incorporate issues of work demands, workload, support and overall satisfaction. These issues are taken up in Chapter Nine.

Conclusion

This chapter set out to review the radical developments in England and the UK since 1997 in respect of childcare policies and statutory family-friendly employment rights. The analysis demonstrated the evolving nature of Labour's agenda and approach. Childcare policy was a major priority, due to the significance of childcare provision to raising mothers' employment rates and improving outcomes for young children. But campaigners called for more attention on issues of quality, parental preferences and the special needs of disabled children or disadvantaged children living outside of deprived areas. Family-friendly employment rights became a critical issue in Labour's second term in office. UK provisions do not lag so far behind other EU15 countries. However, policy developments need effective implementation and realistic investment. Furthermore, we find gender and social inequalities are not comprehensively addressed in these two areas of policy.

Notes
[1] Education Action Zones were local partnerships which strategically reviewed and oversaw educational initiatives aimed at raising educational attainment levels in deprived areas.

[2] The National Audit Office (NAO, 2004) calculated the gross government expenditure on early years from the total of local government expenditure, DfES initiative-based funding, the National Lottery funding, funding for Sure Start and childcare tax credit expenditure.

SEVEN

Parental and family support services

Introduction

This chapter examines developments in parental and family support services from 1997 to 2010. Informal family support refers to the multiple ways people care for one another and provide support for family roles (ie by providing emotional, practical, financial, advisory or childcare support). Informal social support within families and social networks builds social bonds and capital and is associated with practical and emotional support for parents and parental and child well-being, particularly maternal mental health (Quinton, 2004). In contrast, 'formal family support services' are services 'explicitly aimed at supporting parents, families and carers in fulfilling their roles and responsibilities for caring and raising children' (Barlow et al, 2007). In practice, formal family support services may see their aims and objectives in ways that relate to service silos, professional specialisms and boundaries (Penn and Gough, 2002). Formal services are provided by statutory and voluntary sector agencies (and may include funding for 'semi-formal', 'self-help' or 'community' groups or organisations (Williams and Churchill, 2006)). A distinction can be made between 'parenting services' and 'family support services'. According to Barlow et al (2007, p 5), the former refers to 'interventions aimed at increasing parenting skills, improving parent–child relationships, improving parental insight, attitudes and behaviour, and increasing parental confidence', that is, interventions that seek to 'enhance parenting'.

Chapter Four highlighted the 'neoliberal' approach to family support in the 1990s in the UK. Statutory family support services were for children and families in need or 'children at risk' of harm (Children Act 1989). However, during the 1990s the 'refocusing' debate called for more preventative family support measures, including parent education (DH, 1995). From 1998, Labour developed a more explicit family policy aimed at 'supporting parents and parenting', 'reducing child poverty', 'supporting working parents', 'reducing social exclusion' and 'promoting child well-being'. Since 1997 a number of policies have created 'new sites of family and parenting support' (Featherstone, 2004). This chapter charts the evolution of Labour's policy agendas and developments in this field. It shows how policy objectives were informed by Labour's overarching economic and social policy objectives: to raise productivity via higher employment rates and reduce social exclusion via family support reforms and child-centred investment. Informing these objectives was the agenda to revise the social contract between families, citizens and the state to promote active, responsible citizenship (and for parents to raise future active citizens). The analysis in this chapter follows a slightly different format to Chapters Five and Six. Policy impacts are assessed alongside the narrative of policy developments, due to the extent of initiatives introduced. The chapter recognises the significance of the major reform of children's and family services since 2004 and the development of new sites of family and parenting support. However, high levels of unmet need remain, and more attention on 'families and children' in policy terms has been accompanied by behavioural explanations for social problems and has led to extensions in parental responsibilities for children's outcomes. Likewise, in the context of the new Conservative-Liberal Democrat Coalition government, the Conservatives seek to extend this approach and return to highly targeted services for 'disadvantaged and dysfunctional' families (Conservative Party, 2010).

Policy developments

A new era in British family policy

On Labour's first coming to office in 1997, it was concerns about youth behaviour and offending that led to a review of family policy. The Home Office set up the Ministerial Group on the Family in 1997 'to develop a coherent strategy to increase the support and help available to families' (Home Office, 1998). By the time the Green Paper *Supporting families* (Home Office, 1998) was published, the review of family policy was informed by the broader social exclusion, employability and early intervention agendas. The Green Paper set five priorities to Labour's family policies:

- 'Financial support for families'
- 'Helping families balance work and home'
- 'Better support and services for parents'
- 'Strengthening marriage'
- 'Improving support for serious family problems' (Home Office, 1998).

This chapter focuses on the last three objectives.

The Green Paper highlighted four gaps in children's and family services and support: (1) authoritative parenting advice; (2) support for new first-time mothers; (3) integrated early years services for families with young children at risk of long-term poverty and social exclusion; (4) support for serious problems (Home Office, 1998). Parenting advice services were viewed as a universal need. The Home Office (1998) sought a shift in British culture from family support services aimed at problem and needy families, to expert parenting advice, so that seeking advice was seen 'as a sign of responsible parenting rather than an admission of failure' (Home Office, 1998). The Home Office increased funding for Parent-line (a national advice line for parents and families) and established the National

Family and Parenting Institute (NFPI) (to promote good practice, advise on policy and undertake research on family and parenting support issues). Parenting became a public issue. This was because children's outcomes, and social problems, were directly linked to good parenting: 'good parenting provides children with the best possible start in life', 'improves their health, schooling and prospects in later life', and 'reduces the risks of serious problems such as truancy, offending and drug misuse' (Home Office, 1998, p 6). *Supporting families* stated that health visitors would carry out more weekly home visits in the post-natal period, could 'offer parents more advice on child welfare issues' and were well placed to identify child welfare problems (Home Office, 1998). The Sure Start programme sought to improve access to services for families with young children in deprived areas.

Supporting families sought to reduce 'serious family problems' (Home Office, 1998). It focused on problems of school truancy and exclusion, youth offending, teenage pregnancy and domestic violence. Policies subsequently clarified and extended parental responsibilities for young people as well as statutory responsibilities. The School Standards and Framework Act 1998 required all schools to introduce home–school contracts (agreements signed by parents that set out the expectations for their support of children's learning and homework) and work in partnership with parents of children with additional learning needs. The government sought to reduce school truancy and exclusions by a third by 2002. The Criminal Justice and Court Services Act 2000 extended parental responsibilities by making it an offence for a parent to know that their child is truanting from school but not to try to get them to attend. If found guilty, a parent could be fined or receive a three months' prison sentence. Better parenting and a punitive approach to youth crime were 'the solutions' to youth offending. The Crime and Disorder Act 1998 reduced the age of criminal responsibility to 10 years, established the Youth Offending Teams (YOTs) to work with young people at risk and their families, and introduced new powers aimed at compelling parents to take more responsibility for young people's behaviour. These included: Parenting Orders, which required parents to attend parenting classes or parent counselling sessions, and Child Safety Orders and Child Curfews, which required parents to escort a child around the neighbourhood or keep a child at home during certain hours. These proposals reflected continuities with the punitive approach to youth crime developed in the 1980s and 1990s. However, Scotland had historically developed a more 'youth welfare' model which sought to work with young people who became involved in the criminal justice system in ways that steered them away from crime through youth work, welfare and educational supports.

The discussion about the relatively high rates of teenage pregnancy in the UK also emphasised family responsibilities as well as promoting new public programmes to address the problem. Families were described as failing to provide adequate sexual health education and advice about relationships for young people. Educational underachievement was further highlighted as a major cause of teenage pregnancy. Teenage pregnancy became a priority issue for the Social

Exclusion Unit (SEU). By 1999, the Teenage Pregnancy Strategy was published and targets were set to reduce rates of teenage pregnancy among girls under 16 years old, to halve the rate of conception among girls under 18 years old by 2010 and for 60% of mothers aged 16 to 19 years to be in education, employment or training by 2010. Little mention was made of teenage fathers. The discussion of domestic violence recognised that women, adults with learning disabilities and older people were particularly vulnerable. The 'solutions' were more help and support for victims, the need to raise awareness of the problem and improvements in reporting and conviction systems. However, feminists highlighted the lack of critical analysis of the dynamics of power and dependency within gender and generational relations (Featherstone, 2004).

The other major theme in *Supporting families* was to 'strengthen marriage'. New Labour stated that marriage was associated with better outcomes for children but 'the role of government was not to pressure people into one type of relationship' (Home Office, 1998, pp 2–3). Rather, New Labour sought to 'encourage a responsible approach to parenthood, marriage and divorce' in ways that 'put children's welfare first' (Home Office, 1998). Proposals included: (1) granting automatic parental responsibility to all unmarried fathers named on a child's birth certificate; (2) the promotion of pre-marriage contracts whereby couples agree their respective rights and responsibilities as future spouses; (3) investment in marriage and relationship counselling services; (4) family law reforms aimed at promoting child welfare and fairness between adults. The latter aimed to reduce the confrontational nature of divorce proceedings. Changes in family law are not examined in depth in this book. However, two major legislative changes have been noted in previous chapters. The Children and Adoption Act 2002 enabled single adults and same-sex partners to be considered suitable adopters and the Civil Partnership Act 2004 granted same-sex couples similar rights and responsibilities to married couples.

Supporting families reflected considerable new departures in British family policy, but also limited change (Maclean, 2002; Featherstone, 2004). The reform of social services was not linked to the Green Paper's overall strategy, even though many families involved with social services suffer from the 'serious problems' identified. Feminists raised concerns that the focus on 'parenting' in practice led to a focus on mothers, unless policies actively encouraged (a) services to engage with fathers and (b) fathers to take on more childcare (Featherstone, 2004). However, *Supporting families* did identify 'work with fathers' as a future policy priority and referred to the role of grandparents. From 1999 to 2004, the Home Office/Lord Chancellor's Office funded family support projects involving work with fathers. Fathers Direct was established to give advice and information on fatherhood issues and provide advice, consultancy and dissemination on engaging with fathers and promoting their rights.

Sure Start

The previous chapter described the development of Sure Start. The Sure Start initiative was based on the premise that poverty and social exclusion were not merely a matter of relative low income and material deprivation but related to growing up in families and neighbourhoods deprived of services and opportunities. The government was impressed by the cost-effectiveness of US early years programmes, such as the Head Start programme aimed at disadvantaged young children and their families, where it was estimated that for every $1 spent per child $7 was saved in the long run, due to the reduced need for remedial measures when a child was older (SEU, 2001). Sure Start aimed to:

> work with parents to be, parents and children to promote the physical, intellectual and social development of babies and young children – particularly those who are disadvantaged – so that they can flourish at home and when they get to school, and thereby break the cycle of disadvantage for the current generation of young children. (www. ness.bbk.ac.uk)

Important features of SSLPs were that they were: set up in deprived neighbourhoods; open to all families with children under 4 years old living in the neighbourhood; non-stigmatising and responsive; designed and coordinated by local Sure Start Partnerships, which involved statutory early years services, voluntary sector agencies, community organisations and parent/community representatives; and emphasised community and parental involvement (Belsky et al, 2006). SSLPs were required to meet centrally defined targets for children's early development. They were also expected to provide the following 'core services': outreach and home visiting; support for families; good-quality play, learning and childcare for young children; primary and community healthcare, and support for families in need. Belsky et al (2006) noted that in the early days of Sure Start the flexibility afforded to SSLPs generated varied outcomes among programmes, and a few years later the government took a more prescriptive approach to defining the 'core offer'. In the first four rounds of funding, 260 SSLPs were established. In 2000 the government announced that 500 programmes would be in operation by 2004 to expand the reach of Sure Start to a third of poor children. SSLPs also became subject to stricter targets for reducing re-registration rates for the Child Protection Register, reducing rates of maternal smoking and reducing the numbers of workless families.

Sure Start was accompanied by an internationally renowned evaluation programme. The National Evaluation of Sure Start (NESS) carried out a comprehensive evaluation of the first 260 SSLPs. NESS carried out an analysis of the local context of need and provision in each neighbourhood; an impact study of children, family and community outcomes; in-depth case studies of

SSLPs, and thematic studies. The impact studies collected longitudinal data about children, families and neighbourhoods served by SSLPs and compared this with children, families and neighbourhoods elsewhere. The initial impact evaluation findings showed small but significant improvements in early child development and parenting within Sure Start areas but less positive outcomes for lone-parent and teenage-parent headed families (Belsky et al, 2006). There was much variation in performance and impacts between SSLPs and Sure Start areas (Belsky et al, 2006). More recent findings reported substantially better outcomes for children, parents, families and communities (Melhuish et al, 2008). Two NESS thematic studies examined family support services and outcomes for parents: one on *Parental empowerment in Sure Start* (Williams and Churchill, 2006) and one on *Family and parenting support in Sure Start* (Barlow et al, 2007). Several Sure Start Centres were found to contribute to parental empowerment, particularly individual empowerment, due to their individualised support for parents and quality services as well as via providing resources and opportunities for individuals and groups to support one another and work together to improve their neighbourhood (Williams and Churchill, 2006). Likewise, Barlow et al (2007) found much good practice in family support services in SSLPs and highlighted the significance of working in empowering and responsive ways with individuals, families and groups. Box 7.1 summarises these findings.

Box 7.1: Family and parenting support in Sure Start Local Programmes

Barlow et al (2007) conducted an evaluation of family and parenting support services in SSLPs. This study defined family and parent support services as 'services that reduce the stresses associated with parenting' and that could include 'informal activities that provided social contact and support, relaxation and fun, as well as programmes to develop confidence and self-esteem in parents themselves – adult learning programmes for example' (Barlow et al, 2007, p 2). 'Parenting support' was defined as 'services that enable parents to enhance their parenting', which included 'formal and informal interventions to increase parenting skills, improve parent/child relationships, the insight of parents, their attitudes and behaviours and their confidence in parenting' (Barlow et al, 2005, p 2). Barlow et al's (2007) study examined services across 59 SSLPs and conducted more intensive case study research into six SSLPs. They found that:

- Involving, supporting and working with parents and families was key to the Sure Start ethos and approach, although SSLPs varied in the extent to which they prioritised and were successful in engaging with fathers and extended family members.
- 649 family and parenting support programmes were in operation. On average, the SSLPs delivered 11 different types of family and parenting support services.

- The majority of services fell into the category of 'parenting support', while around a third of services involved broader family support work.
- Parenting support services mainly consisted of: (1) parenting courses (mainly courses designed by Sure Start practitioners that aimed to improve parent–child relationships and parenting knowledge, attitudes and practices); (2) home visiting schemes; (3) perinatal programmes (such as antenatal health clinics, breastfeeding advice, baby massage groups and parenting classes aimed at new mothers); (4) early learning programmes (groups for parents with young children or access to resources such as books and educational toys).
- Family/parent support services included therapeutic, adult learning and general support services for families and parents (social/support groups, counselling, cognitive behaviour therapy, family therapy and art therapy, basic and adult education, English language courses, welfare rights advice and back-to-work guidance).
- Beneficial outcomes for children and improvements in parent–child relationships and indicators of parenting.
- Key processes and factors promoting good outcomes for children and families included: (1) focusing on the relationship between parent and child; (2) staff modelling good relationships with parents and children; (3) theoretically informed practice; (4) evidence-based interventions; (5) measures that improved the accessibility of services; (6) good staff development and training; (7) non-judgemental and empowering relationships with service users.

Modernising social services and improving child welfare assessments

From 1997, the Department of Health introduced measures to 'modernise social services'. In the context of scarce resources and increasing rates of referral, social services were criticised for establishing high thresholds for support services and retaining a narrow 'forensic' approach to child protection. Within this framework, the needs of many vulnerable children and families were left unmet, often after families were subject to intrusive and distressing investigations (DH, 1995). New Labour incorporated these concerns into plans to improve 'the cost-effectiveness and management of social services' (DH, 1998). For example, the Quality Protects programme, launched in 1998, required social services to improve outcomes for children and young people in need, particularly those in the care system. Social services were required to develop Quality Protect Action Plans which identified children's outcomes and matched service provision to children's needs. The Department of Health (DH) also introduced new systems to collect and store information about young people in the care system.

As part of the drive to improve services, the DH introduced the Framework for the assessment of children in need and their families (commonly known as 'the Framework') (DH et al, 2000). This sought to improve and standardise needs assessment processes (Rose, 2009). The Framework was informed by a (partial) adoption of an ecological approach whereby children's own views, the quality of parenting in the family, parental welfare and the wider home, family and community issues were addressed. The Framework established three assessment foci:

- the child's developmental needs (requiring an assessment of a child's health, education, emotional and behavioural development, identity, family and social relationships, social presentation and self-care skills);
- parenting capacity (requiring an assessment of parenting and caregiving in the family in respect of basic care, ensuring safety, emotional warmth, stimulation, guidance and boundaries and consistency);
- family and environmental factors (requiring an assessment of family history and functioning, wider family issues, housing, employment, income, social integration of the family and community resources) (DH, 2000).

Rose (2009, p 39) argued that effective implementation would require social workers to undertake detailed assessments; make professional judgements; provide regular and consistent contact with, and observation of, children and their families; and practise effective multi-agency working. However, scarce resources, high caseloads, and staff recruitment and retention problems generated counter-pressures towards prioritising the protection of children in the most immediate danger and increased the scope for error (Laming, 2009).

Expanding the preventative agenda

Chapter Four showed that Labour's preventative agenda expanded from 1999, prompted by the work of the Social Exclusion Unit and the historic pledge to end child poverty by 2020 (SEU, 2001). The SEU (2001, p 5) set out a preventative agenda aimed at:

- preventing those at special risk from becoming excluded
- reintegrating those who had become excluded
- improving basic standards in public services so that they were more inclusive.

A strand of policies would target 'children, families and schools'. One such initiative was the Children's Fund. The Children's Fund was targeted at children aged 5–13 years and their families, and aimed to 'prevent children from falling into drug abuse, truancy, exclusion, unemployment and crime' (Morris et al, 2009). With a budget of £450 million from 2000 to 2003, the Fund would be distributed to 150 LAs within England. A Cabinet Committee, the Children and Young People's Unit (CYPU), was established to oversee the Fund. The Children's Fund was not a distinct intervention but an investment in local services and strategic partnership networks, with emphasis on voluntary and statutory sector partnerships. Local partnerships were required to assess local needs, identify priority groups and develop preventative services, and were subject to targets to reduce truancy, raise educational attainment, reduce youth offending and improve outcomes for young people in care. By 2008 there were 149 Children's Fund partnerships operating across England. The national evaluation of the Children's Fund ran from 2003 to 2006. This found that many services funded by the Children's Fund worked with and involved parents and families, but the main focus was on providing services and opportunities to children, including: specialist services for particular groups (disabled children, asylum-seeking and refugee families, Black and ethnic minority children, Traveller and Gypsy families, and children at risk from crime were among the main target groups), social and recreational opportunities for children, and mentoring and counselling (Edwards et al, 2006). However, the national evaluation found that some local partnerships did not grasp the preventative agenda and utilised the funds to provide their usual services (Edwards et al, 2006). Services and partnerships were criticised for not consistently working in partnership with young people and families and not consistently adopting a joined-up approach – two issues that mean services are more limited in addressing the multiple risks in young people's lives or issues of stigma and discrimination (Edwards et al, 2006).

2002 Children at risk review

A few months into Labour's second term, the Treasury announced a review into services for 'children at risk'. The review echoed the findings and proposals set out by the SEU (SEU, 2001). The review concluded that 'a substantial minority [of children] face a combination of problems which result in persistently poor outcomes in terms of educational achievement, employment, health and anti-social behaviour' (HM Treasury, 2002c, p 153). The review recognised that 'children at risk' form a diverse group, but highlighted 'poor parenting, disability and poor health, and poverty' as major risk factors. It argued that 'despite extensive investment in services for children, most services were not having the desired positive impact on disadvantaged children' (HM Treasury, 2002c, p 153). The 'solutions' were:

(1) measures to improve strategic coordination across local children's services via the establishment of Children's Trusts (local strategic partnerships of service providers which coordinate service provision and establish multi-agency objectives); more systematic identification, referral and tracking systems for information sharing about young people at risk; and more coordinated packages of services for children with additional needs;

(2) reforms to mainstream services so they 'better serve children with additional needs' and reforms to social services so that they 'focus more on prevention and early detection of problems as well as crisis and acute interventions';

(3) 'filling the gaps' in services, which primarily meant more 'parenting support and education'. The 2002 CSR announced the establishment of the Parenting

Fund with a budget of £25 million between 2002 and 2006 for voluntary sector parenting support and investment in training parenting practitioners.

The 2002 *Cross-cutting children at risk* review therefore adopted a broader concept of 'child at risk' as compared to the Children Act 1989 definition. Government policy seemed primarily concerned with preventing and reducing: child abuse and neglect; youth offending; and educational underachievement.

The Anti-Social Behaviour Act 2003

Alongside an expanding preventative agenda, the Anti-Social Behaviour Act 2003 extended powers to compel and encourage parents to engage with parenting support. Developments were informed by the national evaluation of the Youth Justice Board parenting programmes and impressive findings of the Dundee Family Projects, which worked intensively with families at risk of homelessness and engaging in anti-social behaviour (Box 7.2). The 2003 Act extended the range of agencies that could apply for a Parenting Order, particularly in relation to concerns about neighbourhood nuisance, school truancy and poor behaviour at school. This legislation also introduced Parenting Contracts, which agencies could apply for and parents could engage with voluntarily. Labour was criticised, though, for inadequate attention to the influence of peers and neighbourhood contexts, and an inadequate analysis of gendered patterns of offending (Morris et al, 2009).

Box 7.2: Positive parenting: the national evaluation of the Youth Justice Board's parenting programme

The Youth Justice Board (YJB) parenting programmes aimed to reduce youth offending by working with parents of young people at risk or involved in the youth justice system (they also intended to undertake direct work with young people, but few achieved this). Parents subject to a Parenting Order were required to participate. Ghate and Ramella (2002) reported on the findings of the three-year national evaluation. Out of the 42 parenting programmes in operation by 2002, 34 were evaluated; 800 parents, 500 young people and 800 project workers participated. The impact study involved a sub-sample of 200 parents. The parents and young people participating in the programme had very high levels of needs. Parents often reported severe debt, health, personal relationship and housing problems. The young people scored highly on standardised measures of emotional and behavioural difficulties. The parenting programmes sought to improve parenting and parent–child communication in families in need and developed additional one-to-one work and therapeutic interventions for families with severe problems. In group parenting courses the following issues were addressed: dealing with conflict and challenging behaviour, supervision and boundary setting with young people and parent–child communication. Of the 200 parents taking part in the impact study: one in

---

six were subject to a Parenting Order, 81% were women (mothers or female carers), 96% were of White British backgrounds, 49% were lone parents and 25% were under 34 years old. The young people of concern were mainly aged 14–15 years. The evaluation found that participants had experienced a range of positive outcomes. Parents reported:

* improved communication with children
* improved supervision and monitoring of young people
* reductions in parent–child conflict and better handling of conflict
* improved relationships with children and more praise/less criticism of young people
* more confidence as a parent.

The study reported similar outcomes for the parents subject to a Parenting Order, although these parents were initially likely to have negative views about the programme. Six per cent of participants reported negative impacts. The outcomes for young people included:

* a 30% reduction in conviction rates in the year after their parent(s) had participated in the programme, as compared to the year previous
* a 50% reduction in re-conviction rates in the year after their parent(s) had participated in the programme, as compared to the year previous.

The Every child matters *reforms*

From 2002 the preventative agenda pointed to more comprehensive reform of children's services. The CYPU (2003) was instrumental in promoting the idea of local Children's Trusts and setting out a vision of 'child well-being'. In June 2003 a new position of Minister for Children, Young People and Families was established. In October 2002, Prime Minister Tony Blair proposed a Green Paper on 'Children at risk'. This became the Green Paper *Every child matters*, which set out major reforms to children's services (Chief Secretary to the Treasury, 2003). The immediate driver of reform was Lord Laming's Inquiry into the Death of Victoria Climbié (Laming, 2003)[1]. The Inquiry concluded that the legal framework guiding child protection was robust but that front-line malpractice and systemic failures in the organisation and management of children's social services had prevented agencies from intervening to protect Victoria (Laming, 2003, p 2). Laming recommended reforms aimed at improving the coordination of child and family policy and children's services at the local level; making children's services more 'outcomes' focused; enhancing managerial accountability; improving recruitment, retention and standards in the social care workforce; and improving the quality and delivery of local services via better coordination and information sharing.

Every child matters (Chief Secretary to the Treasury, 2003) took forward these recommendations and incorporated a wider programme of reform across children's services. Chapter Two stated that children's services were to improve five key outcomes for children and young people: being safe, being healthy, enjoying and achieving, making a positive contribution to society, and economic well-being. In practice, the 'deficit approach' to monitoring and improving child well-being was dominant, focusing on dysfunctional families and human capital deficits (see Chapter Two). Targets were subsequently set to monitor poor outcomes for children in relation to: child poverty and deprivation; physical health; mental health and well-being; child maltreatment, bullying and abuse; children and young people in and leaving care; childcare; child and youth involvement in crime and social disorder; educational disadvantage; neighbourhood deprivation; and social exclusion (Utting, 2009).

Every child matters (Chief Secretary to the Treasury, 2003; DfES, 2004a) proposed a major reorganisation of children's services which had three key themes: (1) better horizontal and vertical accountability and coordination across children's services; (2) early intervention and prevention; and (3) more support for parents and carers. Accountability and coordination were strengthened via the new outcomes-focused approach, institutional reforms and multi-agency working. LAs were required to merge social services and education departments into children's services departments led by a Director of Children's Services. Directors of Children's Services would head up a local Children's Trust, the local strategic partnership guiding local policies and service reforms, with representation from all the main service providers in the authority. Local Safeguarding Boards were to replace Area Child Protection Committees and oversee child protection reform. Proposals for the reform of front-line services included: the introduction of a Common Assessment Framework to be used by practitioners working with children and families to collect basic information about children's and families' needs that could be shared with other practitioners; new electronic information systems with data about children; the introduction of a lead professional to oversee services for children known to more than one agency and specialist agencies; and multi-agency teams based around Sure Start Children's Centres and Extended Schools. The Children Act 2004 placed a statutory duty on LAs to promote the *Every child matters* five outcomes for children and young people and introduce the reforms. LAs were required to produce a Children and Young People's Plan (CYPP) by 2006, setting out local priorities based on a review of local needs and services against the five outcomes for young people and consultation with young people, parents and carers.

In respect of 'supporting parents and carers', *Every child matters* (Chief Secretary to the Treasury, 2003) set out a vision of integrated support across three levels:

(1) universal support and services which consisted of schools, health services and childcare, alongside parenting advice and information
(2) targeted and specialist services to meet additional support needs
(3) compulsory action: statutory measures and parenting orders to protect children and enforce parental responsibility.

Changes to universal services aimed to make services more responsive to parental needs, promote the role of parents in facilitating children's outcomes, engage fathers and families most in need, provide more information and advice to parents and carers, and improve information sharing between services.

Subsequent developments in education and health took forward these proposals. The DfES (2004b) promoted parents' rights as consumer-citizens and the role of parents as educators. The DfES set out 'a parent guarantee' and 'a family guarantee' to increase access to school places in popular secondary schools; to invest more in school refurbishments; to improve attendance and behaviour codes at schools; and to improve parent–school communication via email and web-based information as well as newsletters (DfES, 2004b). Extended Schools and Sure Start Children's Centres would provide access to parental and family support services, as the DfES set targets for every school to be an Extended School and for 3,500 Sure Start Children's Centres by 2010. In response to the disappointing findings from the NESS early impact study, the DfES established a more prescribed 'core offer of services' for Sure Start Children's Centres which included a stronger focus on full-time nursery provision, outreach workers and engagement with fathers. Extended Schools were encouraged to provide advice and support, such as family learning sessions and behaviour management courses, for parents of children with problems at school. Likewise, the role of parents in terms of children's and young people's health was promoted in DH reforms. The National Service Framework for Children, Young People and Maternity Services established standards for 'fair, high quality and integrated health and social care from pregnancy through to adulthood' (DH, 2004). There was a strong focus on the relationship between maternal and child health. The Standards promoted better screening for health problems during pregnancy and post-natal depression. They encouraged health services to engage more with fathers and promote fathers' health. Further, health services were to offer more information, services and support to parents and carers in respect of their parenting role (DH, 2004). The role of universal services was conceptualised as providing support and services, as well as 'raising concerns about child welfare'. New legislation enabled those working with children to raise concerns about a child 'at the point of concern' rather than 'evidence of harm' and recognised 'witnessing the domestic abuse of others in the home' as damaging to children (Chief Secretary to the Treasury, 2003).

Parenting and parental separation

Following many calls for reform of divorce proceedings and courts, the government published *Parental separation: Children's needs and parents' responsibilities* (HM Government, 2004). The proposals were driven by concern about the negative impacts that parental separation and divorce can have on children, due to distress and loss, disruption to family relationships, family conflict and the implications for family income or housing. The paper stated that the Children

Act 1989 remained adequate and reinforced the messages of lifelong parental responsibilities for children and the paramount importance of putting children's welfare first. But changes were introduced: to simplify divorce court proceedings, to improve support services for parents and to extend court powers to 'enforce parental responsibilities [for contact and child maintenance] where necessary' (HM Government, 2004, p 7; see Chapter Five). More support for parents included better access to information about services, parental rights and legal processes; investment in intensive Family Resolution Pilot Projects (to run from 2004 to 2005 in three cities and offer support for parents involved in the court system to reach agreements about parenting, contact and child welfare issues via Relate family relationship groups and parent planning meetings); more access to relationships counselling and mediation services; the promotion of 'parenting plans', where parents agree parenting and contact arrangements; and access to parenting advice and support. The paper stated that parental responsibilities were to minimise the harmful effects of separation and divorce on children and put children's welfare first. It stated that non-resident parents should maintain contact with children, while the resident parent with the main caring responsibilities should facilitate such contact 'as long as this is safe for everyone' (HM Government, 2004). The paper proposed new legislation to strengthen powers to compel parents to adhere to court orders and contact agreements. There was a review of how the court system deals with domestic violence cases, and proposals to establish new domestic violence courts. Beyond advice and support for dealing with the courts, parenting issues and disputes over 'children, money and homes', this paper did not review the social rights of non-resident parents or discuss their support needs.

Extending support and controls aimed at parents and families

Labour's third term in office, from 2005 to 2010, saw major developments in family policy. The 2005 Budget announced funding for the Bookstart scheme (whereby families living in deprived areas were given packs of children's books) and increased investment in Extended Schools, Children's Centres and the Parenting Fund. Under pressure to review services for disabled children, youth services, children's mental health services, health promotion services and social care services for children in care, *Every child matters* was followed by *Youth matters* (DfES, 2005a), *Care matters* (DfES, 2006a) and reviews into services for disabled children and mental health services. The role of parents and parenting in respect of outcomes for older children became a more prominent theme. *Youth matters* (DfES, 2005a) sought to promote 'active responsible citizenship' and better outcomes for young people via more family and parenting support for parents; community services for young people; and volunteering opportunities. *Care matters* (DfES, 2006a) raised concerns that children in care have much lower levels of educational attainment, poorer health and are three times more likely to be involved in the youth offending system than children who have not been in care (DfES, 2006a).

Care matters sought to prevent children entering care, improve the provision and stability of care placements, support children leaving care and improve access to opportunities. Proposals included a higher basic level of maintenance for foster carers, multi-agency packages of family support services, improved training and support for foster carers and adoptive parents, an emphasis on involving children in decisions, and better inspection of provision. Legislation subsequently required LAs to improve educational outcomes for children in care.

The Treasury and DfES published a review of policies and services aimed at parents and families to inform the 2007 CSR. This review marked a significant shift in government thinking about parents and parenting, whereby Labour's social inclusion agenda was more strongly aligned with 'helping parents to meet their responsibilities for children and young people' (HM Treasury and DfES, 2005, p 5). The review set out a more detailed and integrated assessment of the role of families, parents and parenting in determining children's outcomes. Parents and parenting were identified as critical to children's education, health, emotional and mental well-being, behaviour and social integration, transition to adulthood and life chances as adults. Parental employment was associated with higher educational and employment aspirations among children as well as reductions in family poverty. Parental attitudes to education and aspirations for children as well as involvement with schools, consistent encouragement, family/home learning activities, and provision of out-of-school educational and recreational opportunities were all cited as critical to children's educational attainment levels and subsequent participation in further and higher education. Parents were viewed as 'primarily responsible for pre-school learning' (HM Treasury and DfES, 2005, p 24). Parental behaviour, decisions and life-styles were strongly linked to child health trends. Maternal health in pregnancy was closely related to child health, with poor health in pregnancy linked to premature birth and low-weight babies, who were subsequently at a higher risk of long-term health problems. Responsible mothers were cast as those who breastfed; responsible parents as promoting a healthy life-style. Parental behaviour and parenting/communication style were highly associated with children's behaviour. Additionally, warm and authoritative parent–child relationships, and parental and family support for young people, were identified as important protective factors which promoted young people's resilience in the face of adversity and responsible behaviour in the face of peer pressure. The importance of fathers was highlighted with reference to research that demonstrated that 'strong, positive relationships between children and their fathers' are associated with 'better exam results at 16 years, lower criminality and lower drug use' (HM Treasury and DfES, 2005, p 20). The review took an instrumental view of parents and parenting. It stated that 'what parents did with children and the quality of parent–child relationships' was more important than 'the quantity of time spent together' (HM Treasury and DfES, 2005, p 20). In contrast to the earlier focus on younger children, the review stated that 'the influence of parents is greatest when children are very young, but parents matter at every stage of a child's life' (HM Treasury and DfES, 2005, p 20). Alongside a more detailed review of the role of parents and parenting in relation to the Every child matters outcomes for children, the review provided a more informed and expanded view of parental and family support needs. The Family and Parenting Institute (FPI) (formerly the National Family and Parenting Institute, NFPI) had an instrumental role in setting the agenda, as did parenting research and consultation events with parents and family support organisations. Drawing on the findings of FPI surveys and research, the review concluded that parents wanted and needed more support to fulfil their responsibilities for children. Critical issues for parents concerning their children were identified as: the importance of informal support from family and friends, the pressures and stigma arising from poverty, children's public safety and 'online' safety, bullying, peer pressure, work–family conflicts, family conflict, social isolation, parenting teenagers, school–family relationships and consumer pressures (HM Treasury and DfES, 2005, p 23). Below, the discussion highlights how some of these issues, from 2006, did receive more government attention. In terms of specific proposals, the Treasury announced that £21 million would be invested in Parent Support Advisers (PSAs) in 600 primary and secondary schools in deprived areas. PSAs would work with parents whose children were truanting from school or showing signs of difficulty/poor behaviour at school. The 'Families at Risk' review was subsequently announced, to review how far services were reaching 'the most socially excluded groups' (HM Treasury and DfES, 2005, p 29).

With increasing attention placed on the role of parents, families and parenting, and the cost-effectiveness of parental and family-focused interventions, further measures extended compulsory measures. The White Paper *Higher standards, better schools for all* (DfES, 2005b) detailed new legislation to extend the powers of schools to use parenting contracts and orders to engage parents in parent education courses in order to prevent children from becoming excluded from school. In 2006 the Home Office launched the 'Respect' action plan to prevent and reduce crime and anti-social behaviour, where it noted that 85% of the public thought parents were responsible for youth anti-social behaviour. Investment in parent education and support had become one of the main 'policy solutions'. The Respect action plan announced that parenting practitioner posts would be established in local authorities with high rates of youth offending. During 2006/07 £15 million would be invested to establish 50 Family Intervention Project (FIPs) pilots. FIPs were based on the Dundee Family Projects and involved specialist key workers providing tailored services to families, based on a formal agreement (or 'compact') whereby families agreed 'behaviour change' targets. FIPs were targeted at families and youth engaged in anti-social behaviour and at risk of offending and homelessness (Box 7.3). The Plan announced that a National Academy of Parenting Practitioners (NAPP) would be established to train and support parenting practitioners. Further legislation would extend the range of practitioners and services with powers to use Parenting Orders and Parenting Contracts in order to 'take a new approach to tackle the behaviour of 'problem families' by challenging them to accept support

Box 7.3: Family Intervention Projects: an evaluation of their design, set-up and early outcomes

White et al (2008) conducted the national evaluation of Family Intervention Projects (FIPs). These researchers examined how FIPs were designed and implemented, the experiences of practitioners and the outcomes for families. The evaluation examined key features of the 53 FIPs established in England during 2006 and 2007 and the characteristics of practitioners and families, and undertook in-depth case study research into 9 FIPs. FIPs developed three distinct models of delivery: (1) 'the assertive outreach service', in which FIP workers regularly visited and provided support to families in their own homes; (2) 'the dispersed service', where families were supported while living in accommodation managed by the FIP in the community; or (3) 'the core unit', where 'every aspect of family life is scrutinised on a daily basis' while families lived in residential units. FIPs tended to work with families for 6 to 12 months. The FIPs led to positive outcomes for parents, children and families, with significant reductions in anti-social behaviour, offending and risk of eviction by the time families left the project and improvements in young people's school attendance, behaviour and well-being. The evaluation highlighted several key factors which facilitated these beneficial outcomes:

- effective recruitment and retention of highly skilled staff
- small case loads
- a dedicated key worker with some control over the allocation of funding
- a whole-family approach
- the use of sanctions with support
- effective multi-agency working
- the capacity to work with the family for as long as needed.

to change their behaviour, backed up by enforcement measures' (Home Office, 2006, p 3). Soon after, the DfES announced that £3 million would be invested in training practitioners in one of three evidence-based parenting programmes (Triple P, Webster Stratton: Incredible Years and Strengthening Families) who would then deliver these programmes to parents of young people aged between 8 and 13 years at risk from offending and in FIPs.

Developing parenting support at the local level

During 2006, the DfES (2006b) published guidance for LAs to develop 'parenting support strategies'. The guidance stated that 'the significance of parenting to improving child outcomes has become increasingly central to family policy' (DfES, 2006b, p 6). A study commissioned by the DfES on 'the market for parental and family support services' recommended that LAs develop local parenting support strategies and policy makers better integrate and sustain funding streams for parental and family support services (PricewaterhouseCoopers, 2006). The PricewaterhouseCoopers (2006) report particularly found gaps in funding and provision for 'Level 2' provision (specialist and targeted services for families with additional needs that are not catered for by universal services but where there are not safeguarding concerns) and argued for national standards for parent education and support services. This study found that many LAs were unaware of the extent, range or quality of local provision; that provision funded by public money continued to be focused on remedial rather than preventative work; that funding for provision or staff training was insecure and fragmented; that interventions were rarely evaluated; that there was little joint working between agencies and that services continued to work primarily with mothers and primary carers, with an under-representation of fathers, teenage parents and ethnic minorities using services (PricewaterhouseCoopers, 2006). To develop a strategic approach, LAs were encouraged to identify a single commissioner for parenting support services; undertake a review of local services and needs; establish multi-agency parenting partnerships; and produce a local Parenting Support Strategy (DfES, 2006b, p 2). LAs were encouraged to develop a seamless 'continuum of support' ranging from universal parenting advice and services for children and families, to targeted and specialist support services for families with additional and compulsory action. LAs were to consult parents and establish local Parent Forums to inform the Parenting Support Strategy. However, funding for new services remained heavily skewed to the specific programmes and priorities established via the Respect Agenda, other work within the Home Office, the DfES, the SEU and the Department of Health. From 2007, government policy developed in two directions: (1) extending support for parents and (2) developing targeted policies and services for 'the most socially excluded families'.

Every parent matters

The persuasively entitled *Every parent matters* was published in March 2007. It sought to promote a 'national debate on how to support and engage parents' (DfES, 2007a, p 1). In contrast to *Every child matters*, *Every parent matters* did not set out a vision for adult and family well-being but rather, focused on parental needs for support during 'critical stages in children's development' and parental responsibilities for children (DfES, 2007a). *Every parent matters* set out the important role that parents have in 'guiding their children through key transitions', discussed as the early years, the transition to secondary school, adolescence and the transition to adulthood (DfES, 2007a). *Every parent matters* set out proposals to extend Labour's parent-focused interventions in education, health and youth criminal justice policies; ensure that services engage better with families in need and fathers; develop the parenting support workforce; and improve parental involvement in schools. The role of Extended Schools and Children's Centres in engaging families in need was stressed, with proposals to extend the role of outreach workers. Children's Centres were encouraged to engage more with grandparents, disabled parents, step-parents and fathers. Some Children's Centres were to receive additional funding for specialist work with teenage parents. *Every parent matters* stated that 5,690 schools were delivering parenting support in England and 900 schools would have PSAs by 2008. It proposed more parenting programmes for parents of teenagers and more universal forms of parenting advice. This led to the 'Parent Know How' website and increased funding for parent and child help-lines. More investment in family therapeutic, mediation and counselling services was proposed to help 'parents stay together or retain their parenting role post-separation and divorce' (DfES, 2007a). Workforce reforms included new occupational standards for children's services working with parents following the introduction of NAPP.

The commitment to extend support for parents was taken forward by the 2007 CSR, informed by two key reviews: *Aiming high for children: Supporting families* (HM Treasury and DfES, 2007) and *Aiming high for disabled children* (DfES, 2007b). *Aiming high for children* described 'a new partnership with parents': 'to improve outcomes for children, the government would work in partnership with active, responsible parents and empowered communities' (HM Treasury and DfES, 2007, p 3). The 2007 CSR announced more funding for Sure Start Children's Centres, free out-of-school activities for children in receipt of free school meals in Extended Schools, two outreach posts in Sure Start Children's Centres, parent education and FIPs.

Refocusing on the 'most socially excluded'

As Labour's parenting support agenda was expanding, the work of the SEU was being redefined. In June 2006 the SEU was renamed the Social Exclusion Task Force (SETF), with a remit to identify 'the most at risk and hard to reach groups' (Cabinet Office and SETF, 2007a). In September 2006, the SETF published *Reaching out: An action plan on social exclusion* (SETF, 2006). This report set out the progress made under Labour against overarching policy objectives and targets: rising employment rates, significant reductions in child poverty since 1999 and improvements in educational attainments rates at Key Stages 1 and 3. In this context it was argued that the 'persistent and deep seated social exclusion of a small minority stands out ever more starkly' (SETF, 2006, p 8). The narrative running through the report suggested a dominant moral-underclass perspective. The most socially excluded were described as 'shut off from opportunities, choices and options in life', 'behaving in ways which cause disruption and distress to communities', 'a small group of people whose needs are unique and complex', 'who are difficult to reach', 'who fail to fulfil their potential or accept opportunities the rest of us take for granted' (SETF, 2006, pp 8–9). At-risk groups in respect of children were identified as: children in care, teenage parents and groups who underachieve at school. The discourse in respect of adults was much more stigmatising, with an emphasis on chaotic life-styles, anti-social behaviour and drug and alcohol addiction which places children at risk. Earlier chapters have highlighted the limitations and ideological agenda aligned with this approach. The widespread nature of social problems such as drug and alcohol addiction is downplayed and social exclusion is linked to individual problems, attitudes and behaviour rather than complex social processes and personal troubles. The 'policy solutions' were (1) better identification and early intervention; (2) better information sharing and coordination between agencies, especially between adult and children's services; (3) investment in personalised, intensive, multi-agency interventions targeted at families and adults at risk, and based on evidence of 'what works'; (4) the use of conditional forms of support and compacts to engage 'hard to reach' groups (SETF, 2006). Initiatives aimed at families and children included:

- ten health-led home visiting parenting support pilots based on the US Nurse-Family Partnerships model to provide intensive, home-based support for first-time mothers at risk during pregnancy and the first two years of a child's life. The pilots were required to improve mother–baby attachments and breastfeeding rates, reduce smoking during pregnancy, improve maternal health and diet and promote education and employment opportunities;
- Multi-Systemic Therapy programmes piloted in 10 local authority areas aimed at children and parents with severe attachment and mental health problems.
- treatment Foster Care pilots to improve outcomes for children in care;
- training for midwives and health visitors to deliver evidence-based parenting programmes and identify family problems at an early stage;
- a duty on adult services to assess the needs of adults as parents and work in partnership with children's services;
- a revised teenage pregnancy strategy;
- the development of commissioning tools and databases on evidence-based parenting programmes and intensive interventions.

This focus and approach informed the *Families at risk* review. The findings of the review, which included much consultation work and commissioned reviews of research and evaluations, were published in *Reaching out: Think family* (Cabinet Office and SETF, 2007b). *Reaching out: Think family* stated that 2% of British families, around 140,000 families, were severely socially excluded, with 'multiple, entrenched and mutually reinforcing problems' which created barriers to the education and employment opportunities that secured social inclusion and full citizenship (Cabinet Office and SETF, 2007b, p 4). The report continued to stress the primary role of parents and families for children's development and well-being. Parents and families were conceptualised as a 'resource' in children's lives:

> Parents matter in particular because they provide critical early resources that help children to grow, develop and achieve. Family relationships

can provide love, strength and support to get through hard times and overcome problems. (Cabinet Office and SETF, 2007b, p 4)

Parents and families were also conceptualised as 'a risk' to children. This referred to two perspectives. Firstly, a range of risk factors were defined as parental risk factors (such as worklessness, low skills, poor housing, domestic violence, poor mental and physical health, lack of informal support, family conflict, divorce, disability) because they affected parents and required interventions targeted at parents, carers and families. Secondly, parents were deemed a risk to children in the sense of unacceptable behaviour, values and intentions – in the main associated with drug and alcohol misuse, high family conflict, parental neglect, anti-social behaviour and offending. Addressing the growing debate about the 'Broken Society', instigated by the Conservative Party's Broken Society campaign, the *Families at risk* review stated that family structure was not a defining issue – rather, the emphasis was on the degree and severity of risk factors in children's lives. The review set out the need for greater integration between services (especially adult and children's services) and more investment in targeted intensive family interventions akin to the FIPs. To integrate services more, the SETF argued for common objectives across services; clear accountability; better systems for information sharing; common processes and assessment tools; and more multi-agency working and training.

The 2007 Children's Plan

In February 2007 the UNICEF report on child well-being trends across 21 advanced industrialised nations presented damning findings on the UK (UNICEF, 2007). The public and parliamentary debates about the report either criticised the out-of-date data or explained the findings with reference to family and social breakdown or parenting deficits. Some social commentators highlighted the problems of materialism, poverty and economic inequalities (Bradshaw and Richardson, 2009). The press dubbed the UK 'the worst place to grow up in Europe'. In May 2007 Tony Blair resigned as Prime Minister, and Gordon Brown, the former Chancellor, became Prime Minister. One of the first developments of the Brown era was the disbanding of the DfES and establishment of the Department for Children, Schools and Families. The new department had a remit to promote the five outcomes for children and young people aged 0–19 years. Responsibility for further and higher education policy was reallocated to the new Department for Innovation, Universities and Skills (which was also concerned with adult training and skills). The DCSF (2007b) defined its mission as 'making the UK the best place to grow up in Europe', speaking directly to the UNICEF report debates, and announced the development of a Children's Plan, published in December 2007. The Children's Plan (DCSF, 2007b) remained dominated by concerns about educational attainment, offending and 'the most socially excluded families'. But it also extended the notion of 'children at risk' by incorporating concerns about contemporary risks to children symbolic of normative life-styles: work–family conflict, online safety, the commercialisation of childhood, access to recreational opportunities, and sedentary life-styles. Reference was made to children 'enjoying childhood' as well as their transitions to adulthood. Supporting parents and families remained a strong theme but more emphasis was given to 'involving parents in schools and learning'. Greater importance was placed on improving young people's health. Key announcements were:

- funding for two parenting practitioners in every LA in England and Wales by 2010 (£31 million between 2007 and 2010)
- more PSAs in schools
- schools to provide parents with more regular information about their child's educational progress and involve parents more in school management
- the establishment of a Parents Panel to advise government
- funding for facilities and respite breaks for families with disabled children and a Family Fund for services for families with disabled children (£90 million between 2007 and 2010)
- funding for play and recreational facilities and opportunities for young people (£225 million between 2007 and 2010)
- the publication of a 'Play Strategy', 'Child Health Strategy' and 'Staying Safe Action Plan' in 2008
- the DCSF to review progress in reducing youth offending and develop preventative strategies to reduce drug and alcohol misuse among young people
- new legislation to require future governments to stick to Labour's child poverty reduction targets and make Children's Centres a statutory service.

Progress reports on addressing these objectives were published in 2008 and 2009. Positive evaluation findings led to further investment. Findings from the Sure Start evaluation reported further significant impacts on parenting, child development and child and parental health and much good practice (Melhuish et al, 2008). The national evaluation of the FIPs reported equally significant findings (Box 7.3). In 2008 the DCSF announced that a further £18 million would be invested in FIPs. Sure Start Children's Centres became a statutory service. In 2009 the DCSF reported that there were around 3,000 Children's Centres serving 2.4 million children under 5 years old and their families in May 2009; 93% of schools had become extended schools; there was near universal take-up of the free nursery place offer for 3- and 4-year-olds; disadvantaged children aged under 2 years would receive a free nursery place; 2,000 families had been supported by FIPs; 2.5 million parents had logged on to the 'Parent Know How' website and significant progress had been made in improving educational attainment and reducing youth offending (DCSF, 2009a). There was little mention of the upward trend in child poverty since 2005, although there was some discussion of the negative impact that rising unemployment and the economic recession had on families (DCSF,

2009a).The strategies aimed at improving child health, safety and youth offending all stressed the need to engage parents and improve parenting. The distinction between 'parents as consumer citizens with rights to information, support and services' continued to be in tension with the need to be directive and punitive towards 'irresponsible and neglectful parents and families'. However, a renewed emphasis on 'couple and family relationships' emerged. A Green Paper on fFamily relationships stressed the relationship between adult/parental relationships and child well-being – aligned with more attention towards 'adult relationships' in families (DCSF, 2010). It announced that couples' counselling and mediation services would receive additional funding of £3.1 million by the end of 2010.

The Social Work Task Force

The death of 'Baby P', due to fatal abuse, in August 2007 led to an inquiry into child protection procedures in the local social services; a national review of the *Every child matters* safeguarding reforms (Laming, 2009) and the establishment of the Social Work Task Force. Lord Laming's report (Laming, 2009) concluded that the *Every child matters* safeguarding reforms had not been properly implemented and the government needed to invest in effective implementation. The Social Work Task Force had a broader remit than child protection concerns and recommended reforms to child and family social work as well as adult social work across England and Wales (Social Work Task Force, 2009). It focused on workforce reforms aimed at improving front-line services and outcomes for service users via better qualified and supported social workers. In relation to child and family social work, the Taskforce called for a simplification of the Integrated Children's System (to reduce administrative burdens on social workers) and widespread reform to the training, qualification framework, supervision and staff development of front-line social workers and social care managers.

Conclusion

This chapter has charted the evolution of Labour's family and child-focused policies. A child-focused social investment approach was a strong theme running through developments whereby policies aimed at parents, families and children sought to address human-capital deficits, produce active citizens and reduce social exclusion. These agendas led to reformulations of parental rights to support and parental responsibilities for children's health and education outcomes and social behaviour – with policies and services having distinctly classed and gendered effects when the gender division of labour in the family is not challenged. From 2003, Labour established a more coherent 'child well-being' agenda. Departmental policy agendas were given much coherence through a focus on five key outcomes for children. Sweeping organisational reforms sought to reconfigure and integrate children's services so as to be more responsive to children's and families' needs.

In the main, the child well-being agenda continued to be dominated by the need for active, responsible and productive citizens, but policy developments also incorporated an expanding range of child welfare concerns. Several evaluation studies reported that initiatives had significantly achieved their intended outcomes for parents, children and families. However, the challenges for LAs and front-line staff in realising the vision of needs-centred integrated services are enormous. The final report of the National Evaluation of the Children's Trusts Pathfinders (NECTP, 2007) found that while many Children's Trusts were effectively developing and integrating services in ways that were highly valued by front-line professionals and parents, considerable challenges remained. An overall finding was that the *Every child matters* vision was challenging to put into practice. While integrated services could lead to efficiency gains and better outcomes for service users in the long run, in the short term they required significant investment and managed change, the extent of which was not fully recognised by central government and required effective implementation (NECTP, 2007). More collaborative working at all levels of services required much effort, investment, expertise and commitment. The report identified the following problems and constraints: professional silos; staff recruitment and retention problems; a lack of staff training; time-consuming and complex planning and needs assessment issues; lack of service user involvement; and confidentiality concerns (NECTP, 2007). This having been said, parents interviewed for this study highly valued Children's Centres and Extended Schools services, children valued access to after-school activities and young people valued access to specialist and recreational services (NECTP, 2007). Parents, children and young people, however, identified shortages in specialist services for children and families (especially for disabled children) and affordable recreational opportunities for young people (NECTP, 2007). In December 2007 the Labour government established a new government department dedicated to promoting the five key outcomes for children – the DCSF – which developed an expanding notion of 'risks to children'. However, the work of the DCSF was increasingly informed by family and behavioural explanations for social exclusion. On coming to office in May 2010, the new Conservative-Liberal Democrat Coalition government returned the DCSF to the more traditional title of the Department for Education and announced major public spending cuts in October 2010. The database of information about children (Contact Point) was withdrawn and the NAPP disbanded. Proposals so far include more targeted and limited family support services (Conservative Party, 2010). However, heightened concerns about social cohesion, 'the broken society' and family breakdown reflect the ongoing dominance of family-centred and behavioural explanations for social exclusion and child well-being. Both the Conservatives and the Liberal Democrats support further investment in Labour's intensive family interventions for 'disadvantaged and dysfunctional families' (Cameron, 2009).

Note

[1] This Inquiry was established in 2001 following the death of Victoria Climbié, an 8-year-old girl from the Ivory Coast who had moved to London to live with her aunt in 2000 and who died in 2001, due to severe abuse and maltreatment. Subsequently, her aunt and her aunt's boyfriend were convicted of fatal abuse. During the court case it transpired that Victoria's welfare had come to the attention of several agencies and that she had been registered with the local social services department. The actions of the social services department and agencies were investigated by Lord Laming's Inquiry.

Part Three
Research on parental perspectives

EIGHT

Parenthood and parenting in context

Introduction

Part Three analyses social research about everyday perspectives and experiences of parenthood and parenting. This chapter considers issues emerging from a thematic analysis of recent sociological and social policy research about the social constructions of parental rights and responsibilities, and parents' experiences, concerns and practices across a range of social, personal and family contexts and in relation to a range of 'parenting topics'. Everyday accounts of parenthood and parenting are analysed as informed by 'layers of meaning' (Charles et al, 2008) (as well as constructed through the research process). The chapter considers everyday accounts and experiences as, in particular, reflecting 'layers of meaning' about:

- 'family' and parent–child relations
- children and children's needs
- maternal and paternal responsibilities for children
- desirable and normative parenting and childcare practices.

Many parents, in line with policy and legal imperatives, seek caring, loving and authoritative parent–child relationships; construct good parenthood as involving the fulfilment of obligations and responsibilities towards children; view good parenting as meeting children's needs; and construct particular practices as 'desirable parenting practices'. However, what constitutes caring and authoritative parent–child relationships, children's needs, parental responsibilities and desirable parenting practices is contested, context-dependent and dynamic. First, the chapter examines three aspects of parent–child and family relationships: (1) the ethic of care for children, (2) intimacy in parent–child and family relations, and (3) parent–child power and authority relations. Second, the chapter selectively reviews research into particular aspects of parenthood and parenting. Third, it highlights several moral dilemmas that parents and families negotiate.

Parent–child and family relations

Key themes in everyday accounts of parent–child and family relationships are: an ethic of care, intimacy and power relations.

An ethic of care towards children

The child welfare paradigm orientates parent–child relations towards the care, nurture and protection of children. A distinction can be made between 'care as work, labour and activity', 'caring about' children and 'care as an ethical orientation' (Williams, 2004a; Doucet, 2006). Chapter Two drew on Sevenhuijsen's (1998) notion of an ethic of care as 'motivation towards and sensitivities to the welfare needs of others'. The ESRC Care, Values and Future of Welfare research group (CAVA) undertook in-depth studies of 'the values that matter' to people in their personal and family lives (Williams, 2004a). In the context of changing family formations, the research examined family relationships in lone-mother headed families, post-divorce families and same-sex couple headed families. Participants expressed strong beliefs in 'fairness, respect, care, communication and trust in coping with changes in their family lives' (Williams, 2004a, p 8). Williams (2004a, p 8) argued that these ethics of care within families and personal networks 'helped people to cope with change and enabled resilience'. The CAVA studies highlighted the difficulties parents and family members faced in living up to their ideals of family life, but found that commitments to sustaining family and parent–child relationships were more prominent than popular theories of 'excessive individualism' suggested (Williams, 2004a). Where parents do not uphold an ethic of care towards children, Chapter Three highlighted the social problems parents face and the 'cultural supports' for negative and oppressive attitudes towards children. Critical questions for social policies become how to promote an ethic of care alongside an ethic of justice, across society (Williams, 2004a).

Other studies have highlighted more everyday ethics of care such as 'putting children first', 'putting family first', 'being there' and 'doing your best as a parent'. Ribbens McCarthy et al (2000) argued that 'putting children first' was portrayed as a 'non-negotiable moral imperative' within their interview study with step-families. Their study found 'overwhelming consensus, adhered to whatever the parenting status of the narrator, that children's needs come first' (Ribbens McCarthy et al, 2000, p 791). 'Putting children first', in the context of step-families, could relate to 'taking responsibility to work out how to do the right thing in developing new or different relationships with children', 'treating step and biological, resident and non-resident children fairly', 'building trust and warm relationships with children', learning 'how to listen and be aware of children's feelings' and 'giving children time' (Ribbens McCarthy et al, 2000). 'Putting children first' referred to ways of relating to, thinking about and treating children in particular ways relevant to the step-family situation. This ethic encompasses relational competences and exchanges of resources, such as time and emotional labour. Measuring up to these ideals, however, is another matter. Much research finds that the majority of parents fear they are not 'doing a good enough job' (Edwards, 2004; NFPI, 2001). Ribbens McCarthy et al (2000) theorised parental narratives as 'moral tales' and found that, where respondents reported not living up to these ideals, moral identities were salvaged by emphasising the vulnerabilities of adults, overwhelming constraints and lack of choice (Ribbens McCarthy et al, 2000). Moral identities were retained by portraying effort towards 'putting children first'. Another theme in Ribbens McCarthy et al's (2000) analysis was how personal discourses of, and responsibilities for, children's needs were informed by factors such as parental status, gender, social class and ethnic identity. For example, mothers' accounts were 'more organised around accepting care responsibilities for children', and 'the creation of a stable family unit was a strong moral theme in several women's accounts, requiring considerable emotional work, mediation of relationships and organisation skills' (Ribbens McCarthy et al, 2000, p 793). The male respondents did not perceive 'putting children first' in such demanding 'caring for' terms, but rather referred to constraining their leisure, social or paid work aspirations in order to 'be there' for step and birth children, often in the evenings or at weekends. However, some did 'allude to a tension between taking responsibility for children and the pursuit of individual goals' (Ribbens McCarthy et al, 2000, p 792). These reflect the moral dilemmas of responsible parenting.

An additional everyday ethic can be described as 'putting family first' (Backett-Milburn et al, 2008). This ethic can be complementary to 'putting children first' but can also encompass competing demands and 'webs of obligations' within the broader context of kin, family and personal networks (Backett-Milburn et al, 2008). Backett-Milburn et al (2008) described the significance of this ethic for the working-class women working in retail outlets interviewed for their study:

> For most interviewees, family coming first was expressed and appeared to be experienced both as a choice and an obligation; as such, it seemed to be part of the taken for granted framework of normative familial behaviour. Putting family first was also a means of laying claim to a moral identity as a good family member; this was simply something you did as a good mother or a good daughter/family member. (Backett-Milburn et al, 2008, p 481)

For the women in their study, 'putting family first' influenced numerous aspects of their lives such as their 'choice' of employment (with a preference for employment that 'fits round family commitments' and the informal use of 'trusted and known' family members for childcare); their residential location (to be near family); daily domestic and caring responsibilities, and availability to provide support. 'Putting family first' placed considerable demands on the women's daily lives and was not always compatible with the demands of being 'good reliable employees' and their breadwinning responsibilities:

> Managing webs of obligations at the intersection of work and family could sometimes, however, result in competing priorities and challenges to the belief that 'family comes first'. Several women explained that

their partners or children sometimes expressed negative sentiments about their jobs or the hours they worked. This might suggest tensions between women putting their families first by providing financially for them, but at the same time not providing them with enough time or attention. Interviewees tended to respond to such potential challenges to their claims that 'family comes first' by explaining that that they allocated particular time-slots or did activities with their children. (Backett-Milburn et al, 2008, pp 483–4)

'Putting family first' can express a family focus rather than a child focus (Barns et al, 2006; Phoenix and Hussain, 2007; Pugh, 2009). Phoenix and Hussain (2007) reviewed studies of parenting across ethnic groups. They concluded that there is a dearth of research that sufficiently examines generational change and differences within and across ethnic categories. There are particular gaps in research on smaller ethnic minorities, 'mixed ethnicity families' and minority White ethnic groups (Phoenix and Hussain, 2007). Some ethnographic and qualitative studies sought to fill such gaps and have examined child-rearing practices across ethnic groups. Barns et al (2006) described the less individualistic cultural heritage among non-Western cultures and the value placed on children 'fitting into' the family unit, parental authority over children and child training, as opposed to Western perspectives on 'individualised intensive child-rearing' and 'smaller family sizes'.

'Being there for children' has figured in many studies as an important everyday family value (Ribbens, 1994; Kempson, 1996; Graham and McDermott, 2005; Charles et al, 2008; Dermott, 2008). Lupton and Barclay (1997, pp 121–2) generated qualitative data on the experiences of first-time fathers and found that:

> Many fathers used the phrase 'being there' in their interviews to describe a 'good father'. 'Being there' appeared to be a term that has entered the popular vernacular [...] It is a powerful phrase, which is somewhat amorphous and open to a wide range of interpretations.

'Being there' was associated with parental presence in children's lives, parental availability for children, providing emotional support to children and parental supervision of children's behaviour, activities and well-being. The sentiment is further informed by notions of family as involving reciprocal support ('being there for each other') or forming a family household ('being there' by co-residing with children) or 'being there' for family occasions (ie weekends, school events, religious holidays or birthdays). Ribbens McCarthy and Edwards (2002) argued that mothers with young children were likely to associate 'being there' with the role of primary carer and as constant availability for children. Dermott (2008) found that the fathers of secondary school-age children in her study expressed strong commitments to 'being there' for their children. The fathers associated being there for children with 'being around' at home, doing activities with children, building close relationships with children and 'being there' for specific occasions or times. Southerton (2006) concluded that moralities of 'being there' and 'putting children first' have a 'stronger temporal impact on mothers' daily lives than fathers", indicating how gender cultures infuse parental responsibilities.

Another everyday ethic of care towards children is that of 'doing your best for your children'. This phrase refers to parental efforts to fulfil responsibilities to and support children – resonating with the theme raised earlier about the morality of good intentions. Focus group research with parents (Counterpoint Research, 2007) found that participants often referred to 'doing your best' as an indicator of committed parenting. This phrase in part expressed concerns about being judged an inadequate parent and the context-dependent nature of parenting:

> They [the parents participating in the focus groups] were loath to discuss 'childhood' as a concept. They [the parents] argued that every child is different which means that what makes one child happy might not make another child happy; parenting skills are relative, and they would be loath to judge another parent in absolute terms; and therefore you can't objectify 'childhood', there are no guarantees, only *'your best efforts'*. (Counterpoint Research, 2007, p 14; emphasis in original report)

'Doing your best for your children' expressed a deep sense of parental responsibility for children's welfare:

> It's down to us [parents] to do the best we can (Father, aged 20–35). (Counterpoint Research, 2007, p 30)

'Doing your best' acknowledged the parental efforts in the context of 'few guarantees' and 'many constraints and uncertainties' (Counterpoint Research, 2007). While policy discourses talk about 'children's outcomes', this lay discourse highlights 'being committed to your children' and 'good enough parenting' in the context of limited control and influence over children's lives and outcomes. Parents felt that siblings, peer groups, neighbourhoods, schools, the media and popular culture particularly had powerful influences on young people:

> You just do your best and hope it all turns out ok (Mother, aged 20–30). (Counterpoint Research, 2007, pp 16–17)

> 'You do your best and you just hope it works out for the best ...' (2nd respondent) '... they say that, don't they, there are no guarantees with children!' (Single mothers, aged 20–30). (Counterpoint Research, 2007, p 17)

> You bring them up as best you can, and just hope they don't get in
> with the wrong crowd and they get a reasonable school (Single mother,
> aged 20–30). (Counterpoint Research, 2007, p 43)

Intimacy in parent–child relations

The *Good childhood inquiry* (Layard and Dunn, 2009, p 15) stated that 'above all
children need to be loved'. In the author's interview-based research with lone
mothers and parents using Sure Start services, respondents often referred to the
importance of 'caring about' their children, and related 'caring about' to a range of
values and practices, such as: being warm and empathetic towards their children,
valuing their children, recognising their child's individuality and individual worth,
loving their children, knowing and understanding their children, 'being on their
side when they get into trouble at school or with the police', and appreciating
their child's strengths (Williams and Churchill, 2006; Churchill, 2007). The
quality of parent–child relationships is deeply affected by the relational dynamics
in households and families, across and within generations (DCSF, 2010). The
Counterpoint Research (2007) study discussed earlier found that parents not
only valued close parent–child relationships in terms of children's emotional
well-being (and the personal emotional rewards of parenthood) but emphasised
how 'knowing your child' and 'good parent–child relationships' were at the heart
of 'good parenting'. Participants talked about good parent–child relationships in
terms of mutual respect, warmth, empathy and intimacy. Participants reported
that 'all else flows' from parent–child and family attachments, such as children's
self esteem, aspirations and behaviour (Counterpoint Research, 2007).

As reviewed in Chapters Two and Three, father–child relations are thought of
as being more intimate in contemporary times (Dermott, 2008). Leaving aside
the lack of comparative historical research to support these claims (Smart, 2007),
many fathers refer to these generational differences in fatherhood. Stephen
Williams' (2008, p 498) interview-based study with fathers found that 'building a
relationship with children that moved beyond the traditional model of fathering
was expressed in virtually all the interviews'. Doucet (2006) used the term
'emotional responsibility' to refer to parental commitments to children's emotional
well-being. Erikson (2005) conceptualises 'emotional work' within parent–child
and family relationships as a two-way process involving all family members.
Erikson (2005) in particular highlights how mothers in her research undertook
'activities that are concerned with the enhancement of others' emotional well-
being and with the provision of emotional support' (Erikson, 2005, p 338), and
listed the following examples: monitoring children's moods; comforting children;
expressing positive feelings; expressions of caring about and loving your children;
more open two-way communication between parents and children; offering
encouragement; showing appreciation; listening closely to children and expressing
empathy (Erikson, 2005, p 339).

Much research has examined the quality of family relationships in the context of parental separation and divorce. Several studies have found that when adults are able to maintain functional and supportive relationships during and after divorce, non-resident parents in the post-divorce context are more likely to remain in contact with children – this usually relates to non-resident fathers (Lewis and Lamb, 2007). Economic issues critically impact on patterns of residence and contact between non-resident parents and children. Non-resident fathers living on low incomes can face burdensome financial costs associated with sustaining contact with children. Speak et al (1997) interviewed young non-resident fathers who detailed the way poverty, material deprivation and unpredictable employment impinged on their capabilities to provide for their children, sustain contact and participate in recreational activities with their children.

Smart et al (2003) carried out several studies of parents' and children's experiences of divorce and post-divorce parenthood. Their earlier research explored the experiences and narratives of parents, while subsequent research explored children's voices, concerns and experiences – with one longitudinal study involving the same sample of families (Smart et al, 2003). Smart et al (2003) found that fairness, care and respect were important to children in describing desirable parent–child relationships. In particular, children needed reassurance and support, and felt powerless and anxious when parents argued, kept information from them and involved them in adult conflicts. Parents tended to refer to 'minimising harm and disruption for children'. Smart et al (2003) found that at times parents could be pre-occupied with their own problems or seek to protect their children in ways which children found less acceptable or which left children more powerless and anxious. Parents could be uncertain about 'when, how and to what extent' to involve children and talk to them about problems and issues. Parents and children could differ in their judgements about whether parents 'ignored the wishes of children', 'involved them too much', 'manipulated them' or 'protected them' (Smart et al, 2003, p 144).

Some studies capture diverse perspectives about intimate parent–child relationships. For example, some fathers may see their role as being more limited to breadwinning and paternal authority. A small-scale study based on focus group interviews with first-generation and second-generation South Asian immigrants found that older fathers (first-generation migrants) tended to continue to see their role in more traditional ways: 'first generation fathers were more inclined to see [father absence] as a norm'; while the younger fathers (second-generation migrants) tended to problematise 'fathers being absent in their sons' early years and adolescence' (Fathers Direct and An-Nisa Society, 2008, p 4). Moreover, the second-generation fathers spoke about a 'major vacuum in their lives' when they judged they did not have enough time or contact with their children (Fathers Direct and An-Nisa Society, 2008, p 4). Other studies found that notions of gendered parental responsibilities and gendered childhoods shape relational practices. In a review of research on parenting adolescents, Henricson and Roker

(2000) found that several studies reported young people had more intimate and confiding relationships with mothers than with fathers and that mothers more often report higher levels of anxiety and concern about their children's emotional well-being.

Alongside parental feelings of responsibility, love and empathy for children, there is a need to recognise negative and difficult emotions in parent–child relationships. For example, Sevon (2007) interviewed first-time mothers and examined the highly charged nature of transitions to motherhood. In her longitudinal qualitative study, Sevon (2007) found that mothers often, over time, gained expertise in caring for their babies, especially when they were well supported and in good health. But she also found 'tiredness, guilt, shame, anxiety, anger and aggression' were often part of the experience of meeting the demands of childcare and adapting to parenthood (Sevon, 2007, p 2). The concept of emotional labour captured 'the emotional aspects and work aspect of care from the carer's point of view' (Sevon, 2007, p 2).

Power and authority in parent–child and generational relations

Hierarchy, power and authority are further important dimensions to parenthood and parenting. The MCS (2nd Survey) was conducted during 2003–05 and involved interviews with parents and carers of 18,000 children born in 2000 who were reaching 3 years old. The MCS sample included a disproportionate number of families living in poorer and Sure Start areas. The survey asked general questions about parenting style. Although caution is needed in interpreting the findings about ethnic differences in this study (due to small sample sizes), the MCS data allows for analysis of gender, ethnicity and social class differences. Smith (2007, p 2) reported that the majority of respondents described their parenting style as 'firm discipline with lots of fun'. However, the data generated gender differences, with more fathers subscribing to the view of 'firm rules with fun' and more mothers describing their parenting as 'doing my best':

> The majority of parents reported that their style was either 'firm rules with fun' (42 per cent of mothers and 54 per cent of fathers) or 'doing my best' (50 per cent of mothers and 33 per cent of fathers).

The MCS reported different responses across ethnic groups. For example, half as many Bangladeshi fathers described their parenting as 'firm but fun' as Black Caribbean fathers:

> Only 30 per cent of Bangladeshi fathers reported 'firm discipline with lots of fun' as a parenting style, compared with 60 per cent of Black Caribbean fathers.

Parents were asked about 'rules in the family household'. In analysing the mothers' responses to these questions, Smith (2007, p 2) noted that the Bangladeshi mothers were least likely to report having 'lots of rules' and the Black Caribbean mothers were slightly more likely to report 'lots of rules':

> About a third of mothers (31 per cent) reported that their family had lots of rules, 42 per cent did not have many rules and 27 per cent said that their policy varied. Almost half (49 per cent) added that the rules they did have were strictly enforced. Black Caribbean mothers were most likely to report that they had lots of rules (39 per cent), while Bangladeshi mothers were the least likely (17 per cent).

The MCS asked parents to weigh up the values of children 'thinking for themselves' in contrast to 'obeying parents'. It found that White British parents valued 'thinking for self' while South Asian, African and Afro-Caribbean parents tended to prize 'obeying parents' more highly (Smith, 2007, p 3). Regional differences across the UK were noted, with parents in Northern Ireland more likely to value 'children should obey parents' above children 'thinking for self' (Smith, 2007, p 3). These findings are limited though, as parents were asked morally loaded and general questions. There is a need for more in-depth research (Phoenix and Hussain, 2007).

The Counterpoint Research (2007) study found a keen rejection of both authoritarian and lax parenting (the latter associated with 'allowing children to get what they want'). Participants in this research felt that too much parental control over children was detrimental, but so too was lax or permissive parenting – parenting which 'indulged children' led to 'selfish and self-centred' children (Counterpoint, 2007, p 41). Participants felt that children needed 'tough-love' (Counterpoint, 2007, p 41). Studies with children and young people also found that they prefer 'negotiated and involved decision making' rather than 'always getting their own way' (Madge, 2006; Madge and Willmott, 2007).

Lewis's (2007) study of parenting teenagers found that many parents rejected notions of traditional authoritarian parenting as 'impossible to achieve in practice, damaging to parent–child relationships and likely to encourage children to rely more on their friends'; and supported ideas about 'respect for teenagers' opinions and freedoms' (Lewis, 2007, p 298). The parents in this research reported preferences towards guiding their children via persuasive reasoning and negotiation. Important 'discipline and monitoring practices' were giving children information, guiding their choices, 'monitoring' their children in several ways by directly asking them for information about their activities or 'reading emotional signs of well-being', transporting them to places to ensure they were safe and communicating with other parents to corroborate young people's accounts and monitor their welfare. Problems, dilemmas and anxieties arose for parents. Negotiated parental authority was demanding on parents, and required competences, resources and parent–child relationship qualities; and children were influenced by other agents, such as popular culture, the media, peer groups and the internet. Many parents reported that these approaches were 'difficult' ways of sustaining parental authority and relied on engagement and motivation on the part of children and parents (Lewis, 2007). Some of the participants were anxious about 'being too soft' or 'too hard' on their teenage children.

Children's needs and parental responsibilities

A common theme across many studies is that 'parents view good parenting in terms of meeting the needs of their children' (Borland et al, 1998). Within this definition of good parenting, definitions of children's needs and divisions of responsibility for meeting needs are varied, context dependent and dynamic. The discussion below will examine some key areas of research.

Providing for children

Chapters Two and Three set out the economic necessities underpinning the shift to the dual-earner family norm as well as differences in mothers' and fathers' breadwinning roles. The gendered aspects of parental financial responsibilities lead to concern about sustaining financial responsibilities for children in the context of parental separation, divorce and lone motherhood. The 2006 BSA Survey analysed attitudes to child maintenance and asked its representative sample of the British public: Should a father pay maintenance for their biologically related children when they split up from the children's mother? An overwhelming majority, 88% of respondents, answered 'yes'. The majority view was also that duties to pay maintenance on the part of the non-resident parent should be assessed in relation to the income of both parents. Of the 88% in agreement, though, 89% felt that the level of maintenance should depend on the father's income and 74% felt that the level should depend on the mother's income. These figures show how financial responsibilities for children are considered a joint responsibility. In the context of remarriage and being a step-parent, attitude surveys suggest more ambivalent views, with respondents divided over whether maintenance should continue and how much this depends on the step-parent's income. The BSA Survey asked about the situation of step-fathers and found that just over a half (54%) of respondents agreed that maintenance should continue, but around a third (35%) felt that the level of maintenance depends on the combined household income within the child's main residence (Park et al, 2006). Researchers have called for more recognition of the economic burdens on non-resident fathers responsible for birth and step-children (Lewis and Lamb, 2007). Further, there is a dearth of research that has examined parental responsibilities within the context of financial interactions across families and personal social networks. Grandparents tend to contribute financially to the costs of raising children in families and there are particularly strong expectations for inter-generational transfers in Asian and African cultures (Barns et al, 2006).

Atkinson et al (2006) explored views within focus groups about non-resident fathers' responsibilities for child support and maintenance. They found that considerations about fathers' responsibilities to provide for children were mediated by issues of the fathers' rights to contact and their financial capabilities. In cases of severe poverty, it was felt that non-resident fathers should still pay child maintenance for birth children but this should be set at a low rate. However, in line with the sentiments of the Children Act 1998, many respondents felt that fathers' rights to contact were dependent on such contact not placing children at risk of significant harm, but there was much uncertainty about whether responsibilities for paying maintenance were also dependent on having contact (Atkinson et al, 2006). This research found that the focus of the group discussions tended to deliberate the respective interests, duties and needs of mothers and fathers, but rarely considered 'children's rights to a basic standard of living' or 'children's rights to family relationships' (Atkinson et al, 2006). Discussions about paternal responsibilities for children were related to consideration of the circumstances surrounding paternity. For example, the issue of 'responsibility for the pregnancy' was debated:

> Views about the responsibility to pay child support in the event of an unplanned pregnancy were polarised. Some people felt that all men should be responsible for the consequences of their actions and making their own arrangements for contraception, whilst others felt that if the man had been entrapped by the woman becoming pregnant, he should not be forced to pay maintenance. Nobody considered the rights of the child in such a situation. (Atkinson et al, 2006, p 14)

The circumstances in which parents become parents therefore influence notions of parental responsibilities, with contemporary society divided over the normative expectations associated with different routes into parenthood. Financial responsibilities for children were further explored in relation to different constructions of childhood, which in turn are thought to strongly relate to social class contexts. Based on an ethnographic study of child rearing across middle-class, working-class and poor families in the US, Lareau (2003) argued that social class is a critical context influencing approaches to child rearing. Lareau (2003) argued that middle-class parents appear to be orientated towards 'cultivating individuality' and 'human, social and cultural capital'. She found within her sample of US middle-class families that there was a more self-conscious use of financial resources 'to invest in their child's individuality, talents and skills' in order to enhance their child's future life chances. Lareau (2003) found that more of the middle-class families in her study paid for children to take part in leisure, social and recreational activities which were described as 'educational' and 'developmentally beneficial', as well as for private education and tuition, as compared to the working-class and poor families. Investing in these positional goods and services could place middle-class families under considerable financial strain and compel parents to work long hours, as well as reflect much higher levels of financial capital, income and assets. In contrast, Lareau (2003) argued that working-class and poorer parents in her study had much lower incomes and were under financial constraints. There was a tendency for child rearing to be more focused on looking after children in a day-to-day sense, monitoring children's behaviour and not paying much for leisure, recreational, educational or childcare services. Lareau (2003) felt that child rearing was underpinned by a stronger notion of 'natural child development'. She stated that social class differences were more pronounced in her study than were child-rearing differences related to ethnic, religious or gendered cultural practices. Similar theories have been developed from UK research (Ribbens, 1994; Gillies, 2007). Evidence suggests that parenting remains highly gendered and demanding in better-off families but that having a higher income enhances access to assets, social and cultural capital, and opportunities. Parents in this context can negotiate and seek to sustain a more privileged social status for their children, albeit not one without its own struggles and anxieties (Devine, 2004; Ribbens, 1994). Family expenditure surveys additionally find a strong association between family household income and spending on formal childcare, recreation and leisure (ONS, 2009). However, other studies have found that affordable local leisure and recreational services, and opportunities for parental involvement in children's early education and school learning, are highly valued by working-class parents, who utilise them to promote their child's learning and opportunities (Williams and Churchill, 2006).

Financial responsibilities for children intensify in the context of living in poverty and changing consumption patterns. A survey by the National Family and Parenting Institute (NFPI, 2001) found that 84% of parents felt that there was too much marketing aimed at children. The high rates of family poverty in the UK mean that many parents reported difficulties meeting children's basic living needs (for housing, clothes, food and so on) as well as experiencing financial pressures from the 'more subtle pressures arising from their own and their children's material expectations and demands' (Andersen et al, 2002, p 6). Studies of parenting on a low income have illuminated how 'putting children first' leads to prioritising spending on children (Middleton et al, 1998). Middleton et al (1998) developed the concepts of 'strategic adjustment' (to refer to the strategic choices, responses and behaviours that parents developed to help them to provide for their children while living on a low income) and 'resigned adjustment' (which described the development of fatalistic attitudes) to examine coping strategies. Kempson (1996) identified three main strategies that families deploy to make ends meet: keeping control over finances, living from day to day and paying the most pressing bill first. Families reported managing on a low income via strict financial monitoring and budgeting; restricting spending on items deemed less essential or too expensive;

constant price checking; seeking out bargains; buying in bulk; buying more or less the same items each week; and cooking meals for your children that you know they like and that will fill them up (Kempson, 1996; Attree, 2004). Coping on a low income leads to a daily struggle of attempting to juggle resources so as to pay the most urgent bills or meet immediate subsistence needs (Ghate and Hazel, 2002; Bennett, 2006). Economising where possible is an additional strategy. Economising meant living 'localised lives' and keeping to going to places and using services within walking distance; not owning a car or taking many long journeys on public transport (Middleton et al, 1998). Parents attempt to spread the costs of clothes, presents and household items by using mail order catalogues and buying cheaper and bargain items where available (Kempson, 1996). The Families and Children Survey found that families living on the lowest incomes particularly restricted spending on social activities such as leisure, recreation and sport activities, holidays abroad, staying with friends and relatives, visiting friends and relatives who lived some distance away from them, and adults taking a night out (Connolly and Kew, 2008). However, coping strategies and family practices lead to social exclusion (Ridge, 2002).

Mayo and Nairns (2009) examined how families negotiated 'the commercial world'. Mayo and Nairns (2009, pp 316–18) cited the following parental practices as nurturing values, attitudes and behaviours which help children to become discerning consumers: making children work for their pocket money; encouraging children to save; teaching children about budgeting; discouraging self-identities and definitions of success based on wealth and earning money; encouraging children to give some of their pocket money to charity; encouraging volunteering; encouraging contribution to household chores and rewarding children for helping others; parental commitment to finding out about the internet and marketing strategies; and watching TV/reading magazines together so that they can become 'teaching moments' whereby parents can discuss with their children how marketing and advertising targets them. Studies with children and young people have also found them to be discerning consumers – aware and cynical of obvious marketing strategies and ploys, and often regulating their own desires due to concern about over-burdening their parents and families (Ridge, 2002; Seaman et al, 2007). However, consumption and participation in social and recreational activities are understood as critical elements of 'normative childhoods' (Ridge, 2002). Contemporary consumerism, according to Pugh (2009), had become associated with 'new standards of meeting children's needs through the market place and new stakes for failing to do so [which combine] to make child-rearing consumption urgent, prevalent and fraught with emotional meaning' for parents (Pugh, 2009, p 23). In an ethnographic study undertaken in the US, Pugh (2009, p 5) asked 'how is the commercialization of childhood changing what it means to care for and raise children, and what it means for children to belong?'. Pugh (2009, p 23) examined consumption as driven by desires for social belonging as well as by 'desires for socio-economic status' and 'class specific tastes'. Pugh

(2009) found some general tendencies across families that appeared to link to social class and ethnic differences. In terms of social class, Pugh (2009) argued that affluent families engaged in a process of 'symbolic deprivation', while low-income families engaged in a process of 'symbolic indulgence'. The majority of the middle-class families in Pugh's (2009) study expressed an ambivalent position towards child-orientated consumerism, presenting themselves as in control of their child's consumption desires and selectively consuming goods and services in ways that invested in children's development. However, Pugh (2009) found that few middle-class parents 'resisted' children's consumption desires and many under-reported the cost of purchases such as for birthdays or Christmas. Parents in lower-income families also attempted to meet children's social needs for consumption but emphasised the financial constraints and limitations they faced, while going to great lengths to strategically purchase goods and items that they felt were important for their child's social inclusion. Critical issues underpinning these practices, for Pugh (2009), included the social construction of poverty as an inferior material and social status, and parental experiences of economic disadvantage. In some cases, Pugh (2009) found that parents held cultural and child-rearing values that enabled them to resist commercial pressures. Good parenting in these cases involved 'enforced limits on their children's gratification, even if doing so threatened to impede their children's ability to participate in their social world' (Pugh, 2009, p 156). However, Pugh (2009) additionally found that few parents were unaffected by children's social suffering. Several other studies in the UK context have associated consumption practices with parental concerns about children's opportunities to enjoy the goods and services which their peers enjoy, and fears of bullying, social exclusion and low self-esteem that arise from non-participation (Madge, 2006). Purchasing brand-name clothing, cable television services and electronic games/equipment are practices that have been associated with enabling children to enjoy contemporary childhood (Middleton et al, 1998; Ridge, 2002; Gillies, 2007).

Caring for children

'Being well cared for' was cited as a fundamental aspect of a 'good childhood' among the participants in the DWP study (Counterpoint Research, 2007). What this meant was often understood in taken-for-granted ways or expressed in terms of general principles such as 'ensuring children are well fed', 'providing children with 1 hot meal a day', 'providing a nice home', 'keeping children clean and well dressed' or 'making sure children sleep well'. Doucet's (2006) qualitative research on caring within families distinguished between domestic labour, 'DIY', financial management, subsistence activities, and physical and emotional care. Folbre and Yoon (2007, p 232) argued that definitions of childcare need to incorporate a range of activities such as physical care (ie feeding, bathing, dressing or attending to the physical medical needs of a child); domestic labour arising from having children in the house (such as preparing a meal, doing the laundry, tidying up toys or cleaning the house); developmental care activities (ie activities that stimulate cognitive, emotional or social development, such as talking to your child, parental language use, reading to a child or playing with a child); and logistical and managerial activities (where a parent carries out an activity on their child's behalf, such as arranging social activities, transporting children to activities or communicating with teachers).

Gender cultures shape parental responsibilities for childcare, the make-up of the professional childcare workforce and how parents perceive the care needs of children. Chapter Three illustrated how survey research finds that women continue to carry out the bulk of informal childcare and domestic labour. However, less research has examined fathers' experiences of childcare. Lewis and Lamb (2007) reviewed studies of fatherhood. They found that conventional measures of childcare which focus on the primary carer and physical day-to-day care of children neglect fathers' contribution to childcare. Fathers have been found to take on more responsibility for domestic labour if they hold more egalitarian views about gender (Lewis and Lamb, 2007). Conflict and poor relationships between parents have been associated with lower rates of father involvement in childcare, especially among non-resident fathers (Lewis and Lamb, 2007). Henwood and Procter (2003) found that many fathers with young children described their role as 'supporting maternal care' but did not perceive their contribution to childcare as marginal. Doucet (2006) proposed that men may care differently to women, with an emphasis on play. Dermott (2008), though, felt that fathers are able to 'select more rewarding activities with children', due to childcare or domestic labour being positioned as primarily mothers' work (Dermott, 2008, p 19). However, Lewis and Lamb (2007) found evidence that some studies reported fathers could feel mothers had a 'gatekeeping' role when it comes to children's lives and childcare issues.

Adults with more severe health problems or disabilities, or families with disabled children, are more reliant on social care and health services. Children's services reform has neglected the support needs of adults with disabilities in respect of their parental and childcare roles, although the needs of disabled children have moved up the policy agenda in recent years. Families affected by disability constitute a diverse group but there are higher rates of disability among low-income families and some ethnic minorities. Quinton (2004) noted that South Asian children in the UK are three times more likely to have a learning disability than White British children. Studies have found that health and social care services do not adequately address language barriers that inhibit access to services; do not widely meet religious or cultural needs; and can assume that families can rely on support from family and friends (Quinton, 2004). Parents can report a lack of information and communication from health and social care services that they need to rely on, and experience a lack of access to specialist respite services and equipment (Quinton, 2004). A study of parents' experiences of using specialist health services found a lack of effective multi-agency work and coordination, and shortages in speech therapists, physiotherapy, and educational provision for disabled children (Quinton, 2004). Health and social care professionals can be criticised for adopting a medical model of disability and not attending to disabled children's family, social and education needs, or parents' emotional and support needs (Quinton, 2004).

An under-researched area is children and young people's own contribution to childcare, the care of family members and domestic labour. Chapter Three summarised Olsen and Clarke's (2006) study of 'parenting and disability', which found that young carers constituted a diverse group and 'care' was a 'two-way ethic and activity'. Research has identified young carers' needs for support from health, respite and educational services to combat the detrimental impact that being a young carer can have on children's health, social networks and relationships with peers, and educational attainment; and the lack of awareness and knowledge that young people can have about their rights and the availability of services for young carers (Mayhew, 2005).

'Educational' needs and discourses of child development

This section considers parental involvement in children's education and school life, as well as studies of child development in families. Several studies have examined parental involvement in homework and school life. The Families and Children Survey (FACS), conducted by the DWP and involving a sample of 8,939 families in 2006 (with 7,464 families interviewed for the survey, giving a response rate of 84%), found that parents reported that 7 out of 10 children did their homework regularly (Connolly and Kew, 2008). Families with higher incomes reported higher levels of homework completed, and girls were found to be completing their homework more than boys (Connolly and Kew, 2008). Page et al (2009) found that parents had become more involved in schools and homework supervision, in part due to some of the educational reforms described in Chapters Six and Seven. Children's schoolwork, however, could be a source of conflict in families (Page et al, 2009). Some parents report difficulties in motivating and supporting children (Page et al, 2009). In their research based on interviews with parents and children in five schools in England and Wales, Page et al (2009) found that parents could have difficulties in communication with schools, could feel 'pigeon-holed' and 'judged' by teachers as providing inadequate support for children, and could feel that they lacked sufficient information about schoolwork and school life to effectively support children (especially in relation to secondary schools). Goldman (2005) reviewed studies on fathers' involvement and found that fathers are more likely to be involved when:

> their child's mother is involved in the child's learning and education, they have good relations with their child's mother, they or their child's mother have relatively high educational qualifications, they got

> involved in their child's life early on, their child is in primary school rather than secondary school, their child is doing well in secondary school, and their child's school is welcoming to parents. (Goldman, 2005, quoted in Lewis and Lamb, 2007, p 13)

Devine (2004) argued that parents utilise social, economic and cultural capital to support their children's educational, employment and social opportunities. Through qualitative research informed by social capital theories, Gillies (2007) examined mothers' beliefs, practices, resources and contexts across families from different social class backgrounds. Likewise, Gillies (2007) argued that middle-class parents utilise their 'access to money, high status social contacts and legitimated cultural knowledge' to 'consolidate advantages' for their children through investing in education, out-of-school activities, leisure pursuits and social networks (Gillies, 2007). In her qualitative research, she found that middle-class parents generate resources and opportunities that support children's educational achievements (Gillies, 2007). Gillies' (2007) research examined 'constructions of childhood, parenthood and the self' as imbued with social class consciousness and cultures. In her analysis of identity formations and parenting practices, Gillies (2007) examined how parenting is a crucial site for the moulding of social class dispositions and identities, so that middle-class parents and schools 'mould' children into a 'middle class child' with a sense of confidence, competence and entitlement. Long-term poverty and low income, however, can orientate parenting towards 'preserving limited resources' and equip children with 'survival skills' (Ghate and Hazel, 2002; Gillies, 2007). Working-class parents are more likely to negotiate 'challenges and difficulties that middle class parents worried less about', such as poor housing, living in a deprived neighbourhood, unemployment or employment insecurity – leading them to prioritise their 'protection' role towards their children and manage risks in present time.

Supervision, safeguarding and discipline

There are several studies of parents' experiences of supervising, disciplining and safeguarding children. Stacey and Roker (2005) conducted an in-depth study of parental practices and experiences of supervising and monitoring children. Through in-depth interviews with parents and young people, the study explored how parents and young people negotiated monitoring and supervision in 50 families with children aged between 11 and 16. Parental 'monitoring' of children and young people was associated with keeping 'young people safe and out of trouble and preparing them for independent living as adults' (Stacey and Roker, 2005, p 2). 'Monitoring' involved monitoring children's whereabouts and activities, and their emotional well-being, particularly during 'critical developmental stages' such as starting secondary school, being a teenager or during difficult life events and circumstances such as parental separation, moving house or moving school

(Stacey and Roker, 2005, p 2). Five main parental strategies for monitoring and supervising their children's activities and whereabouts were identified. These included: observing and being attentive to children's emotional well-being and behaviour; establishing rules and setting boundaries; asking for information; checking and tracking; and encouraging open communication. The first strategy involved observing children's behaviour and moods in order to make judgements about their well-being; monitoring emotional stability and change; or providing support or guidance if deemed appropriate. One parent in the study described how she monitored her child's emotional well-being, encouraged her child to confide in others and provided advice during a difficult period of her child's life when her grandfather died.

Strategies for monitoring and supervising children could additionally include asking young people directly about their intentions and activities, and checking and tracking their activities, such as calling them on their mobile phone or corroborating what their children have said against the views of their friend's parents. Stacey and Roker (2005) found that parents placed much importance on nurturing trusting, respectful and open parent–child relationships for effective parental supervision and monitoring; and young people placed importance on being able to 'talk to their parents' in an open and honest way. Equally, young people express stronger commitment to their parents' rules and boundaries when they feel they have a good relationship with their parents, where they respect their parents, receive clear and consistent messages about rules and boundaries, feel listened to and involved, and feel that their parents are good role models 'living the values they expected their children to live by' (Madge, 2006). The effectiveness of specific monitoring and supervision practices relates in part to the broader quality of family relationships and communication:

> You have to impart some knowledge onto your children otherwise they do not learn right from wrong. You can't monitor your children properly unless you actually have a conversation and teach your children how important it is, how they should behave and shouldn't behave and to be a good example to them yourself. (Mother of 13-year-old girl, in Stacey and Roker, 2005, p 2)

In their study, Stacey and Roker (2005, pp 3–4) found that 'mothers were more actively involved in monitoring and supervision', 'bore most of the responsibility for monitoring and supervision, regardless of whether the family had one or two parents [in the household]', and that mothers 'often found [monitoring and supervision] time consuming and stressful'. This was due to mothers' taking the primary role in caring for children on a day-to-day basis and spending more time in the home while fathers were at work or non-resident. The primary role of mothers in caring for children also involved young people talking to and confiding in mothers more, which in turn meant that they tended to talk to their mothers more about their activities and whereabouts.

Stacey and Roker (2005) further explored the factors influencing monitoring and supervision from parents' perspectives. They found that parents spoke much about how their decisions and strategies were informed by judgements about their local neighbourhood and their child's age, gender and individual personality. Fear about safety in the neighbourhood led some parents to 'increase the extent of parental monitoring' of children's activities outside the home and 'decrease the young person's freedom to go out of the family home without their parents' (Stacey and Roker, 2005, p 3). The young person's age was also a key factor that influenced parental strategies. However, general views about children's age and how this related to expectations of behaviour, self-responsibility and independence are clearly balanced against parental knowledge and judgements about children's individual characteristics and personalities. Stacey and Roker (2005, p 4) called for recognition of the complex ways that parents reported 'tailoring monitoring and supervision arrangements to suit each child's personality and maturity'. The way that parents can monitor and supervise boys and girls differently has been a further area of research and was noted in Stacey and Roker's analysis of their interviews with parents. Stacey and Roker (2005) found that some parents explicitly referred to the need to monitor their daughters' activities in terms of safety:

> I do think you worry about girls more when they go out, that is why I try and talk to her about things. You worry about them more. (Mother of 14-year-old girl, in Stacey and Roker, 2005, p 3)

Ghate et al (2003) carried out a representative survey with 1,250 parents with children aged 0–12, to examine attitudes and practices towards 'disciplining children'. In line with earlier surveys, the study found that a sizeable minority of parents, 10% of those responding to the survey, took the view that parents had the right to use physical force to discipline a child. Around half the respondents felt that the use of physical force was 'sometimes' necessary in certain situations – as a 'last resort' to discipline young children (Ghate et al, 2003). Around 50% of parents reported using minor physical punishment in the past year, while 9% had used severe physical punishment. In this study, the use of physical force was correlated with parental age, parental 'stress', parental conflict, social isolation and parents' feeling unsupported in their parenting role, having a toddler, and having children with 'difficult' behaviour (Ghate et al, 2003).

Andersen et al (2002) conducted a major study of Scottish parents' attitudes and behaviours in their use of physical and non-physical methods of disciplining children. The study carried out qualitative interviews with couples, individuals and focus groups, and a nationally representative survey of 692 parents across Scotland, during 2002. The study concluded that:

Although there is some evidence of change over time in the unacceptability of many forms of physical chastisement, the research indicates that specific use of smacking remains deeply embedded in parenting culture within Scotland. But it would be simplistic to characterise parental attitudes as overwhelmingly or straightforwardly pro-smacking. The most common attitude is one of ambivalence – recognising that smacking can have negative consequences and that there are better ways of dealing with most situations. (Andersen et al, 2002, p vi)

The research found that, in terms of change, parental attitudes and behaviour had become less strict towards children and the use of harsh physical chastisement of children has become more unacceptable. There was considerable agreement that parents should not smack very young children or older children. However, the data generated about actual parenting behaviour found it more common for parents to use physical methods of discipline for children aged 3–5 years old, often within 'highly charged' situations or in response to children's challenging behaviour or to safety concerns (Andersen et al, 2002).

Social inclusion and belonging

Children's needs for social inclusion, belonging and recognition figure highly in research with parents, children and families (Ridge, 2002; Madge, 2006; Seaman et al, 2007). Parents from ethnic minority and mixed-race backgrounds negotiate cultural heritage, social belonging and racial disadvantage and discrimination in a range of ways (Barns et al, 2006; Phoenix and Hussain, 2007). Studies of parenting 'mixed race' children have identified diverse approaches and strategies among parents, orientated towards enabling children to develop positive bi-cultural identities and competences and to cope with racism both within their families and in society more broadly (Okitikpi, 2005). However, some young people also report pressure from parents and families to retain traditional or more essentialist ethnic identities (Okitikpi, 2005). Accounts of working-class mothering and fathering can additionally be infused with experiences and anxieties about social difference, exclusion and discrimination (Speak et al, 1997; Gillies, 2007). As discussed earlier, a critical aspect of promoting children's social inclusion is enabling children to 'fit in' with their peers – through purchasing the latest consumer items marketed at children and making sure children wear clothes and do activities which help them to 'fit in' (Ridge, 2002). Likewise, parents raising disabled children express huge concern about their children's social needs – to enjoy normative opportunities and activities (Hobson et al, 2001).

Negotiating contemporary parental dilemmas

This chapter has examined perspectives about normative parent–child relations, parental rights and responsibilities and children's needs. This section argues that situational and moral decisions and dilemmas pervade everyday practices and experiences. Sevon (2007, p 3) argued that, compared to the complexities of lived realities, idealised normative discourses about family relationships are 'too simplistic and do not assist in understanding the multi-layered problems and moral questions inherent in the relations between gender, power, care and ethics'. This final section will highlight several types of moral dilemmas:

- negotiating the changing, holistic and situated nature of children's needs, childhood and parenthood
- negotiating divisions of responsibilities for children
- negotiating care and paid-work responsibilities
- negotiating responsibilities for children, others and self
- negotiating responsibilities and capabilities.

The first moral dilemma relates to parental perceptions of children's 'holistic', changing and conflicting needs and how best to meet children's needs, given the realities of people's lives and situations. For example, Kelley et al (2002, p 19) argued that developmental, intimacy and risk discourses produced tensions in parental accounts of managing risk in their children's lives. Parents negotiated a tension between meeting children's need for protection and their needs for development. Parents reported 'keeping their children safe at home and accompanying their children to places', but feared their children were lacking opportunities for independence, unsupervised play and outdoor play beyond the home. Parents often provided children with play activities, toys and games based in the home and financially invested in a 'family home' with a safe outdoor play space and garden. Yet many parents, especially mothers, drew on a developmental discourse, recognising that 'the home in itself could not meet the welfare and developmental needs of children' (Kelley et al, 2002, p 20), and that children can be harmed by 'over-protective or overly anxious mothering' and a lack of opportunity to learn important social skills.

Related to these points are examples of some uncertainty about issues of parental authority, particularly as children grow older. Lewis (2007) explored this within qualitative interviews with employed parents with children aged between 14 and 16 years living in London. Lewis asserted that 'the main problem for parents of teenagers was negotiating their teenager's independence' (Lewis, 2007, p 297):

> All parents expressed concern about how to negotiate the transition
> to independence with their children, and children often expressed

impatience and dissatisfaction around the same issues. (Lewis, 2007, p 299)

However, this uncertainty was not deemed a matter of parental ignorance or flight from responsibility. Rather, parental uncertainty was linked to tensions between contemporary ideals of parenthood and childhood. Parents report concern over 'getting the balance right' and whether they are 'being too soft' or 'too hard' on their teenage children.

A second moral dilemma for parents relates to negotiating divisions of responsibilities for children in different situations – such as between children and young people themselves, between parents, between parents and families, or between parents and professionals/the state or society more generally. These tensions were alluded to above in the discussion of accessing health services, maternal–paternal responsibilities or parental involvement with schools. A third moral dilemma has been conceptualised as 'negotiating between responsibilities for children, others and the self' (Sevon, 2007; Backett-Milburn et al, 2008). This dilemma is related to broader social processes of individualisation (Beck and Beck Gernsheim, 2002).

A fourth moral dilemma is negotiating responsibilities and capabilities. Williams (2008) exemplifies this dilemma in relation to decisions about paid work, involvement in childcare and 'breadwinning' among the fathers who took part in his study. Williams (2008) argued that whatever the fathers' 'ideals of fatherhood and family' were, their decisions were heavily reliant on their earning capabilities and access to employment opportunities. Such work–family conflicts are discussed in the next chapter.

Conclusion

This chapter has examined everyday understandings of family relationships and parenting, and situated family practices. The analysis set out several 'layers of meaning' within parental accounts and diverse perspectives, but also evidence of shared values and a strong ethic of care towards children. Parental rights and responsibilities were found to be negotiated within a complex process of deliberating 'the right thing to do' and the realities of the economic and social contexts people face (Williams, 2004a). However, fulfilling parental responsibilities can involve family practices which sustain social inequalities and generational power relations. Compared to policy discourses, parents provided accounts of negotiating holistic, contested and changing ideas about children's needs. In-depth qualitative studies of everyday family practices can generate valuable insights into everyday ethics of care and the ways parents and children negotiate contemporary childhoods, adulthoods and social life.

NINE

Negotiating work and family life

Introduction

This chapter reviews research about parental perspectives and experiences of paid work. It highlights discrepancies between parental aspirations and preferences in relation to work–family issues and dominant current policy perspectives which inform welfare to work and family-friendly employment policies. The chapter further finds that, while recent childcare, in-work support and employability reforms have extended support and opportunities to many parents, the framework of support for parents in relation to employment opportunities and experiences does not fully take account of the ongoing difficulties some parents face in taking up and sustaining training and paid employment, or achieving a satisfactory work–family balance.

Family, children and paid work: conflicting obligations and aspirations?

Several research studies debate the 'heterogeneity of work–family preferences' among men and women (Duncan and Edwards, 1999; Hakim, 2002; Bell et al, 2005; Speight et al, 2009). A considerable literature has examined mothers' orientations to paid work, given the historical construction of gendered family roles; increases in maternal employment rates in recent decades; and the lag in lone mothers' employment rates. In an attempt to move beyond 'preference versus structural constraint' debates, Duncan and Edwards' (1999) research examined lone mothers' attitudes to paid work in Britain, Germany and Sweden, combining qualitative, quantitative and comparative research methods and utilising an 'action-context' approach to integrate several analytical concerns, namely:

- the 'micro-level' context of personal subjective experience and beliefs about motherhood, welfare receipt and employment; and individual social location in terms of welfare receipt, social class, ethnicity, age, education and qualifications;
- the 'meso-level' context: lone mothers' social networks and neighbourhoods, which influence individual norms and values, and access to resources, support and opportunities; and
- the 'macro social structural context': such as welfare state contexts, and economic and labour market trends.

Duncan and Edwards (1999) argued that lone mothers' decisions about taking up and sustaining paid work were informed by personal, moral and social understandings about maternal responsibilities for children and children's needs. This challenged the view that welfare-reliant lone mothers were primarily constrained by financial benefit traps, low human capital, a lack of affordable and accessible childcare and a lack of viable employment opportunities. Duncan and Edwards (1999) argued that while these latter factors influenced lone mothers' decisions, they were secondary to moral considerations and imperatives about the appropriate relationship between lone motherhood and employment. Duncan and Edwards (1999, pp 118–19) devised the concept of 'gendered moral rationalities' to refer to 'understandings about maternal responsibilities for children'. They set out three moral discourses that were discernible from their interviews with mothers: the primarily mother, mother/worker integral and primarily worker. The 'primarily mother' orientation emphasised maternal responsibilities for caring for children and putting children first, such that the use of childcare services or engagement in paid work that did not fit around children's needs can reflect badly on a mother and be thought of as placing children at risk. This perspective can endorse views of maternal rights to care full time for children when they are young and children's rights to maternal care. In contrast, the 'mother/worker integral' position emphasised the moral benefits of maternal employment for children and the personal benefits of maternal employment for women, as well as women's rights to employment opportunities. The 'primarily worker' position viewed paid work as a source of personal fulfilment for women and recognised women's rights to employment opportunities (Duncan and Edwards, 1999, p 120). Although these categorisations are similar to those of Hakim's (2000; 2002) framework of 'home-centred', 'work-centred' and 'adaptive' work–family preferences among men and women, Duncan and Edwards' (1999) theory of gendered moral rationalities conceptualised individual attitudes to paid work within the context of gender, social class and ethnic identities and social locations, and local labour markets. Duncan and Edwards (1999, p 122) found that the White working-class lone mothers in their study were more likely 'to give primacy to caring for their children themselves'; while the White middle-class lone mothers tended 'to combine a 'primary mother' gendered moral rationality with elements of a separate identity as a worker'; and the 'White alternative mothers' (mothers who hold more feminist views about gender and motherhood) and the African, African-Caribbean and West African mothers in their study emphasised the benefits of maternal paid work for their children and themselves, indicating more integrated 'mother/worker' identities. The spatial and social patterning of gendered moral rationalities within Duncan and Edwards' (1999) empirical research was explained with reference to the historical development of gender norms and cultures in local labour markets, neighbourhoods and ethnic/religious cultures, as well as broader gender, social class and ethnic inequalities.

This book has already discussed several factors which could lead working-class and poorer women to identify more strongly with more traditional notions of stay-at-home motherhood: poorer and working-class families experience higher rates of poor health and disability; parents living in deprived neighbourhoods and disadvantaged social housing neighbourhoods are more likely to have fewer local labour market opportunities and are concerned to manage risks in their children's lives by prioritising 'being there' for them; working-class women gain respectability and status as mothers; there can be little experience of using formal childcare services and much mistrust towards them; and not 'being there' for children out of school hours is associated with inadequate parenting and parental supervision of children, which in turn is thought to lead to more problems with children's behaviour (DWP, 2007a; Gillies, 2007). A 'primarily mother' norm has further been associated with the cultural and religious values within South Asian communities and cited to explain the relatively low employment rates among Pakistani and Bangladeshi mothers (Aston et al, 2007). Within this context of competing discourses and normative perspectives about good motherhood, mothers negotiate a complex moral and social terrain.

Turning to research on fathers' perspectives, constructions of good fatherhood have similarly been considered. Brannen and Nilsen (2005) explored ideas about fatherhood among four-generational families, interviewing 31 fathers. They distinguished between 'work-focused', 'family-men' and 'hands-on' fathers, noting the degree to which fathers were actively involved in childcare and domestic labour as well as their attitudes to fatherhood and paid work in general. The 'work-focused' fathers identified primarily with paid work and reported 'low involvement with their young children'. Brannen and Nilsen (2005, p 341) found that many fathers of different ages and backgrounds fell into this category:

> They are from all three generations. They include middle-class 'careerist fathers' in managerial or professional jobs providing intrinsic rewards and good pay; and a group of 'provider fathers' in low-skilled jobs with few intrinsic rewards that provided low wages and so required fathers to work long hours in return for a decent wage.

The second approach to fatherhood was that of the 'family man', which tended to be expressed more by the older generations of fathers. This involved being the main breadwinner while 'placing high value on 'being there', and participating to some extent in childcare' and placing 'priority on relationships with their children as well as upon family life' (Brannen and Nilsen, 2005, p 341). The other discernible model for fatherhood was that of the 'hands-on' father – a position expressed by a minority of fathers (four of the men interviewed) who were heavily involved in childcare and domestic labour (three caring for their children full time) and who were not the sole breadwinner in their family. In contrast to notions of uniform social change from the work-focused to the hands-on father, Brannen and Nilsen (2005) noted shifts in multiple directions, with some younger fathers more work focused than previous generations, as well as many fathers sustaining a particular view of the 'family male breadwinner and involved with children father'. Shifts towards being more work focused were explained with reference to broader trends in material expectations, the financial pressures on middle–class families and a culture of long working hours among higher-status occupations.

The coexistence of different ideal models of fatherhood can place pressures on fathers to maintain the main-provider role while additionally being involved in family life and contributing to childcare. Dermott's (2001) research on fathers' take-up of parental leave rights found that men's accounts of taking up leave following a birth in the family differed in relation to normative constructions of the role of fathers in childcare. Dermott (2001, p 154) found that men who did not take up any parental or paternity leave tended to hold a view of 'the role of the father after the birth of a child in terms of supporting the mother of the child' and that it was only when mothers were having their first child or were unable to cope with childcare that fathers should take time off employment, as exemplified by the example of Bill, who did not generally support fathers' taking much leave after the birth of a child:

> Don't get me wrong, if there was a problem with the thing, with the birth, if there was anything like that, clearly one's duty and one's responsibility are with one's wife. But day-to-day when things go straight ... I really think it's unreasonable for people to expect [to take time off]. (Dermott, 2001, p 154)

Other fathers in Dermott's study who took up parental leave, however, expressed the importance to them of 'bonding with their children and being involved in childcare'. These fathers 'emphasised developing a bond with their child(ren) and frequently mentioned the emotional aspects of their relationship with the child' (Dermott, 2001, p 158). These fathers viewed 'fatherhood as an ongoing commitment involving active caring for children, which will necessarily impact on other areas of their life including their paid work' and invested in building the 'type of relationship they desired with their children' (Dermott, 2001, p 158). Between these two perspectives, other fathers in Dermott's study expressed the view that fathers should 'be there' for their children and 'be involved' in childcare, although not to the extent of 'substantial and equal involvement in the upbringing of children', exemplified by an extract from William, below:

> I think principally what's important is being available. What I mean is being able to go to the sports days and parents days ... If you need to collect [from school] or whatever. (Dermott, 2001, p 156)

These studies of maternal and paternal orientations to paid work illustrate the ways social expectations of motherhood and fatherhood influence paid–work decisions. There is further evidence that some parents' values and perspectives on the appropriate relationships between paid work and responsibilities for children can change over time, following a 'positive employment experience'. Himmelweit and Sigala (2004) investigated the dynamic nature of parental attitudes by conducting longitudinal research to see how attitudes and behaviour changed over time. These researchers examined maternal attitudes to and engagement with paid work and childcare services over time and found that maternal attitudes and behaviour changed considerably. Himmelweit and Sigala (2004) hypothesised a 'feedback effect' between lived experiences and personal values, and illustrated how, over time, mothers who experience good-quality childcare, benefits for children and satisfaction from their employment can become more positive about working full time when children are young.

Childcare

Chapter Six reviewed progress towards 'accessible, affordable and quality' childcare provision, primarily in England. Although the provision of day care and out-of-school childcare provision has expanded in line with the objectives of the NCS, sustainability of provision has been a problem. Gaps in provision remain for: families with disabled children, atypical working hours, school holiday provision and childcare/youth services for secondary school children (Speight et al, 2009). Many researchers and campaigners have called for more government action to make formal childcare more affordable. The 2010 Cost of Childcare survey (Daycare Trust, 2010) found that:

- there had been an above-inflation rise in average childcare costs. For example, the cost of a full-time nursery place for a child under 2 years had increased by 5.1%, compared to the 2009 Costs of Childcare survey;
- parents in London reported paying the highest childcare costs, with parents paying up to £11,050 per year for 25 hours of childcare per week;
- there had been a growth in all forms of childcare, but a fall in out-of-school childcare in Scotland and Wales;
- 58% of Family Information Services (which provide information about local childcare services) reported a lack of childcare in their area, and high levels of unmet need for parents with older children and disabled children;
- the average award through the childcare element of the Working Tax Credit was £68.69 a week, an increase of £3.89 from 2009.

These figures indicated the financial shortfall between childcare costs and tax credit support. In the survey, more than two-thirds of parents living in England reported a lack of affordable childcare in their localities, with parents in London particularly citing 'lack of affordable and appropriate childcare' as a major barrier for taking up or sustaining paid work (Daycare Trust, 2010).

The current policy emphasis on early education and formal childcare provision has been criticised for not recognising the significance of 'trust' issues for parents and preferences for informal childcare arrangements. The FACS, which is overly represented by low-income families, found that families used informal childcare more than formal services (Conolly and Kew, 2008). Childcare decisions can be complex ones. In-depth studies of parental attitudes to childcare find that many are aware of the potential positive advantages for children from quality formal childcare services, but they also feel there are disadvantages in using formal childcare (Bell et al, 2005). Parents report valuing formal childcare services where provision meets their needs for childcare and provides social and developmental opportunities for their children (Deforges and Abouchaar, 2003). For example, Pakistani and Bangladeshi women are often represented as overwhelmingly 'pro-family care'. However, Aston et al (2007) found that Pakistani and Bangladeshi women found childcare decisions 'complex ones to make'. The women interviewed for their study expressed many benefits of using informal family childcare such as: they had female relatives living nearby who 'were keen to help' with childcare; informal childcare was cheaper; beliefs that children would be 'with their own family', 'speaking their mother tongue' and 'with known and trusted family members' (Aston et al, 2007, p 62). However, many felt that 'their child might learn more in formal childcare' and negotiated childcare options provided by local mosques and Muslim organisations as well as other local providers (Aston et al, 2007, p 62). Aston et al (2007) concluded, though, that the expectation to use informal childcare was 'starting to change', particularly among younger Pakistani and Bangladeshi mothers. The younger women, those in their 20s and 30s, were 'more open to the idea of using formal childcare', but other factors, such as the cost and availability of childcare, limited the options available to them. It was also important for the mothers that formal childcare provision should both encourage their children to 'mix' with children from different ethnic and religious cultures and 'help them to learn English', but that they should also mix with children from similar cultural backgrounds so that they could 'improve their language skills, and be taught in line with religious beliefs'. Factors such as whether a childcare provider supported their diet, dress and religious events were important considerations for some (Aston et al, 2007, p 65). In using informal childcare, some women expressed concern about 'burdening grandmothers too much as they too had their own lives' (Aston et al, 2007). The qualitative data in this study provides evidence of complex social attitudes towards informal and formal childcare. It was not the case that informal childcare was unproblematic or readily available for these mothers nor was it the case that they were unaware of the social and educational benefits of mainstream, formal childcare for children. It was, rather, the case that these mothers negotiated conflicting moral imperatives about the right thing to do – not only for their children, but also for themselves and other family members – and were limited to choosing between the available and affordable childcare options within their social networks and localities.

Negotiating employability

Chapter Five reviewed developments in welfare to work reforms. Research undertaken by the Institute of Employment Studies indicated the need for training and employability schemes to be tailored to the diverse needs of parents (Dench, 2007; Dench and Bellis, 2007). For example, the evaluation of the Care to Learn scheme aimed at young parents aged between 16 and 20 years and reliant on out-of-work welfare benefits found that the scheme was successful in raising the educational and employment aspirations, skills and prospects of the young parents because of the flexible and responsive childcare, financial and educational support that was provided (Dench et al, 2007a, p 3). The research carried out a survey in 2006/07 with 1,000 parents who had taken part in the scheme (representing a third of the 2004/05 parent intake). The percentage of parents with no qualifications fell from 39% at the start of the course to 20% by the end (Dench et al, 2007a, p 1). Among the participants, 88% said they would not have attended a training course if it had not been for the personalised support offered to them in the Care to Learn scheme (Dench et al, 2007a, p 1). Dench and Bellis (2007) further carried out a qualitative study interviewing 51 young mothers aged between 16 and 20 years who were not in education or employment, and which identified several common themes for mothers. The mothers talked about their negative experiences of primary and secondary school and their fears that further education or training would be similar. Dench and Bellis (2007) found that only a minority of the young mothers in their study were positive about their educational experiences and that many 'had not enjoyed school', 'had not got on with teachers', 'felt teachers were not interested in their progress or difficulties', 'found school boring' and 'had experienced bullying'. To overcome these issues, the mothers required support, understanding and sensitive professional learning and basic skills support and training. Short practical courses, delivered in accessible locations, with on-site childcare and that related to the mothers' everyday needs, concerns and aspirations were valuable as 'first steps' back into education or employment.

Considerable barriers to taking up training, further education and employment have been identified in many studies. Coping with the stresses, strains and demands of being a full-time mother or father highly involved in caring takes up much time, commitment and energy – stresses which are compounded by the short-termism of coping on a day-to-day basis when living on a low income. Flexibility, empathy and understanding about these issues among training and education providers are highly valued (Dench and Bellis, 2007). The extent of poor health, disability and health concerns among those not in paid work has been extensively researched. Casebourne and Britton (2004) found high levels of health-related problems and concerns among their sample of welfare-reliant and employed lone parents. The parents in this study discussed their needs for employment advice services, employers and training schemes to provide additional support to help them access health- and disability-related benefits or to accommodate their needs to enable them to sustain and progress in employment. Limited knowledge about the educational and employment opportunities that are available and what skills, qualifications and experiences are needed for different types of work and careers (cultural and social capital) curtails individual opportunities. The study with young parents by Dench and Bellis (2007, p 4) found that the young people varied in their capabilities to 'think and talk about their future in any concrete terms'. While the young mothers overwhelmingly aspired to provide a better life for their children and be in some form of further or higher education or employment within five years and once their children were at school, the women 'varied in the extent to which they had clear ideas about what course or job they wanted to aim for, or the route through which this could be achieved' (Dench, 2007, p 4).

Studies with fathers in prison, lone mothers and unemployed fathers also reported a similar theme of ample aspiration but a lack of concrete and realistic awareness about how to accrue the necessary skills and experience to achieve their aspirations (Quinton, 2004; Churchill, 2007). Initiatives such as the recently piloted Skills Coaching scheme have been found to be beneficial in helping those in need of job search and options advice. Page et al (2009) evaluated 20 pilot schemes which were targeted at adults who were aged over 20 and in receipt of out-of-work benefits. The clients of the pilot schemes reported that the skills coaching had 'improved their understanding of the labour market, understanding of available jobs and careers, the skills and qualifications needed to undertake specific jobs, and of what employers require from CVs and interviews' (Page et al, 2009, p 2). However, schemes were found to be restricted by their remit and funding. Further, the focus on skills as the only barrier to finding work was limited in addressing the 'multiple barriers' that clients faced (Page et al, 2009).

Practical, family and financial issues affect parental experiences of completing further education and training, and sustaining paid employment and progression in the labour market. Students with caring responsibilities report higher levels of financial problems in further and higher education (Barnfield and Brookes, 2006).

A process of 'skill devaluing' additionally restricts employment opportunities for parents. Although the business case for valuing the 'soft skills' and 'transferable skills' that one learns as a parent and in everyday life has been made, the emphasis on more formal forms of qualification, work experience and training discriminates against these skills being recognised. More overtly, the skills, experience and qualifications of those who have migrated to the UK can be devalued and unrecognised by employers (Platt, 2007). This can compound other difficulties that migrants face in securing employment, such as lack of fluency in English, lack of familiarity with job-searching skills, lack of knowledge about job-search agencies and social discrimination.

Negotiating occupational and workplace settings

The specificities of occupational, organisational and workplace cultures and contexts are important 'work-related' factors that influence work–family patterns and practices and the take-up of employment rights. Warhurst et al (2008) challenged the assumptions that abound about 'work' and 'family' as distinct social spheres of experience and argued for more empirical analysis of work–life boundaries and practices. Work–life boundary theory encourages researchers to empirically assess the ways that people perceive, experience and manage work–family boundaries and the multiple personal, family and work-related factors that generate work–family integration or conflict. Warhurst et al (2008) posed theoretical, empirical and policy questions by asking how people perceive work–family boundaries; how people seek to integrate or separate their working and family lives; and how occupational and workplace contexts influence the opportunities, constraints and risks individuals and families negotiate as part of their 'boundary work' and work–family practices. Work–life boundaries are influenced by several dimensions of work and family life, for example, in terms of temporalities, spatialities, social networks, tasks and rationalities (McKie, 2005).

Several studies have explored women's experiences of working in the female-dominated UK retail industry (Backett-Milburn et al, 2008; Yeandle et al, 2002). Backett-Milburn et al's (2008) research was based on qualitative interviews with women working in food retail outlets. Recognising the female-dominated nature of the industry and the reputation that retail work has for flexible and part-time employment opportunities, Backett-Milburn et al (2008) found that the women they interviewed did not talk about their employment as a matter of 'personal fulfillment or aspiration' but as a means of providing for their families and balancing their paid-work and family responsibilities. The researchers found that, to some extent, the workplace cultures within local retail outlets expressed values similar to the family values discussed above: assuming women's family responsibilities and emphasising the importance of putting family first, the reciprocal obligations between employees and employers, pulling together, and employee loyalty and the development of informal relationships based on knowledge about each others' lives, reciprocity and flexibility:

> It appeared that many of the values expressed by these low paid women regarding their family lives were carried over into the workplace. (Backett-Milburn et al, 2008, p 487)

However, even within this female-dominated context, where staff, supervisors and managers were often women with family responsibilities and many flexible employment options were actively promoted, the temporal, spatial, instrumental and hierarchical logics and nature of the employment produced conflicts and tensions for individuals. Some flexibility could be negotiated in relation to changing shift times or places, but shifts had to be covered, work was carried out in specified shops, shops had to open for business during pre-determined times, retail performance had to be sustained and 'timeframes may be tight and demands made on workers at short notice' (Backett-Milburn et al, 2008, pp 490–1): 'it was evident from the interviews that sometimes work had to come first, (and that family raised objections), especially in a work setting where flexibility was at a premium'. The women's accounts of their work–family lives were orientated around presenting themselves as good mothers, loyal friends and reliable paid workers:

> The women's accounts and the employers' interviews gave similar assessments of what constituted a 'good worker' in food retailing (and therefore one whose request for emergency time off would be treated seriously). These included: how flexible employees were; how good their absence record was; how long they had been working for the company; how well they knew their managers; how well their managers knew them; and whether their managers were aware of their family situations. All of these factors came into play when requests around flexibility, time off and emergencies arose. (Backett-Milburn et al, 2008, p 490)

Within these 'webs of obligations' many factors influenced assessments of how acceptable a request for time off for family responsibilities was – including an employee's record as a worker and whether the request was deemed worthy. Some interviewees felt that often child-related requests were taken more seriously and supported more than requests for other kinds of caring responsibilities. Further, when family emergencies arose:

> What constituted 'an emergency' required assessment and legitimation, mothers described instances of evaluating how sick a child really was and how much a parent's presence was really needed. (Backett-Milburn et al, 2008, p 486)

When employees covered the shifts or time off for other employees' emergencies, there was an expectation that such support would be reciprocated sometime in the future:

> Just as the moral identity of being a good mother or relative had to be sustained over time and continuously maintained, so too did that of being a good worker. This also involved learning what and how much you could ask for and expect from the workplace, summed up in the following quotation as 'as long as you don't push it' (Backett-Milburn et al, 2008, p 489)

Backett–Milburn et al (2008) illustrated how women working in retail outlets negotiated competing discourses and demands, and how low-income working women have 'far fewer material resources' with which to 'navigate or escape webs of obligation'.

Other research has explored the experiences of women in male-dominated occupations and the experiences of men. Gatrell's (2005) interview study of professional women's experiences of working in high-status and senior positions found occupational hierarchies and cultures unsympathetic to the needs and aspirations of women as mothers. Wattis et al (2006) conducted qualitative research into mothers' experiences of employment in the UK and the Netherlands. They found that women in the UK experienced higher levels of work–family conflict than women in the Netherlands (although work–family patterns and experiences remain highly gendered in the Netherlands). They found that the UK had a more substantive 'work-first' culture with a long-hours culture (in comparison to a 'reduced hours' culture for parents, especially mothers, in the Netherlands) and informal organisational cultures (the social expectations and attitudes that employees face in their day-to-day lives) that stressed 'work-first' rather than 'family-first' values. Research with senior-level men and women employed in various sectors in the UK has found that both men and women would ideally prefer greater flexibility in their working hours, working conditions or workload, but that their jobs do not afford them such opportunities, or such opportunities would 'damage their careers and incomes'. For example, research in the IT industry found that senior managers in principle wanted greater flexibility at work:

> 93% of women and 81% of men wanted more flexible job roles and working practices. However, these senior employees felt that conducting their job on a more flexible basis would bring with it lower pay, diminished promotional opportunities and less interesting project work and activities. (Flexecutive, 2002, p 6)

In this survey it was found that 36% of the sample overall stated that they were 'dissatisfied with their work life balance' (Flexecutive, 2002, p 15), although a higher percentage reported an unsatisfactory work–family balance in relation to specific family roles:

> 50% of all respondents (vs. 75% of people working more than 10 hours per week) agree that they don't get involved with their family as much as they would like; 53% of all respondents (56% female and 49% male – 73% of those working longer than 10 hrs) feel that it is difficult to get involved in school activities; 49% of respondents, (55% of female and 40% of male), with children feel that they miss out on their children's development; 43% of all respondents (vs. 51% of people

aged 20–24) believe that they don't have enough holiday time with their families. (Flexecutive, 2002, p 15)

This study surveyed 1,001 employees in the UK IT industry, of whom 65% of respondents were female and 35% male, and 88% of respondents were employed full time and 11% part time. The long-hours culture in the industry was exposed, with 35% of respondents regularly working out of hours; 13% regularly staying away from home overnight; 65% working up to 10 hours a day and 11% working more than 10 hours a day – with the latter figures related to seniority and levels of reward. In the survey, 52% of those reporting working long hours, both women and men, stated that they believed 'late or weekend meetings are an integral part of their job' (Flexecutive, 2002, p 16). Further, 75% of respondents overall agreed that 'there was a long hours culture in their organisation' and 67% of senior managers agreed that 'their workload is too much to accommodate flexible working hours' (Flexecutive, 2002, p 17). Those in senior positions highlighted many constraints that made flexible working an unattractive option to them, including the views that flexible or part-time working did not 'offer respite from the pressures associated with full time hours: Some 62% of all respondents (and 70% of those earning £50k+) agree that part-time roles result in senior managers trying to cram 5 days work into fewer days' and would 'put an end to their careers' (Flexecutive, 2002, p 14). Work–life balance policies are found to be poorly implemented, unsupported and inadequate in some organisations, with organisational cultures and employment demands impinging on family and other life aspirations.

Negotiating employment rights

Chapter Six detailed how employment rights to parental leave and flexible working have been introduced and extended in recent years. By 2007 the DWP and DIUS claimed the right to flexible working had promoted family-friendly employment and changed 'attitudes and behaviour' in the workplace (DWP/DIUS, 2007, p 18). However, studies present a more mixed picture of change.

Yeandle et al (2002) carried out their research before the extensions in rights to request flexible working. Their study, however, highlighted some common themes across the experiences of employees in six organisations in two English cities (Sheffield and Canterbury) representing large supermarket chains, local government and retail banking. Similar to the discussion earlier, this study found that supermarket employers had more progressive, family-friendly policies, but that in practice local organisations, managers and employees faced conflicting pressures in implementing family-friendly policies or actively taking up entitlements. The national 'official' picture of family-friendly policies within the six organisations indicated support for a range of family-friendly employment policies above the statutory rights to leave. Organisational policies included: 'compassionate leave, carers' leave, flexi-time, voluntary reduced hours, 'responsibility breaks', emergency leave and shift-swap' (Yeandle et al, 2002, p 2). Entitlement to these measures, however, depended on length of service and type of contract; were in most cases available on an unpaid basis; and were mediated by the local organisation's 'formal and informal' policies and practices. In line with other studies of organisational and individual perspectives, the research found that there was considerable lack of awareness at the local level among both employees and managers about national organisational family-friendly policies (Wattis et al, 2006; Crompton, 2006). The research found that managers and employees in the supermarkets had higher levels of awareness, but that those working in local government reported 'lower than expected' levels of awareness of their employment rights, given that they worked within the public sector (Yeandle et al, 2002, p 2). The study found that managers had a critical role to play in promoting family-friendly policies and their uptake – with managers in the supermarkets found to be more likely to be women with caring responsibilities themselves and more sympathetic to employees' requests. Consistent with much research in the field, the study argued that 'policy implementation occurred on an informal, flexible basis, and reflected reciprocity between managers and employees' (Yeandle et al, 2002, p 3; Wattis et al, 2006; Backett-Milburn et al, 2008). Managerial discretion was both valued and criticised, as flexibility was felt to be important but some employees felt that individuals within and across organisations could be treated unfairly. Managers and employees reported conflicting pressures: managers were concerned to balance family-friendly policies against organisational staff and resource cut-backs and considerable pressure to meet steep service provision and delivery standards and targets. Managers in general were in support of the business case for family-friendly policies but felt that some employees would abuse the system; there was a lack of staff resources to cover any leave and a lack of 'training, guidance, consultation and communication' within their organisation on how they were to implement family-friendly policies. Employees sought to meet their caring and paid-work responsibilities. Carers of children 'mainly used options which gave them time flexibility' and were concerned about conflicts between their working schedules and school timetables; namely in the late afternoons, evenings, weekends and school holidays. Carers of adults and disabled people expressed different needs and were more concerned with gaining help with unexpected demands on their time in order to respond to sudden illness or meet appointments. Among carers, work pressures, a lack of awareness about their entitlements, the double-edged informal nature of flexible arrangements and the unpaid basis of leave were significant barriers to take-up of family-friendly policies (Yeandle et al, 2002).

According to recent surveys there has been a general increase in requests for flexible working and requests granted by employers since 2003, but problems in accessing flexible working options remain. Common types of flexible working options include part-time working; flexi-time working (having some element of choice in when to work); annualised hours (hours are worked out on an annual basis); compressed hours (working fewer days but similar hours); staggered hours (starting or finishing the working day at different times); job sharing and home working. The Third Work–life Balance Survey (Hooker et al, 2007) found that, compared to the two previous surveys, 'employee awareness, take-up and satisfaction of flexible working arrangements' had increased (Hooker et al, 2007, p 13). The survey involved telephone interviews with a representative sample of 2,081 employees working in organisations with five or more employees across the UK. Overall, the survey found that:

> 87% [of respondents] said they were satisfied with their working arrangements, an increase of 6% points from the 2002 survey. 90% of employees reported their employers offered at least one flexible working opportunity and these mainly consisted of part-time working, reducing hours or flexitime. (Hooker et al, 2007, p 1)

The most common arrangements used by employees were part-time working, working from home and flexi-time, with figures showing an increase in the percentage of employees making such arrangements. Nevertheless, the survey also found significant levels of 'unmet demand' for flexible working:

> There remained considerable levels of unmet demand, however, particularly for flexible arrangements to cover school holiday periods. (Hooker et al, 2007, p 1)

> The highest level of unmet demand was for flexitime (29 per cent) and a compressed working week (27 per cent). In addition 21 per cent of all employees would have liked the opportunity to work from home on a regular basis, and the same proportion of employees were attracted to the idea of reduced hours for a limited period. One in five would have liked the chance to work an annualised hours arrangement. There was less unmet demand for working term-time only (14 per cent), for part-time working (13 per cent) and for job-sharing (11 per cent). (Hooker et al, 2007, p 4)

The study highlighted several persistent problems and limitations with requests for flexible working: 'a number of factors put off individuals from taking up flexibilities which might improve their work–life balance', which included:

> perceived impact on career prospects; incompatible organisational cultures, such as unsupportive attitudes and behaviours of senior managers, line managers and colleagues; heavy workloads making it difficult to see how an alternative way of working would work; individuals often lacked knowledge of what was available and feasible, especially when the employer relied on the creativity of the

individual to identify solutions for themselves; the infrastructure and technology was often not in place which would support the uptake of such initiatives as working from home; and the downward impact on earnings of some flexible working arrangements. (Hooker et al, 2007, p 12)

There are considerable financial risks involved in working part time, risks which disproportionately impact on women, particularly women in lower-income jobs. Warren (2004) analysed data from the British Household Panel Survey to assess the financial circumstances of women working part time, compared to those working full time. She concluded that:

The financial risks associated with working part-time are considerable [...] Earning just over £4 an hour, part-time manual workers were the lowest waged employees. Their median hourly wages were only slightly above the minimum wage that came into force for most workers in that year (£3.60). Their household incomes were the lowest of the sample too, at 75 per cent the median for all the women. They were in the least subjectively comfortable financial positions, and were faring particularly poorly in their accumulation of financial, housing and pension assets. (Warren, 2004, pp 111–12)

Comparative research has further examined women's attitudes towards and experiences of key policy initiatives, such as in the areas of parental leave, childcare and flexible working arrangements in Britain, as compared to other European countries (Crompton, 2006). Several studies have found less awareness of parental rights to parental leave and the right to request flexible working hours in the UK, and less active promotion of family-friendly policies and practices within informal organisation cultures, as compared to the knowledge, awareness, attitudes and experiences of women and men in many other European countries. Wattis et al (2006) detailed how informal organisation policies differed from their official policies in many UK organisations. Women were well aware of the informal organisational policy, but less aware of the formal. In addition, 'even when women were aware of parental leave, some expressed the view that they were unlikely to use it and that it would not be acceptable in their workplace' (Wattis et al, 2006, p 18).

Other research has highlighted the use of informal arrangements whereby employees take time off paid work for family reasons or emergencies (Yeandle et al, 2002). In terms of employment support and family-friendly policies, the fathers in Dermott's (2001, p 161) research valued the 'idea of some flexibility to take time away from work for shorter periods of time, either for scheduled events such as the school play, or for occasions which were not able to be planned in advance such as a child's illness'. However, Dermott's study and others found that formal organisational policies often did not afford fathers such flexibility and did exclude some from contributing to childcare or responding to family demands (Dermott, 2001).

Conclusion

This chapter has reviewed research about parental experiences of negotiating family life and paid work. Recent social policy reforms have been criticised for not respecting mothers' choices about full-time motherhood and not going far enough in promoting fathers' aspirations for active fatherhood. Childcare reforms were criticised for not recognising the complexity of childcare decisions and providing more information about the quality of care. Further, employability reforms need to be sensitive to parental needs and employment reforms need to do more to tackle labour market disadvantages and discrimination.

Part Four
Policy implications

TEN

Conclusion: rights and responsibilities for child, family and social well-being

Introduction

This book has reviewed the shifting and contested nature of parental rights and responsibilities for children in several spheres of English and UK social policy since 1997 and contrasted official policy perspectives with social research on parental views and experiences of parenthood, parenting and family support needs. This concluding chapter aims to provide an overview of policy change under New Labour and critically assess these policy changes in relation to revisions to the roles, rights and responsibilities of parents and families versus those of the state in respect of child and family well-being. In addition, the chapter reviews the contemporary era and the major revisions in welfare state support for families with children under way following the indecisive 2010 General Election and the forming of a Conservative-Liberal Democrat Coalition government. Since coming to office in May 2010, the new Coalition government has introduced unprecedented public spending cuts and begun a radical programme for welfare state reform. The programme for reform, in the context of economic recession and the increase in the national public deficit since 2007, consists of withdrawing some aspects of welfare state support for citizens and families, 'reducing the size of the welfare state', promoting private sector growth and promoting 'a greater role for citizens, communities, the private sector and the third sector in commissioning and delivering public services' (HM Government, 2010). The Coalition government has stated that it will 'protect disadvantaged families and vulnerable children' and is committed to meeting the government's child poverty reduction targets set out in the Child Poverty Act 2010. However, the Institute for Fiscal Studies has forecasted significant increases in child, family and working-age poverty in 2011 due to the combined effects of job losses, price increases and tax and benefit changes (Brewer and Joyce, 2010), and many councils have announced cuts to children's services in 2011–12. In contrast to withdrawing support for families and children, however, I argue for a more supportive relationship between parents, families, young people and the state to promote better care for children and young people as well as broader family and social well-being. A number of approaches to social policy for social well-being provide useful frameworks from which to review child and family policies, including public health approaches to promoting child, adult and family well-being, and arguments for social policies to more comprehensively promote an ethic of care (Williams, 2004a; Utting, 2009). These principles and priorities, and their more specific policy implications, will be detailed below in two stages – firstly, in relation to the new policy context and the approach to policy and sociological analysis taken in this book, and, secondly, in relation to developments in the five policy areas.

The broader policy context

Chapter Two set out influential frameworks for conceptualising and monitoring child, family and social well-being (Babington, 2007; Bradshaw and Richardson, 2009; Stieglitz, 2009). In developing comprehensive visions of child well-being, the chapter argued for policy makers to draw on policy frameworks informed by a combined child development and children's rights perspective. Within the 'domain-based' approach, these frameworks seek to monitor and promote children's and young people's: economic well-being; quality of housing and neighbourhood context; physical, mental and emotional health and well-being; physical safety and emotional security; pro-social behaviour and healthy lifestyles; 'objective' and 'subjective' well-being; citizenship; immediate family, peer and social relationships; and their experience of childcare, educational and institutional settings (Bradshaw and Richardson, 2009). Child well-being is not only conceptualised in terms of individual normative child development, and personal health and well-being, but also in terms of the 'proximate and distal' contexts, settings and relationships within which children negotiate their everyday lives. These perspectives consider the degree to which children's immediate and broader social contexts promote child welfare and respect children's rights. More profoundly, social constructionist approaches recognise the context-dependent nature of childhood and family practices, and promote collective and cross-cultural dialogue about children's needs and family responsibilities. These perspectives challenge adult-centred and 'top-down' models of the policy process, emphasising the importance of inclusive and deliberative policy processes which take children's and young people's views seriously. A critical debate in the current policy context is whether governmentsin advanced welfare states should pursue a more targeted 'deficit' approach, which focuses investment on families and children most in need and seeks to protect children from significant risk or whether the role of government should be to invest more extensively in early intervention and prevention at the individual, family and community level to promote better cost-effectiveness in the long run via better outcomes for children, families and communities.

Chapter Two argued for more integrated child, family and social well-being policy and research debates. Akin to debates about child well-being, concepts such as 'family and social well-being' are inherently contested. The 1950s' idealised notion of 'family' – defined in terms co-residency and bounded household units, two-generational households, ethnic uniformity, lifelong marriage, gendered family roles and generational hierarchies – does not reflect everyday notions of 'family' or adequately describe the variety of family formations. Family formations in recent decades have diversified and family relationships changed in dramatic ways. While conservative assessments of family change often portray change as crisis and the breakdown of the traditional 1950s' model, social attitudes research finds much evidence of enduring commitment to marriage and long-term couple relationships as well as considerable commitment to parental responsibilities among parents who have separated or divorced (Williams, 2004a). Further, empirical studies find family type, as a single dependent variable, a poor indicator of child welfare outcomes (Bradshaw and Richardson, 2009). Rather, children at risk of the poorest outcomes are those who experience long-term poverty from an early age and who face multiple disadvantages, risks and problems related to their family lives and immediate social contexts. Notions of family well-being therefore need to move beyond ideological and idealised notions of the traditional family form. They should be informed by child and family welfare research as well as an engaging national debate about: what constitutes family well-being; what should be the role of families, policy agencies and other agents such as employers or community organisations in promoting family well-being; and what should be the major family policy priorities in contemporary times and in the context of multi-cultural Britain (Commission on the Family and Well-being of Children, 2005). Although in its early stages, conceptualisations of family well-being call for a social policy agenda informed by the following principles and objectives: (1) to promote shared responsibility for family well-being (such as among families; employers; government departments; schools; communities; and trade unions); and (2) to monitor and promote family well-being using 'objective and subjective' indicators in terms of: (a) individual child and adult well-being attentive to the need to address issues of generational and gender-based power relations and inequalities in families; (b) the degree to which families are part of wider communities and family members have the opportunity for social connections beyond family ties; (c) equality of opportunity between social groups (such as in relation to education, employment, recreational and civic participation opportunities); (d) positive, supportive, caring, loving and non-violent family relationships; (e) family and household economic security; (f) work–family balance issues; and (g) access to family support, community services and public services (Babington, 2007; Wollny et al, 2010). Beyond this, the ethic of care perspective encourages the posing of questions such as: how can the state better serve human welfare needs? And how can the state better support families and communities to improve the care of children and young people? Child well-being research suggests that authoritative parenting approaches (which promote mutually respectful, democratic, warm and authoritative parent–child relations) produce better outcomes for children and young people across a variety of social contexts. However, a wider public debate about, and engagement with, the complexity of everyday understandings of 'good parenting' and the complexity of the micro-negotiation of care, rights and responsibilities across family and social contexts is needed. From more of a child development perspective, an integrated approach to 'child, family and social well-being' is also evident in the public health model which seeks to improve care, health and well-being via investment in the full spectrum of prevention, early intervention and remedial approaches targeting individuals, families and communities. To move beyond solely expert-led public health initiatives, it is important to engage individuals, families and communities in the process of establishing priorities for campaigns, interventions and services.

Notions of social well-being link economic, social and human development, and affirm the importance of collective and community well-being to child and family well-being. Chapter Two drew on several theoretical and political standpoints that integrate child, family and social well-being agendas, such as ecological theories of human development, human rights approaches and ethic of care perspectives. These perspectives call for social policies to intervene across the social 'ecology' of children's and family life; to recognise universal social welfare needs and to enhance universal entitlements to social, economic, cultural and political rights (Doyal and Gough, 1991; Williams, 2004a; Dean, 2010). However, ethic of care critiques of social democratic and human rights campaigns highlight individualistic tendencies and call for a progressive agenda which recognises the significance of care to human needs and rights. Feminist ethic of care debates are particularly pertinent to the critique of New Labour's child and family policies. Feminist ethic of care critiques highlight social injustices related to the unequal distribution of care responsibilities (such as the gendered division of labour in the domestic sphere and the gendered nature of the childcare and social care workforce); the low status afforded to care work and capabilities; and the inadequate entitlements in the UK to childcare and social care services, and paid parental and carers leave (Williams, 2004a). These perspectives further highlight human rights and social justice issues related to systematic forms of social inequality and abuses of power within and beyond families (Williams, 2004a).

Chapters Three and Four of the book went on to assess child, family and social well-being trends and research in the UK context, and highlighted fundamental differences in welfare and family policy regimes across advanced welfare states. Empirical research demonstrates a positive correlation between relatively higher levels of public spending among EU countries on family, child and youth services and benefits, and overall 'national scores' for child well-being (although there remain differences in child and family outcomes between countries with similar levels of public spending – indicating the need to assess the cost-effectiveness of different policy options) (Bradshaw and Richardson, 2009). Part Two of the book analysed recent policy developments in welfare to work, financial support for families, childcare, family-friendly employment measures and family support and child welfare services. Overall, in several respects, the New Labour era heralded extensions in welfare state support for families with children. Social policy took a decidedly 'child-centred' turn and citizens were 'partially de-familialised' (Hantrias, 2004). Social policy developments contributed to reductions in child poverty between 1998/99 and 2003/04; increases in maternal employment rates; improvements in child and maternal health; reductions in youth crime; and higher rates of educational attainment and developments in children's rights. In particular, there were major developments in state support for children and young people classified as most at risk of social exclusion, families with young children, working parents and (deserving) low income families. Furthermore, state responsibilities for children's well-being and rights were enhanced. Policy developments were informed by four overarching policy agendas: (1) to reduce child poverty; (2) to facilitate social inclusion; (3) to achieve full employment, and (4) to promote child well-being. New Labour's policies promoted citizen and family responsibility as well as state responsibility for these social objectives. Policies contributed to the responsibilisation of citizens and families alongside rights recognition for some social groups. The child poverty reduction agenda led to more financial support for (deserving) low income families with children but was also orientated towards reducing welfare dependency and promoting paid-work responsibilities. Full employment in turn was central to New Labour's approach to economic policy and welfare rights were more conditional on back-to-work activities, engagement in further education or training, or labour market participation. Likewise paid work was emphasised as a primary citizen duty among adult citizens and a key route for social inclusion. New Labour's approach to promoting child well-being then, in turn, emphasised investment in 'the future' and investment in human capital. Further, growing up in a 'workless' family household was viewed as detrimental to child well-being, and maternal as well as paternal employment viewed as beneficial to children in financial as well as developmental terms. Alongside this economic and labour market focused perspective of social inclusion, a symbolic element of New Labour's Third Way approach to social welfare was to draw on behavioural, cultural and individual explanations for social problems as well as address economic and material disadvantages. Policy discourses often fuelled fears about the social threats posed by a deviant underclass. In the context of rising employment rates and reductions in child poverty in the late 1990s and early 2000s, policies focused attention on those groups who 'were left behind', who were thought to remain reliant on out-of-work benefits due to 'chaotic lifestyles' and an unwillingness to take up 'opportunities the rest of us take for granted' (SEU, 2007). In the same vein, in the context of slow progress on some indicators of child well-being, parental and family level explanations for child welfare gained prominence, and child well-being policies and interventions increasingly sought to promote parental and family responsibility, and 'responsible' parenting (DfES, 2006; PMSU, 2007). So while children's rights agendas and initiatives individualised children and recognised children as citizens in their own right, New Labour's family interventions and measures aimed at promoting parental responsibilities familialised children and young people – reinforcing children's dependency on parents and families, and parental and family responsibility for young people. In many respects, New Labour's policies contributed to improvements in child, family and community well-being according to many social indicators. However, measured against explicit policy objectives and targets, policies were more effective in particular areas and contexts compared to others. Further, in light of social democratic, feminist and children's rights concerns, policy discourses, agendas, frameworks, developments and outcomes were limited. Policy measures led to clear 'winners and losers' and, in effect, amplified and sustained income, health and educational inequalities. For example, outcomes among the poorest and better-off children widened along some indicators; disabled people, children and young people in care, some ethnic minorities, and asylum-seeking and refugee families remained at a much higher risk of poor outcomes; and young people and those with the lowest qualifications saw their employment prospects worsen. In effect, during the New Labour years, the category of 'disadvantaged children and families' remained strongly equated with 'dysfunctionality and deviance'. On more subtle levels, child and family policy discourses were infused with middle-class and culturally specific notions of family, community, childhood and parenting – Part Three of this book illustrated the complex, relational, negotiated and socially situated nature of family relationships and parenting practices (Gillies, 2007). Political rhetoric and social inclusion policy discourses sought to gain populist support by appealing to tabloid-led media discourses about social problems – dampening the perceived fears of 'middle England'. However, social attitude surveys to some extent question this view of popular attitudes and suggest there is considerable support for more progressive social and economic policies (Parks et al, 2006). Further, an increasing proportion of the population feel that Britain is becoming more materialistic, prejudiced and unequal with damaging personal, social and ecological consequences (Lloyd, 2009; Mayo and Nairns, 2009).

Since coming to office in May 2010, the new Coalition government set out 'a radical programme for government' (HM Government, 2010). This programme includes unprecedented public spending cuts and significant shifts in family and child policy. While the Coalition government claims welfare state reform will seek to protect the poorest families, early assessments of the Coalition's programme for reform predict further increases in child, family and working-age poverty over the next few years and highlight the disproportionate effects of the spending cuts on social groups, such as women, families with children and public sector workers (Brewer and Joyce, 2010). In addition, the new era of family policy is set to sustain behavioural moralising discourses whereby 'disadvantage' equates with 'immorality and dysfunction' while also returning us to a more discriminatory discourse towards alternative family forms (Cameron, 2009). The concluding discussion below turns to a more in-depth assessment of New Labour's policy developments and the new policy context under the Coalition. The discussion sets out some alternative priorities for the review of child and family policy in the current policy context. In essence the review of child and family policy should seek to promote one of the key principles in the Children Act 1989 – that parents and families should have access to family support entitlements and services and that timely and appropriate family support enables and empowers parents and families to fulfil their responsibilities for child and family well-being. The review of child and family policies likewise needs to take seriously the views of children and young people, promoting children's rights to be involved in the policy process and contribute to the 'negotiation of childhood and family relationships' (Williams, 2004a).

Future policy issues in the five policy areas

Welfare to work measures

Welfare to work measures under Labour sought to reduce long-term welfare reliance and raise employment rates (Brown, 1999). Policy developments made welfare benefit receipt more conditional on back-to-work requirements and participation in welfare to work schemes. Developments revised distinctions between 'those for whom paid work is not possible' and 'those for whom paid work is a duty' (Matravers, 2007, p 7), with the former group being reduced to lone parents with children under 1 year old and claimants with the most severe long-term health problems and disabilities as assessed by a medical assessment. Welfare rights became more conditional on participation in welfare to work schemes, the labour market and employability schemes. The JSA regime came to encompass imperatives to take up job opportunities identified by Jobcentre Plus as suitable for claimants. Partners of out-of-work claimants also had enhanced responsibilities to engage in welfare to work measures. Failure to comply with back-to-work requirements was deemed to reflect a lack of willingness to 'work your way out of poverty' (Freud, 2007), and could lead to benefit sanctions. These developments defined active citizenship in narrow terms as formal paid work. With slow progress in reductions in long-term welfare reliance, particularly among lone parents and those on disability benefits, Labour's third term in office led to extensions in both conditionalities and support for these groups (DWP, 2006a).

From a human rights perspective, however, and against the findings of research that has accessed parental perspectives and experiences, several criticisms were levelled against these policy agendas and developments. To some extent welfare to work and associated measures, such as childcare reforms, had successfully enabled many to move from welfare into paid work. However, for claimants with higher support needs, the financial/childcare and back-to-work support measures were insufficient. MacInnes et al (2009) and Gregg (2008) argued that rebalancing conditionality regimes with more generous and tailored forms of support would enhance the effectiveness of welfare to work schemes. Welfare to work reform requires a more comprehensive analysis of claimants' aspirations, needs and local employment opportunities. Welfare to work schemes could more effectively utilise the skills and expertise of family support practitioners, for example, in carrying out comprehensive back-to-work needs assessments that attend to childcare and family support issues as well as employability and back-to-work issues. Further, many claimants, particularly lone parents and families affected by disability, continue to face 'benefit traps', whereby they are unable to find paid work that pays more than benefits. Gordon Brown (1999) described New Labour's approach as 'ensuring work pays more than benefit' via tax credits, increases in Child Benefit and back-to-work financial incentives. However, lone parents reliant on out-of-work benefits gain additional support via lower prescriptions costs and free school meals that need to be covered by their income if they are in paid work, and families affected by disability often incur extra living costs. Welfare to work measures could be supported by more extensive benefit reforms and child maintenance reforms that offer a tapered approach that ensures claimants have financial incentives and financial security as they gradually take on paid work, from working a few hours a week to longer hours.

The social values underpinning welfare to work reforms, however, were challenged by the research on parental perspectives. Chapter Eight highlighted tensions and competing pressures on parents as they seek to fulfil children's different needs. A number of tensions and pressures within parental roles were identified, such as between cultivating child development and promoting natural growth; recognising children's rights while nurturing responsibility; children's dependence and independence; universal children's needs and children as individuals; being there for children and being there for others; hierarchy and equality in families; emotional intimacy and distance; provision and resource constraints; parental responsibility for children and the limits of parental influence. Ambivalence further emerged from parenthood being only one dimension of people's lives and identities. Prominent social values such as 'putting children first' and 'family comes first', which express an ethic of care and moral duty towards children and family, are negotiated alongside other social imperatives such as 'putting work first', 'being a good worker', 'being a good friend', being a 'supportive partner' or being there for other family members and friends. Mothers, in particular, are expected to assume responsibility for the day-to-day physical and emotional care of children and family members. The universal adult worker model downplays the persistence of gender cultures, whereby mothers continue to place much emphasis on 'putting their children first' and maternal rights to care full time for children, especially when children are young or having difficulties. The contribution made by parents as parents could be more recognised as a form of active citizenship, and forms of voluntary and community work recognised among claimants. Further, low levels of social security provision make it very difficult to invest in one's social, financial and human capital while in receipt of welfare. In addition, access to employability and training schemes for claimants to further their skills should be an essential element of the review of careers and skills accounts.

Further reform to the welfare to work system is under way in the new era of the Conservative-Liberal Democrat Coalition government. Some measures build on New Labour's policies developed in its third term, particularly in relation to re-organising welfare to work schemes into an overarching programme and outsourcing employability schemes to private sector providers. The Coalition government's programme for reform published in June 2010 set out the following intentions for welfare to work reform:

- to re-organise the welfare to work programmes aimed at different claimant groups into one programme for all;
- to make out-of-work welfare benefit receipt conditional on willingness to work, participation in employability schemes and participation in work-search activities;
- to refer all JSA claimants with training and support needs to an intensive back-to-work programme when they start to claim JSA rather than after one year of benefit receipt (except for claimants under 25 years old, who will be referred once they have claimed JSA for six months);
- to outsource back-to-work training and support to private and voluntary sector providers, who are paid by 'results' in terms of moving claimants from welfare into paid work and reducing the claimant count;
- to provide more support for claimants seeking to start their own business, such as via start-up business grants, support and advice;
- to set up local 'work clubs' which encourage claimants to help and support one another in their search for work;
- to review and simplify the out-of-work benefits system to reduce benefit traps and remove the financial disincentives and risks in moving from welfare into paid work.

These reforms take forward several strands of policy development under New Labour and the recommendations of major policy reviews such as those undertaken by Freud (2007) and Gregg (2008). For example, the reforms address concerns about the administration costs of running different welfare to work programmes targeted at different claimant groups. Further there is a stronger focus on needs assessment and referral at the start of a claim in relation to more intensive back-to-work training and support rather than the system of support being based on length of claim. The Coalition's approach moves further away from a categorical approach to welfare to work schemes whereby schemes were targeted at different claimant groups based on different work-related conditions and assumptions. In some respects this could engender a more tailored approach, especially as reform of the welfare to work system is accompanied by reform to the benefits system, based on a more individualised assessment of back-to-work aspirations and support needs. However, a critical issue will be the extent to which back-to-work support providers are orientated and resourced to provide tailored back-to-work support responsive to claimants' needs and aspirations. In line with the Coalition government's interest in promoting more self-help and personal responsibility, these early welfare to work reforms include the setting up of 'work clubs' for claimants to provide help for one another. This initiative could provide valued support and motivation among claimants. However, the larger macro-economic issues – such as issues of local job availability and average wage levels – are understated in these reforms. A more robust welfare to work programme would integrate more individualised and tailored back-to-work support with a comprehensive local strategy for job creation, economic regeneration, economic investment and skills investment. The Coalition government has announced stricter work-related conditionality measures in the benefit system and more extensive financial penalties for claimants found making fraudulent claims or not engaging with back-to-work requirements – which further emphasises an individualised conceptualisation of benefit reliance (HM Government, 2010). Essentially, the 'work-first' approach has been extended and benefit reliance continues to be explained with reference to low employability or lack of willingness to take up paid work. There remains little recognition of the moral, financial and practical dilemmas faced by parents and those with caring responsibilities when moving from welfare into paid work, and of the difficulties claimants face in finding desirable family-friendly employment opportunities.

Financial support for families

Tax and benefit reforms under New Labour sought to reduce child poverty, increase financial incentives to take up paid work and recognise the costs of raising children. Parental rights to in-work financial support (as long as they worked more than 16 hours a week and were on a low household income) were extended. The financial responsibilities of non-resident parents have been enforced. Levels of financial support to families with children have increased. Chapter Four detailed the significant reductions in child poverty between 1999 and 2004 that were associated with the combined effects of increases in Child Benefit, Income Support, tax credits and the National Minimum Wage (Stewart, 2009). However, the child poverty reduction targets were narrowly missed in 2004/05 and extensively missed in 2010.

Problems with the system of financial support for families under New Labour were that out-of-work benefits continued to provide an insufficient family income, and financial support measures retained divisions between notions of the deserving and undeserving poor. Welfare rights have been withdrawn and restricted for certain immigrant groups. The safety net entitlement does not 'provide economic security to those who cannot work' and is limited in the context of differential and rising living costs associated with consumerism, housing costs, family size and disability. Against dominant policy agendas, the review of research into the lived experience of providing for children revealed that families are under pressure from rising costs associated with childhood and basic living costs, the commercialisation of childhood and materialistic aspirations.

Chapter One highlighted cross-party consensus in the 2010 General Election on the need to reduce public spending, albeit within the context of wide-ranging political, public and expert debate about the balance between alternative strategies for reducing the national debt (such as the balance between income tax changes, changes to indirect taxes, changes to National Insurance, changes to welfare benefits or reductions in public expenditure); what constituted priority and lower priority public spending; and the timing, scale and speed of public spending reductions. Labour argued for a more long-term and less severe programme of public spending reductions over the course of the next Parliament, an increase in NI contributions in 2011/12, increases in corporation taxes, and public service efficiency savings (Labour Party, 2010). The Liberal Democrats set out plans for tax and benefit reforms which sought to reduce bureaucracy, fraud and administration costs in the public sector and stated they would introduce a cap on public sector pay increases in 2011/12 (Liberal Democrat Party, 2010). Included in the list of welfare benefits and forms of public financial support for families for which spending was to be cut or significantly reduced were tax credits for higher-earning families and Child Trust Funds (Liberal Democrat Party, 2010). There were several policies aimed at increasing taxes on the banks and 'the wealthy', such as via a new banking levy whereby the banks indebted to the public purse would start to pay back their emergency bail-out loans, and a 'mansions tax' related to the value of elite properties (Liberal Democrat Party, 2010). The Conservative Party likewise campaigned for severe public spending cuts to reduce the public deficit, and reform to the tax credit and benefit system to reduce administration costs, benefit fraud and entitlements for higher-earning families (Conservative Party, 2010).

Alongside cross-party consensus on the need for public spending cuts, however, was a cross-party commitment to work towards the child poverty reduction targets set out in the Child Poverty Act 2010. In the 2010 General Election campaign, the Liberal Democrats' main anti-poverty measure was to propose an increase in the income tax threshold to £10,000. In contrast, the Conservatives did not champion redistribution changes in the taxation system but rather promised to favour married couples more in the tax and benefit system, supporting the traditional family form (Conservative Party, 2010). On coming to office, the Coalition government announced an Emergency Comprehensive Spending Review, which was published in October 2010. The Spending Review set out radical departures in economic and social policy. The Coalition government stated that 'reducing the public deficit' was the overarching social and economic priority (HM Treasury, 2010b). This was to be achieved by a programme of departmental spending cuts of between 14% and 25% by 2014/15 (with lower cuts in departmental budgets for education, health, defence and overseas aid), welfare state reform and private sector growth stimulated by reductions in corporation tax, investment, lower interest rates and low inflation (HM Treasury, 2010b). The spending cuts included cuts in welfare state support for families with children and for young people. Key measures were:

- £113 billion of cuts in public expenditure by 2014/15;
- a two-year pay freeze for public sector workers earning over £21,000 per year;
- an increase in VAT by 20% from 4 January 2011;
- the abolition of the following benefits for families with children in 2011: the Health in Pregnancy Grant, the Sure Start Maternity Grant, Child Trust Funds and Education Maintenance Allowance;
- changes to eligibility and levels of Working Tax Credit (WTC). To claim WTC from April 2011 claimants will need to be in paid work for 24 hours a week rather than the current 16 hours a week. There will also be a freeze on levels of basic and 30-hour WTC, and a 10% reduction in the help that WTC claimants receive for childcare costs (reduced from an 80% to a 70% tax credit contribution);
- the withdrawal of the following forms of financial support to middle- and higher-earning families: Child Benefit; WTC and Child Tax Credit;
- changes to Housing Benefit which seek to reduce levels of state contribution to social and private renting costs and increase the financial contribution paid by claimants;
- reform to incapacity and disability benefits, including the removal of mobility payments in Disability Living Allowance awards, aimed at reducing levels of long-term benefit receipt;
- reductions in Council Tax Benefit;
- a new cap on the total income a household can receive in state benefits so that this income should not be above £26,000 a year or the average household income from employment (HM Treasury, 2010b).

The changes to Child Benefit break with the commitment to provide a universal child and family allowance benefit to families with children, which has been part of the benefit system since the 1970s. The principles of progressive universalism have been usurped by a return to targeted financial support reserved for the poorest families. In the latter respect, the Spending Review announced increases in Child Tax Credit for the families on the lowest incomes in 2011 and 2012. Tax changes also included some addition support for lower earners – with an increase of £1,000 to the income tax threshold in April 2011 to £7,475 (HM Treasury, 2010b). The proposal for a tax break for married couples was not introduced although Sarah Teather, the new Minister for Families and Children, stated that this proposal will be revisited later on in the parliamentary session (FPI, 2010).

Given the relatively high levels of child and family poverty in the UK context; the stress on family relationships, parenting and family life caused by financial worries, debt, unemployment and poverty, and the major association between poor outcomes for children and young people and growing up in poverty, the nature and scale of the Coalition government's spending cuts do not equate to family-friendly economic and social policies. Moreover, the distributional impact of the spending cuts serves to place individuals and groups who already suffer a disproportionate risk of living in poverty – such as benefit claimants, women, lone parent families, families headed by young parents, lower paid workers and disabled people – more at risk. A recent report by the Institute of Fiscal Studies analysed the economic impacts of the 2010 Spending Review on families with children and working-age adults (Brewer and Joyce, 2010). This report estimated the combined impact of the benefit cuts and tax changes for a family on the median household income, with one child and two full-time earners. Brewer and Joyce (2010) estimated in 2011 that such a family would be £800 a year worse off. The combined effect of job losses, public sector pay freezes, rising living costs (including increases in VAT, petrol prices, public transport charges and food prices) and rising childcare costs place increasing financial pressures on lower- and middle-income families (Brewer and Joyce, 2010). Brewer and Joyce (2010) predicted increases in child poverty over the next three years and increases in working-age poverty. A gendered analysis of the 2010 Spending Review reveals women are disproportionately affected, as women are more reliant on public sector employment, family welfare benefits and tax credits (Brewer and Joyce, 2010). The withdrawal of Child Benefit and Child Tax Credit from middle- and higher-income families is likely particularly to increase financial insecurity for women and men in two-parent families where there is only one main earner and one adult does not have an independent source of income from paid work. Other changes, such as the changes to Housing Benefit and reduction in state support for childcare costs, will widen income inequalities and the risk of poverty between different individuals and family types such as in relation to family size, locality, house prices and childcare costs. These concerns led the Family and Parenting Institute to state there is an urgent need for the Coalition to carry out policy impact assessments for each proposal set out in the 2010 Spending Review to assess the economic impact on different family types, men and women, and different generational groups (FPI, 2010). Following this, the Fawcett Society won its case in the High Court in December 2010 for the 2010 Spending Review plans to be subject to the Equality Duty and assessed in terms of gender discrimination.

There are likely to be detrimental knock-on effects from the financial pressures on families. Below the discussion will turn to the Coalition's vision for supporting parenting and families in the early years of a child's life and for shared parenting in families and a more equitable gender division of labour in family households. However, Chapters Eight and Nine illustrated how financial pressures and poverty place additional demands on parents and stretch coping resources. These chapters further illustrated how economic pressures can encourage women to return to paid work sooner after having a baby than they would prefer and can discourage men from taking up parental or paternity leave entitlements.

The 2010 Spending Review further introduced major reform to working-age benefits from 2013. The proposals were then developed in a consultation paper on welfare reform led by Iain Duncan Smith, the new Minister at the Department for Work and Pensions (DWP) and an independent review of policies for reducing child poverty and improving life chances, led by Frank Field. These policy reviews, while informed by the overarching economic policy of reducing public expenditure on welfare, build on New Labour's recent proposals for reform to working-age benefits and have gone some way to addressing some of the problems in the British benefit system set out by policy analysts such as Freud (2007), Gregg (2008) and Sainsbury and Stanley (2007). A critical issue in benefit reform debates has long been the complexity of the system whereby several types of benefits operate targeted at different categorical groups such as disabled people, lone parents or single adults. The complexity of the benefit system is associated with higher administration costs, benefit dependency and benefit traps. For the new Coalition government, the benefit system is inefficient and wasteful and generates disincentives to take up paid work. To increase work incentives in the benefit system, reduce administration costs and simplify the system, from 2013, the DWP will introduce Universal Credit – the name given to the new integrated single benefit for working-age benefit claimants. It will replace Income Support, WTC, Child Tax Credit, Housing Benefit, JSA and the Employment and Support Allowance. It will be a benefit paid to working, unemployed and economically inactive claimants with additional entitlements and assessments for housing, caring responsibilities, children and disability. The benefit will be fully administered and managed by the DWP, removing the current role of HM Revenue & Customs for the tax credit system. A key feature of the new reforms is a gradual reduction in benefit as claimants take up paid work – whether this is for one hour a week or moving to full-time hours. This new system could, in addition, offer a more responsive and flexible approach to benefits so that claimants are more able to take up part-time or temporary paid work that fits with their caring responsibilities or health needs. Furthermore, scope for recognising volunteering and civic engagement could be recognised in this system. Critical issues in the development of welfare reform, raised in Chapter Five, include the stricter system of work-related conditionalities and benefit fraud measures which will be introduced alongside the Universal Credit, and the level of benefit entitlements for claimants.

Childcare

The National Childcare Strategy under New Labour sought to make childcare services more affordable, of better quality and accessible to parents and families. The state has taken on much more responsibility for regulating standards in childcare provision, subsidising suppliers and providing pre-school places for 3- to 4-year-olds. Parents have gained new rights to access childcare services as paid workers.

Policy effectiveness was considerable. The Daycare Trust (2010) found near-universal take-up of free nursery places for 4-year-olds and over 80% take-up for 3-year-olds; significant increases in day care and out-of-school services; increases in mothers' employment rates; quality in early years settings had improved (even among private sector providers, although quality tended to be most variable in the private sector); some increase in the number of qualified childcare practitioners; and better financial support for parents (Daycare Trust, 2010).

However, the cost, quality and availability of childcare services remain critical issues for many parents, with prices rising in the recession as well as family incomes falling (Caluori, 2009). There are ongoing concerns about the quality of childcare services, and these concerns are related to matters of workforce reform: pay levels, the status of the childcare profession and levels of training and qualifications among childcare staff. There remains a limited supply of childcare for parents working atypical hours, and of childcare that is 'disabled-friendly' or is available in the school holidays, particularly for older children. The recession has led to major sustainability problems for many providers (Caluori, 2009).

The new Conservative-Liberal Democrat Coalition reflects ongoing cross-party support for the National Childcare Strategy. The Coalition has stated a commitment to sustain the free, part-time nursery provision for pre-school children. There have been further suggestions on developing more extensive policies to give more recognition to the role of grandparents and to promote a better gender balance in the childcare workforce (HM Government, 2010). However, a comprehensive programme of reform that recognises the ongoing problems of variable quality, high costs, unmet needs and lack of availability has not been an early priority. Further, reductions in public spending entail reductions in investment in early years services and a refocusing towards more targeted provision for higher-need families (HM Treasury, 2010b). In the context of strict cuts in public spending, state subsidies to providers appear to be under threat (Caluori, 2009).

Part Three highlighted how childcare decisions are complex for parents. There are many trade-offs and a careful balancing up of issues, including family versus formal childcare; affordability versus quality; children's educational versus emotional needs; care responsibilities versus financial responsibilities. There remain strong preferences for full-time maternal care for children aged under 3 years, and there needs to be more comprehensive public debate about how to support families in the early years with a more extensive range of locally accessible services, early education, childcare and play activities – across and beyond formal childcare providers.

Family-friendly employment

There were major developments in family-friendly employment policies under Labour, with the new Coalition government set to extend flexible parental leave measures and rights to flexible working. There were increases in statutory maternity, paternity and adoption leave and pay, and in parental leave. The new Conservative-Liberal Democrat Coalition government has stated that it will extend rather than repeal these rights – with a promise to extend flexible working rights to all employees (Cabinet Office, 2010). The issue of poor levels of paternity leave and pay in the British context are critical to address. Policy developments further need to recognise the challenges parents face in accessing their entitlements. Occupational cultures, career aspirations and family financial pressures mitigate against the uptake of flexible working practices. For these many reasons, mothers, fathers and carers are often unable to realise their work–family aspirations and take up employment rights.

There were considerable reforms. Rights to request flexible working were introduced, as were the EU Directives for part-time workers, time off for emergencies, and limits on working hours. However, more comprehensive gender quality goals were not an explicit part of the policy agenda and the social research reviewed in Part Three illustrated a range of work–family pressures and conflicts for parents, carers and families. From a critical perspective, the right to flexible working placed decision-making powers more squarely with employers and contingent on a viable business case, while the UK was found to take the path of minimal compliance with EU Directives and work–family balance policy agendas (Lewis, 2009). In other respects, the length of maternity leave was considerably extended and maternity pay increased during the New Labour years, particularly from the second term in office, driven by the multiple policy agendas at work: to reduce child poverty, to promote full employment (in particular mothers' employment) and to encourage employers to develop more family-friendly employment practices. By 2010 the gap between entitlements for UK mothers and those for mothers in EU member states with more generous provisions had closed somewhat. However, the UK continues to provide relatively limited maternity pay. Moreover, entitlements for paternity leave and pay are particularly low, with fathers still only entitled to two weeks' leave in their own right. The system, in the context of rising living costs and economic recession, sustains major trade-offs between fulfilling aspirations as a parent and an adult worker citizen, and between economic considerations and caring commitments and responsibilities. Once more, even from a business case perspective, there is evidence that some employers are unable or unwilling to grasp the economic potential for modernising working practices (via enhanced flexibility for employees and the use of technology) providing employees with choice and support to work in ways which fit more appropriately with their preferred work–family balance. From employees' perspectives, however, enhanced flexibility needs to be accompanied by appropriate levels of workload and a major cultural shift away from attitudes and practices that support a long-hours and work-first culture. As with welfare to work and anti-poverty measures, New Labour attempted to balance the employment agenda with the child and family well-being agenda. By 2010, work–family balance policies promoted a more flexible system of maternity leave and pay, developing new legislation to enable mothers to pass their entitlements over to fathers if they returned to work before the end of their maternity leave period. From a child welfare perspective, parents have gained more rights to care full time for their child in the first year of their life. Fathers, though, have not gained these rights independently. Rather, mothers and fathers have gained rights to share maternity entitlements, placing the UK system within the 'adult worker model' and limiting the extent to which statutory provisions promote the 'universal caregiver model' (Frazer, 2000). Policy, therefore, seems to rest heavily on the economic case for family-friendly employment and more flexible working practices.

Family and parenting support

There were major reforms in family and parenting support services under New Labour. Firstly, new sites of family support were developed, primarily in relation to the development of parent education initiatives and, in Labour's third term in office, an array of 'family level interventions' targeted at families in need, families with multiple problems or families with young people involved in the criminal justice system. Within education policies, parental involvement in children's schooling was a major priority. From 2004, New Labour embarked on a major reorganisation of children's and family services which sought to clarify responsibilities, provide a common framework for promoting children's outcomes, integrate services and make services more 'needs-led'.

Pro-family rhetoric accompanies the Coalition government's approach to family support and children's services reform. Both the Liberal Democrat Party and the Conservative Party revised their family and child policies extensively while in opposition during the New Labour years. Chapters One and Four set out the priorities for the Liberal Democrats in the 2010 General Election as: reform of the child protection system; investment in child and family social work training and social work reform; investment in parent education services for families in need; investment in childcare and integrated early years services for families; investment in health visitors; investment in couple mediation services; and family law reform to promote child welfare and shared parenting among separated and divorced parents. The Conservative Party continued to promote marriage as the best environment for child rearing with the 'Broken Britain' campaign identifying family breakdown and lone parenthood with poor outcomes for children and family instability and aligning marriage with better outcomes for children and 'strong and stable families' (Cameron, 2009). Key to both parties' anti-poverty measures was free pre-school nursery and early education provision for 2-year-olds from poorer families. More recent policy announcements indicate many pending changes to parental and family support services due to changing family and child policy priorities, the wider programme of reform for public services and the impact of the public spending cuts on services.

One month after coming to office, the Coalition government announced a Childhood and Families Task Force Review, which would include four members of the Cabinet including Prime Minister David Cameron and Deputy Prime Minister Nick Clegg. With Nick Clegg taking a leading role, this Task Force was to review 'child and family policies' and 'the barriers to a happy childhood and successful family life' (Clegg, 2010a). The Task Force was due to report in autumn 2010 but by December 2010 was yet to deliver a report, generating parliamentary concern about the progress of this review. However, there are clear family and child policy priorities emerging under the Coalition government, which include: returning to more targeted early years services and policy framework for Sure Start Children's Centres, with a greater emphasis on engaging disadvantaged families and neighbourhoods, and improving outcomes for disadvantaged children via the provision of tailored and integrated parent education, family support and early education and childcare provision; measures (such as the flexible parental leave option) to help parents balance paid work and family responsibilities; child protection reform; targeted support for poorer children in the education system to boost social mobility; investment in health visitor provision; a review of the family justice system; and a campaign against the commercialisation of childhood. Front-line services, however, are facing the prospect of severe public spending cuts, although the 2010 Spending Review did announce additional funding for social care, health visitors and voluntary/community sector service providers (HM Treasury, 2010). There is likely to be more diversity in the mixed economy of provision in line with the Coalition's public service reforms. The Coalition government seeks more devolved public services; less direct state provision; greater involvement in service provision from private and voluntary sector agencies; greater use of contracts with service providers whereby funding is contingent on effective service outcomes; reductions in bureaucracy and central government regulation for front-line staff, and more support for communities, citizens and volunteers to participate in the commissioning, planning and delivery of public services (HM Government, 2010; HM Treasury, 2010b). Local council funding from central government is to be radically reduced but councils will be provided with more autonomy and control over local budgetary decisions. In part such devolution could be about placing difficult budget cut decisions in the hands of local councils. However, comprehensive and appropriate devolution measures could generate more responsive and locally tailored services, designed with the input of local citizens and stakeholders (Kenny, 2010).

Critical features of progressive reform to family and parental support services would include recognition that most families rely on and utilise welfare state support and have family support needs; comprehensive local and 'whole family' needs assessment; a review of the spectrum of universal, targeted and specialist provision; support for all families in their diversity and considerable involvement of services users in service review. A broader vision of family support beyond targeted services for families in need is required. For example, Pugh et al (1994, p 2) defined family and parenting support as 'help for parents, prospective parents and family members which help parents and carers to understand their own social, emotional, psychological and physical needs and those of their children and enhance the relationship between the them' and 'support and services which help families and communities to support a network of services within local communities and help families to take advantage of them'. This vision for family support services could inform the current review of child and family policy priorities and re-orientate services towards the support needs of adults, children, families and communities.

Utting (2009) set out a more comprehensive and inclusive approach to needs assessment and resource allocation in the development of local authority Parenting Support Strategies and Children's and Young People Plans. Utting (2009, p 133) made recommendations for needs assessment and resource allocation processes in local authorities to be informed by felt needs, expressed needs, normative-comparative needs (expert opinion and objective measures of parental, family and children's needs) and extrapolated-comparative needs (needs based on analysis of population and area socio-demographic data). Expressed needs for parent and family support include needs for support and services to meet different types of needs, different levels of need, multiple needs and critical periods of need in families. Utting (2009, pp 130-1) recommended that local authorities review parental support services via systematic reviews of local needs and service provision, seeking to identify unmet needs and gaps in services. Such reviews often find local services could better address: practical needs and support (information and advice for families and young people, advocacy in dealing with public services); financial support; housing problems; childcare issues; parenting concerns and problems (low confidence in parenting skills; guidance and advice on parenting; difficulty in relation to difficult personal and family events or stages of childhood such as raising toddlers or parenting adolescents); conflict in family, adult and parent–child relationships; emotional, physical and mental health problems; the challenges and costs of living with a disability in a disabling society; coping with difficult child and youth behaviour; coping with problems at school; dealing with loss, trauma, addiction or bereavement; protecting children from harm; and tackling issues arising from asylum or refugee status. Local council 'Parenting Support Strategies' should become 'family support strategies', reflecting a broader focus on family support needs beyond parenting education. This strategy document should inform CYPPs and Community Plans and review the range of family and parenting support needs in the local population, informed by extensive service user and public consultation.

Part Three sought to reflect on child and family well-being debates and on policy developments, via an analysis of social research which examined parenthood and parenting as a lived experience. These chapters conceptualised 'parenthood' as a complex social location and 'parenting' as a relational and situated social practice. Parent–child relations were analysed as constructed through layers of meanings about childhood/adulthood, family and normative parenting practices. Everyday accounts of family relations and functions reflect consensus, conflict and ambivalence about normative family relationships and child rearing. In general terms, parents widely constructed 'good parenting' as taking responsibility for one's children and meeting children's needs. Many parents, in line with policy and legal imperatives, appeared to seek caring, loving and authoritative parent–child relationships; construct good parenthood as involving the fulfilment of obligations and responsibilities towards children; view good parenting as meeting children's needs; and have views about 'desirable parenting practices'. In terms of consensus, there is evidence of widely held social values in relation to parental and family responsibility for children; children as dependants; and children's needs for care, love, socialisation, encouragement and guidance. Much conflict, however, arises over what constitutes 'parental responsibilities' and 'children's needs'. Conflicting viewpoints exist about how to fulfil parental responsibilities, conflicts that arise from the situational and diverse nature of children's needs, as well as from conflicting social discourses. Conflicting viewpoints also exist about how responsibilities should be allocated and shared between mothers, fathers, children and young people, relatives, professionals and the state – and how these change as children grow up and develop. There are many blurred boundaries in the division of responsibilities for children and young people. Different perspectives relate to different life experiences and social/situational contexts. Complexity, ambivalence and uncertainty emerged from the more dynamic, holistic and complex engagement parents develop about their children's needs and the micro-level of everyday social relationships and settings. Being a parent is often talked about in terms of 'getting the balance right' between conflicting needs, rights and responsibilities within families.

Policy discourses need to recognise these complexities to parenting practices. Services could, in turn, provide information, support and advice to aid parental and family decision-making.

Rebalancing parental rights and responsibilities: strengthening rights to timely and appropriate family support

This section examines the shifting and contested nature of parental rights and responsibilities in the UK context. Since the 1990s many social policies have clarified and extended parental responsibilities. Under Labour, notions of parental responsibilities for children's outcomes and behaviour informed education, health and criminal justice reforms. Alongside these revisions of parental responsibility, this section argues for more effective parental rights to welfare state support. The Children Act 1989 and the UNCRC, as well as empirical evidence from child and family well-being studies, recognise that parental rights to public support and services enable parents to more effectively fulfil their responsibilities for children and young people. However, some policy developments in the New Labour years raised concern about UK standards for welfare, social, economic, civil and political rights. New Labour extended punitive policies towards undeserving groups, which increased their risk of poverty and social exclusion. Some human rights groups further criticised New Labour for infringements of civil and political rights. The Joint Committee on Human Rights (JCHR) raised concerns about the following policy developments: the erosion of rights to assembly and protest; infringements on civil rights to privacy (via state and corporate monitoring of personal communication; client information databases in children's services; the proposals for ID cards and the National Identity Register); the use of child curfews; the punitive implications of Parenting Orders; the use of eviction notices from social housing against citizens deemed anti-social; and the use of punitive benefit sanctions in welfare to work and criminal justice policies (JCHR, 2008). The JCHR (2008) further highlighted the negative treatment of asylum seekers and refugees; the limited health provision for failed asylum seekers; the use of school exclusions; and inadequacy of educational provision for detained children (JCHR, 2008, p 56).

Parents, children and families gained important new rights under Labour, such as the right to access childcare provision for working parents, children's rights to a Children's Commissioner and family rights to financial support among (deserving) low-income families. However, parental rights to welfare state support were also related to notions of desert, or dependent on employment status. Some developments in welfare state support were based on the construction of the 'consumer-citizen'. For example, rights to access childcare provision continued to be based on ability to pay. Statutory family-friendly employment rights were criticised for offering rights to request flexible working options, rather than more extensive rights to part-time work or flexible working options. Family-friendly employment rights were, in addition, criticised for offering limited rights to fathers and partners, and did not recognise the rights of non-resident parents to support. Furthermore, rights to a range of family and parenting support services remain limited in the UK. Family support services are, in the main, offered to families in response to 'family and parental failure', and are hence highly stigmatising. Koffman (2008) set out the social justice implications of the use of parenting contracts and orders, and associated legislation. Koffman (2008, p 121) argued that Labour extended legal definitions of parental responsibility within anti-social behaviour legislation in ways that add up to 'an imposition of a legal responsibility on parents to control children', representing 'a shift in state intervention from focusing on children's welfare and needs to focusing on their behaviour'. Parenting Orders and Parenting Contracts were introduced as enforcement and punitive measures compelling parents to engage with YOTs, parenting courses and family interventions, with the threat of housing eviction or loss of benefit a possibility. For Koffman (2008, p 118), 'a legalistic and punitive approach has been pursued at a time when there ought to have been a renewed effort to improve family support services, reduce poverty, and to invest more heavily both in recreational facilities for children and young people, and in counselling, health and mental health services'. Although Parenting Orders and Parenting Contracts can lead to targeted and specialist services and support for parents and children, Koffman (2008, p 118) argued that 'it is difficult to understand why a case should need to progress to the stage of a court order, with the threat of imprisonment for breach to the child or young person, and (frequently) the threat of eviction from their homes to their parents, before the appropriate remedial action and support is provided to families'. Beliefs in the primacy of parental responsibility for children's and young people's outcomes led to policies which sought to enforce responsibility. However, the missing piece in Labour's overall approach is to establish more effective social rights to timely, tailored, responsive and appropriate support and services for families and young people in need. In the severe economic context of the Coalition government's spending cuts, family and parental support services are further under threat.

The case for a national statement of parental rights and responsibilities

This book and this concluding chapter have set out the shifting and contested nature of parental rights and responsibilities. Of much relevance to the current review of family and child policy is the debate about a national statement of parental rights and responsibilities.

Several policy analysts have called for such a statement (CSJ, 1996; Henricson and Bainham, 2003; Henricson, 2003; 2007; Commission on Families and the Well-being of Children, 2005). The Report of the Commission for Social Justice (CSJ, 1996, p 320) framed this in terms of 'a national statement of parental responsibilities'. Such a statement was deemed necessary, due to the complexity and variety of legal definitions of parental rights and responsibilities in the UK and to (1) develop 'a far stronger acceptance of the importance of parenthood and the responsibilities that go with it'; (2) set out the expectations and responsibilities that being a parent entails in an accessible and coherent way; and (3) bring UK policies into line with other European countries (CSJ, 1996, p 320). To generate consensus and raise awareness, the CSJ argued that the national statement should evolve through a 'process of extensive consultation, drawing on the work of legal experts and the work of organisations concerned with all aspects and stages of family life' (CSJ, 1996; Henricson, 2007, p 150). It would act as 'a family covenant to be entered into by parents at the birth of a child' (CSJ, 1996; Henricson, 2007, p 150). Likewise, these campaigners stress that a national statement should be supported by state–family partnerships and policies which aim to 'ensure children grow up in families and communities that are enabled to meet their physical, emotional and intellectual needs'; promote a more equal distribution of labour and responsibility within families between mothers and fathers – empowering women to share the financial responsibilities for children as well as the emotional and practical; and enabling men to share the emotional and practical as well as the financial responsibilities associated with parenthood (CSJ, 1996, p 313).

Others have promoted the idea of a national statement of parental rights and responsibilities and related this to the rebalancing of parental rights and responsibilities in the UK context (Henricson and Bainham, 2003; Henricson, 2003; 2007; Commission on Families and the Well-being of Children, 2005). Clem Henricson has been a fervent campaigner for a national statement. Henricson (2003) argued that the development of a national statement on parental rights and responsibilities, based on expert and public input, could stimulate a review of the inconsistencies and tensions across family and child welfare policies and generate dialogue and more open discussion about the complexities of contemporary parenting and the contested nature of the respective roles of governments, parents and families. Henricson (2007) argued that New Labour developed 'a governmental role in family relations' but lacked a 'fully articulated strategy' with a 'comprehensive statement of the relationship between citizen and the state' in the family sphere (Henricson, 2007, p 150). The solution, in Henricson's (2007, p 150) view, was to learn from policy developments in other EU countries, including Scotland, and to engage policy communities, practitioners, agencies, parents, families, children and young people in a 'fuller and more transparent discussion of parental responsibilities and attendant rights'. The Commission on Families and the Well-being of Children (2005) further called for a national statement of parental rights and responsibilities to bring together recent legislative changes and to review policies against international principles in children's and human rights. All of these reports and commentators recognised the counter-arguments to developing such as statement. For example, Henricson (2007) stated that the counter-arguments were that a national statement by itself would do little to change policy or parenting practices and that much would depend on the political will to review parental rights to welfare state support. The statement could, in the current climate, be more orientated towards clarifying parental responsibilities for children rather than state responsibilities for family support. The latter process could risk alienating groups and individuals and reinforce the ethno-centric and middle-class assumptions that pervade policy discourses (Henricson, 2007).

However, there are compelling arguments for the development of a national statement of parental rights and responsibilities. Crucially, though, this process should be informed by a deliberative democratic process; open up public discussion about the complexities of parenthood and parent–child relations; review social and family policies in terms of promoting child, adult and family well-being; and be informed by human rights and children's rights perspectives. The Equalities Review approach to public consultation appears to offer a useful model and approach (Equalities Commission, 2007). The Equalities Review generated a framework for monitoring equality of autonomy, process and outcome that was informed by international legislation on universal social, economic, cultural and political rights, and from a citizen consultation exercise that consisted of:

(1) general public consultation events and (2) interviews with individuals and groups vulnerable to social exclusion and discrimination, and with community representative associations and lobby groups (Burchardt, 2008). The national statement should further seek to balance parental rights with children's rights and promote a diverse notion of 'parent' and 'family', recognising family diversity and the contributions to care made by non-resident parents and intergenerational patterns of care. The limitations of a national statement, however, are that abstract principles have a wide variety of meanings and engage little with the moral and situational dilemmas associated with fulfilling parental responsibilities and the granting of parental rights in specific real-life situations and relations. The national statement could play a major role in clarifying family rights to support and resources, as well as responsibilities for children and expectations on parents and families. It will be critical, however, that parents, families and children are engaged in a meaningful dialogue and provided with support (perhaps through the use of a website/telephone helpline or expert advisers, family support workers and counsellors) when making real-life decisions and when concerned about parenting issues.

References

Alcock, P. (2006) *Understanding poverty* (3rd edn), Basingstoke: Palgrave.

Andersen, E., Murray, L. and Browlie, J. (2002) *Disciplining children: Research with parents in Scotland*, Edinburgh: Scottish Executive.

Aston, J., Hooker, H., Page, R. and Willison, R. (2007) *Pakistani and Bangladeshi women's attitudes to work and family*, Research Report No. 458, Leeds: Corporate Document Services.

Atkinson, A., McKay, S. and Dominy, N. (2006) *Future policy options for child support: The views of parents*, Research Report 380, Leeds: Corporate Document Services.

Attree, P. (2005) 'Parenting support in the context of poverty: a meta-synthesis of the qualitative evidence', *Health and Social Care in the Community*, vol 13, no 4, pp 330-7.

Babington, B. (2006) *Family well-being in Australia: A Families Australia vision*, available at: www.familiesaustralia.org.au/publications/pubs/policy-familywellbeing.pdf (accessed 8 August 2010).

Backett-Milburn, K., Airey, L. and Hogg, G. (2008) 'Family comes first or open all hours? How low-paid women working in food retailing manage webs of obligation at home and at work', *Sociological Review*, vol 56, no 3, pp 474–96.

Bainham, A. (1999) 'Parentage, parenthood and parental responsibility: subtle, elusive and yet important distinctions', in Bainham, A., Day Sclater, S. and Richards, M. (eds) *What is a parent? A socio-legal analysis*, Oxford: Hart.

Ball, S. and Vincent, C. (2005) 'The "childcare champion"? New Labour, social justice and the childcare market', *British Education Research Journal*, vol 31, no 5, pp 557–70.

Bamfield, L. and Brookes, R. (2006) *Narrowing the gap: The final report of the Fabian Commission on Life Chances and Child Poverty*, London: Fabian Society.

Barlow, J. and Stewart-Brown, S. (2000) 'Review article: behaviour problems and parent training programs', *Journal of Developmental and Behavioral Pediatrics*, vol 21, no 5, pp 356–70.

Barlow, J., Kirkpatrick, S., Wood, D., Ball, M. and Stewart-Brown, S. (2007) *Family and parenting support in Sure Start programmes*, NESS/07/FR/023, London: DfES.

Barns, R., Ladino, C. and Rogers, B. (2006) *Parenting in multi-racial Britain*, London: National Children's Bureau.

Beck, U. and Beck-Gernsheim, E. (2002) *Individualisation: Institutionalised individualism and its social consequences*, London: Sage.

Bell, A., Finch, N., La Velle, I., Sainsbury, R. and Skinner, C. (2005) *A question of balance: Lone parents, childcare and work*, DWP Research Report 230, London: DWP.

Belsky, J., Barnes, J. and Melhuish, E. (2007) *The national evaluation of Sure Start: Does area-based early intervention work?*, Bristol: The Policy Press.

Ben-Arieh, A. (2002) 'Beyond welfare: Measuring and monitoring the state of children: New trends and domains', *Social Indicators Research*, vol 52, no 3, pp 235-57.

Ben-Arieh, A. and George, R. (eds) (2006) 'Indicators of child well-being: Understanding their role, usage and policy influence', Social Indicators Research, Dordrecht: Springer.

Bennett, F. (2006) 'Paying for children: current issues and implications of policy debates', in Lewis, J. (ed) (2006) *Children, changing families and welfare states*, Cheltenham: Edward Elgar.

Beresford, B., Sloper, T. and Bradshaw, J. (2005) 'Physical health', in Bradshaw, J. and Mayhew, E. (eds) *The well-being of children in the UK*, London: Save the Children/University of York.

Bertram, T. and Pascal, C. (2000) *Early Excellence Centre Pilot Programme: Annual evaluation report 2000*, London: DfEE.

Bertram, T., Pascal, C., Bokhari, S., Gasper, M. and Holterman, S. (2002) *Early Excellence Centre Pilot Programme: Second evaluation report 2000–2001*, Research Report RR361, London: DfES.

Black, C. (2008) *Working for a healthier tomorrow, Dame Carol Black's review of the health of the British working age population*, London: TSO.

Blair, T. (1998) *The third way: New politics for the new century*, London: Fabian Society.

Bonoli, G. and Powell, M. (2004) 'One third way or several?', in Lewis, J. and Surrender, R. (eds) (2004) *Welfare state change: Towards a third way?*, Oxford: Oxford University Press.

Borland, M., Laybourn, A., Hill, M. and Brown, J. (1998) *Middle childhood: The perspectives of children and parents*, London: Jessica Kingsley Publishers.

Bourdieu, P. (1990) *In other words: Essays towards a reflexive sociology*, Cambridge: Cambridge University Press.

Bradshaw, J. (2005) 'Child poverty and deprivation', in Bradshaw, J. and Mayhew, E. (eds) *The well-being of children in the UK*, London: Save the Children/University of York.

Bradshaw, J. and Mayhew, E. (eds) (2005) *The well-being of children in the UK*, London: Save the Children/University of York.

Bradshaw, J. and Richardson, D. (2009) 'An index of child well-being in Europe', *Child Indicators Research*, vol 2, no 3, pp 319–51.

Bradshaw, J., Hoelscher, P. and Richardson, D. (2006) 'Comparing child well-being in OECD countries: concepts and measures', Innocenti Working Paper, IWP-2003-06, Florence: UNICEF.

Brannen, J. and Nilsen, A. (2005) 'Individualisation, choice and structure: A discussion of current trends in sociological analysis', *Sociological Review*, vol 53, no 3, pp 412–28.

Brannen, J., Hepstinstall, E. and Bhopal, K. (2000) *Connecting children: Care and family life in middle childhood*, London: Falmer Press.

Brewer, M. and Joyce, R. (2010) *Child and Working Age Poverty from 2010 to 2013*, IFS Briefing Note 115, London: Institute for Fiscal Studies.

Bridgeman, J. and Keating, H. (2008) 'Introduction: Conceptualising family responsibility', in Bridgeman, J., Keating, H. and Lind, C. (eds) *Responsibility, law and family*, Farnham: Ashgate.

Bridgeman, J., Keating, H. and Lind, C. (eds) (2008) *Responsibility, law and family*, Farnham: Ashgate.

Bronfenbrenner, U. (1979) *The ecology of human development*, Cambridge, MA: Harvard University Press.

Bronfenbrenner, U. and Morris, P. (1989) 'The ecology of developmental processes', in Damon, W. and Lerner, R. (eds) *Handbook of child psychology: Volume 1: Theoretical methods of human development* (5th edn), New York: Wiley.

Brown, G. (1997) 1997 Budget Speech, available at: http://archive.treasury.gov. uk/pub/html/budget97/speech.html.

Brown, G. (1998) 1998 Budget Speech, available at: http://archive.treasury.gov. uk/pub/html/budget98/speech.html.

Brown, G. (1999) 1999 Budget Speech, available at: http://archive.treasury.gov. uk/budget/1999/speech.html.

Burchardt, T. (2008) 'Monitoring inequality: putting the capability approach to work', in Craig, G., Burchardt, T. and Gordon, D. (eds) *Social justice and public policy: Seeking fairness in diverse societies*, Bristol: The Policy Press.

Cabinet Office (2002) *Inter-departmental childcare review*, London: Cabinet Office.

Cabinet Office and SETF (Social Exclusion Task Force) (2007a) *Reaching out: Progress on social exclusion*, London: Cabinet Office.

Cabinet Office and SETF (2007b) *Reaching out: Think family: analysis and themes from the Families at risk review*, London: Cabinet Office.

Caluori, J. (2009) *Childcare and the recession*, Policy Insight Paper 3, London: Daycare Trust.

Cameron, D. (2009) Speech to the Conservative Party Conference, Manchester, 6 October 2009.

Carpenter, M., Freda, B. and Speeden, S. (2007) *Beyond the workfare state: Labour markets, equality and human rights*, Bristol: The Policy Press.

Casebourne, J. and Britton, L. (2004) *Lone parents, health and work*, DWPRR214, London: HMSO.

Castles, F.G and Obinger, H. (2008) 'Worlds, Families and Regimes: Country Clusters in European and OECD Area Public Policy', *West European Politics*, vol 31, no 1, pp 321-44.

Cawson, P., Wattam, C., Brooker, S. and Kelly, C. (2000) *Child maltreatment in the UK: A study of the prevalence of child abuse and neglect*, London: NSPCC.

Charles N., Davies, C.A. and Harris, C. (2008) *Families in transition: Social change, family formation and kin relationships,* Bristol: The Policy Press.

Cheal, D. (2009) *Families in today's world: A comparative approach*, Abingdon: Routledge.

Chief Secretary to the Treasury (2003) *Every child matters*, Cm 5860, London: Stationery Office.

Churchill, H. (2007) 'New Labour versus lone mothers' discourses of parental responsibility and children's needs', *Critical Policy Analysis*, vol 1, no 2, pp 149–62.

Churchill, H. and Clarke, K. (2009) 'Investing in parent education: A critical review of policy and provision in England', *Social Policy and Society*, vol 9, no 1, pp 39–53.

Clarke, J. (2005) New Labour's citizens: activated, empowered, responsibilized, abandoned?, *Critical Social Policy*, vol 25, no 4, pp 447–63.

Clegg, N. (2010a) Speech on supporting families and children, 17 June 2010, available at: www.libdems.org.uk/speeches.aspx?view=RSS.

Clegg, N (2010b) Nick Clegg's New Year message to Liberal Democrat members, 22 December 2010, available at: http://www.libdemvoice.org/nick-cleggs-new-year-message-to-liberal-democrat-members-22563.html

Commission on Families and the Well-being of Children (2005) *Families and the state: Two-way support and responsibilities – an inquiry into the relationships between the state and the family in the upbringing of children*, Bristol: The Policy Press.

Connell, R.W. (1987) *Gender and power: Society, the person and sexual politics*, Cambridge: Polity Press.

Conolly, A. and Kerr, J. (2008) *Families with children in Britain: Findings from the 2006 Families and Children Study*, Research Report No 486, Leeds: Corporate Document Services.

Conservative Party (2010) *Invitation to join the government of Britain, Conservative Party Manifesto 2010*, London: Conservative Party.

Counterpoint Research (2007) *Child well-being: Qualitative research study*, Research Report DCSF-RW031, London: Counterpoint Research.

CPAG (Child Poverty Action Group) (2008) *Child poverty: The stats*, London: CPAG.

CPAG (2009) *Child well-being and child poverty: Where the UK stands in the European table*, London: CPAG.

Crompton, R. (2006) *Employment and the family*, Cambridge: Cambridge University Press.

Crompton, R. and Lyonette, C. (2007) 'Are we all working too hard? Women, men and changing attitudes to employment', in A. Park, J. Curtice, K. Thomson, M. Phillips and M. Johnson (eds) *British Social Attitudes 23rd Report*, London: Sage.

CSJ (Commission on Social Justice) (1996) *Social justice: Strategies for national renewal*, London: Vintage.

CYPU (Children and Young People's Unit) (2003) *An outcomes framework for a national strategy for children and young people*, London: CYPU.

Daly, M. (2004) 'Changing conceptions of family and gender relations in European welfare states and the third way', in Lewis, J. and Surrender, R. (eds) *Welfare state change: Towards a third way?*, Oxford: Oxford University Press.

Daly, M. and Rake, K. (2003) *Gender and the welfare state*, Cambridge: Polity Press.

Daycare Trust, (2002) *Childcare costs survey 2002*, London: Daycare Trust.

Daycare Trust (2008) *Childcare futures*, Policy Insights Paper 2, London: Daycare Trust.

Daycare Trust (2009) *Childcare costs survey 2009*, London: Daycare Trust.

Daycare Trust (2010) *Childcare costs survey 2010*, London: Daycare Trust.

DCSF (Department for Children, Schools and Families) (2007) *The Children's Plan: Building brighter futures*, Cm 7280, London: The Stationery Office.

DCSF (2009a) *The Children's Plan two years on: A progress report*, London: DCSF.

DCSF (2009b) *Looked after children in England*, available at: www.dcsf.gov.uk/rsgateway/DB/SFR/s000878/index.shtml (accessed 11 December 2009).

DCSF (2010) *Support for all: The Families and Relationships Green Paper*, Cm 7787, London: DCSF.

Deacon, A. (2002) *Perspectives on welfare*, Buckingham: Open University Press.

Dean, H. (2010) *Understanding human need: Social issues, policy and practice*, Bristol: The Policy Press.

Dench S. (2007) *Impact of Care to Learn: Tracking the destinations of young people funded in 2003/04*, Report 442, Brighton: IES.

Dench, S. and Bellis, A. (2007) *Learning for young mothers*, Report 441, Brighton: IES.

Dermott, E. (2002) 'New fatherhood in practice – parental leave in the UK', *International Journal of Sociology and Social Policy*, vol 21, no 6, pp 145–64.

Dermott, E. (2001) *Intimate fatherhood: A sociological analysis*, London: Routledge.

Desforges, C. and Abouchaar, A. (2003) *The Impact of parental involvement, parental support and family education on pupil achievement and adjustment: A review of the literature*, Research Report RR433, London: TSO.

Devine, F. (2004) *Class practices: How parents help their kids get good jobs*, Cambridge: Cambridge University Press.

DfEE (Department for Education and Employment) (1998) *Meeting the childcare challenge: A framework and consultation document*, Cm 3959, London: DfEE.

DfES (Department for Education and Skills) (2002) *Extended schools: Providing opportunities and services for all*, London: DfES.

DfES (2004a) *Every child matters: Change for children*, London: DfES.

DfES (2004b), *Choice for parents, the best start for children: A ten year childcare strategy*, London: TSO.

DfES (2005a) *Youth matters: next steps, something to do, somewhere to go, someone to talk to*, London: DfES.

DfES (2005b) *Higher standards, better schools for all*, Cm 6677, London: DfES.

DfES (2006a) *Care matters: Transforming the lives of children and young people in care*, London: DfES.

DfES (2006b) *Parenting support guidance for local authorities in England*, DfES-04027-2006, London: DfES.

DfES (2007a) *Every parent matters*, London: DfES.

DfES (2007b) *Aiming high for disabled children: Better support for families*, London: DfES.

DH (Department of Health) (1995) *Child protection: Messages from research*, London: HMSO.

DH (1998) *The Quality Protects Programme: Transforming children's services*, LDC (98): 28.

DH (2000) *Assessing children in need and their families: Practice guidance*, London: Stationery Office.

DH (2004) *National Service Framework for Children, Young People and Maternity Services*, London: Department of Health.

DH, DfEE and Home Office (2000) *Framework for the assessment of children in need and their families*, London: Stationery Office.

Disability Alliance (2007) *Disability Alliance's broad policy response to current welfare proposals*, available at: www.disabilityalliance.org/welfare.htm (accessed 26 March 2010).

Doucet, A. (2006) *Do men mother? Fathering, care and domestic responsibility*, London: University of Toronto Press.

Doyal, L. and Gough, I. (1991) *A theory of human need*, Guildford: Guilford Press.

DSS (Department of Social Security) (1998) *New ambitions for our country: A new contract for welfare*, Cm 3805, London: DSS.

DTI (Department of Trade and Industry) (2000) *Work and parents: Competitiveness and choice: A Green Paper*, Cm 5005, London: DTI.

DTI (1998) *Fairness at work*, Cm 3968, London: HMSO.

Duncan, S. and Edwards, R. (1999) *Lone mothers, paid work and gendered rationalities*, London: Macmillan.

Duncan, S., Edwards, R., Alldred P., Reynolds, T. (2004) 'Mothers and childcare: policies, values and theories', *Children and Society*, vol 18, no 4, pp 245–65.

Duncan Smith, I. (2007) *Breakdown Britain*, London: Centre for Social Justice.

DWP (Department for Work and Pensions) (2004) *Households below average income: An analysis of the income distribution 1994/95–2002/03*, Leeds: Corporate Document Services.

DWP (2005) *Opportunity and security throughout life: Five year strategy*, Cm 6447, London: TSO.

DWP (2006a) *A new deal for welfare: Empowering people to work*, Cm 6730, London: HMSO.

DWP (2006b) *A new system of child maintenance*, Cm 6979, London: DWP.

DWP (2007a) *Ready for work: Full employment in our generation*. Cm 7920, London: TSO.

DWP (2007b) *In work and better off: Next steps to full employment*, Cm 7130, London: TSO.

DWP (2008a) *Households below average income: An analysis of the income distribution 1994/95–2006/07*, Leeds: Corporate Document Services.

DWP (2008b) *Raising expectations and increasing support: Reforming welfare for the future*, Cm 7506, London: DWP.

DWP (2010) *Household below average income: An analysis of the income distribution 1994/95–2008/09*, London: DWP.

DWP and DIUS (Department for Innovation, Universities and Skills) (2007) *Opportunity, employment and progression*, Cm 7288, London: TSO.

Dwyer, P. (2004) *Understanding social citizenship: Themes and perspectives for policy and practice*, Bristol: The Policy Press.

Edwards, L. (2004) *The Lever Faberge Family Report 2004: Parenting under the microscope*, London: IPPR Trading Ltd.

Edwards, A., Barnes, M., Plewis, I. and Morris, K. (2006) *Working to prevent the social exclusion of children and young people: Final lessons from the National Evaluation of the Children's Fund*, DfES Research Report 734, London: DfES.

Eekelaar, J. (2006) *Family law and personal life*, Oxford: Oxford University Press.

Equalities Commission (2007) *Fairness and freedom: The final report of the Equalities Review*, London: Crown Copyright.

Erikson, R. (2005) 'Why emotion work matters: sex, gender and the division of household labor', *Journal of Marriage and Family*, vol 67, no 2, pp 337–51.

Esping-Andersen, G. (1990) *The three worlds of welfare capitalism*, Cambridge: Polity Press.

Esping-Andersen, G. (1999) *The social foundations of post-industrial economies*, Oxford: Oxford University Press.

Esping-Andersen, G. (2009) *The incomplete revolution: Adapting to women's new role*, Cambridge: Polity Press.

Esping-Andersen, G., Gallie, D., Hemerijcke, A. and Myles, J. (2002) *Why we need a new welfare state*, Oxford: Open University Press.

Etzioni, A. (1993) *The spirit of community: Rights, responsibilities and the communitarian agenda*, New York: Simon and Schuster.

Etzioni, A. (1996) *The parenting deficit*, London: Demos.

Eurostat (2008) *Living conditions in Europe 2003–2006*, Luxembourg: Office for the Official Publications of the European Communities.

Family and Parenting Institute (FPI) (2010) *Family policy and the new government: The 2010 conference: the full report*, available at: www.familyandparenting.org/Filestore//Documents/PolicyDiscussionPapers/conference_rep_2010_final.pdf

Fathers Direct and An-Nisa Society (2008) *In conversation with Muslim dads*, London: Fatherhood Institute.

Featherstone, B. (2004) *Family life and family support: A feminist analysis*, Basingstoke: Palgrave.

Featherstone, B. (2010) 'Gender, rights, responsibilities and social policy', in Wallbank, J., Choudhry, S. and Herring, J. (eds) *Rights, gender and family law*, Abingdon: Routledge.

Ferguson, C. and Hussey, D. (2010) *2008–9 citizenship survey: Race, religion and equalities topic report*, London: Communities and Local Government.

Fernstein, L., Duckworth, K., and Sabates, R. (2008) *Education and the family: Passing success across the generations*, London: Routledge.

Finch, N. and Searle, B. (2005) 'Children's lifestyles', in Bradshaw, J. and Mayhew, E. (eds) *The well-being of children in the UK*, London: Save the Children/University of York.

Finer, M. (1974) *The Finer Report on one parent families*, Cmd 5629, London: HMSO.

Flexecutive (2002) *Work–life balance or career death? Issues and paradoxes facing marketing and human resources professionals*, London: Flexecutive.

Folbre, N. and Yoon, J. (2007) 'What is childcare? Lessons from Time Use surveys of major English speaking countries', *Review of Economics of the Household*, vol 5, no 3, pp 223–48.

Foley, P. and Rixon, A. (2008) *Changing children's services: Working and learning together*, Bristol: The Open University and Policy Press.

Fraser, D. (1997) *The evolution of the British welfare state* (2nd edn), London: Macmillan.

Fraser, N. (2000) 'After the family wage: a post-industrial thought experiment', in Hobson, B. (ed) *Gender and citizenship in transition*, Basingstoke: Macmillan.

Freud, D. (2007) *Reducing dependency, increasing opportunity: options for the future of welfare to work*, Leeds: Corporate Document Services.

Furlong, A. and Cartmel, F. (2007) *Young people and social change*, Buckingham: Open University Press.

Gatrell, C. (2005) *Hard Labour: The sociology of parenthood*, Buckingham: Open University Press.

Gauthier, A.H. (1996) *The state and the family: A comparative analysis of family policies in industrialised countries*, Oxford: Clarendon Press.

Gauthier, A.H. (2002) *Family policies in industrialized countries: Is there policy convergence?*, available at: http://depts.washington.edu/crfam/Symposium1/Gauthier.pdf (accessed 3 June 2010).

Ghate, D. and Hazel, N. (2002) *Parenting in poor environments: Stress, support and coping*, London: Policy Research Bureau.

Ghate, D. and Ramella, M. (2002) *Positive parenting: The National Evaluation of the Youth Justice Board Parenting Programme*, London: Youth Justice Board.

Ghate, D., Hazel, N., Creighton, S., Finch, S. and Field, J. (2003) *The national survey of parents, children and discipline in Britain*, London: Policy Research Bureau.

Giddens, A. (1992) *The transformation of intimacy*, Cambridge: Polity Press.

Giddens, A. (1998) *The third way*, Cambridge: Polity Press.

Gillies, V. (2007) *Marginalised mothers: Exploring working-class experiences of parenting*, London: Routledge.

Glennerster, H. (2007) *British social policy 1945 to the present* (3rd edn), Oxford: Blackwell.

Goldman, R. (2005) *Fathers' involvement in their children's education*, London: Family and Parenting Institute.

Golombok, S. (2000) *Parenting: What really counts?* London: Routledge.

Gornick, J.C. and Meyers, M. (2001) 'Lesson-drawing in family policy: media reports and empirical evidence about European developments', *Journal of Comparative Policy Analysis: Research and Practice*, vol 3, no 1, pp 31–57.

Graham, H. and McDermott, E. (2005) 'Qualitative research and the evidence base of policy: insights from studies of teenage mothers in the UK', *Journal of Social Policy*, vol 35, no 1, pp 21–37.

Gregg, P. (2008) *Realising potential: A vision for personalised conditionality and support*, London: DWP.

Guo, J. and Gilbert, N. (2007) 'Welfare state regimes and family policy: a longitudinal analysis', *Journal of International Social Welfare*, vol 16, no 4, pp 307–13.

Hakim, C. (2000) *Work–lifestyle choices in the 21st century: preference theory*, Oxford: Oxford University Press.

Hakim, C. (2002) 'Lifestyle preferences as determinants of women's differentiated labour market careers', *Work and Occupations*, vol 29, no 4, pp 428–59.

Hanafin, S., Brookes, A., Carroll, E., Fitzgerald, E., Gabhainn, S.N. and Sixsmith, J. (2007) 'Achieving consensus in developing a national set of indicators', *Social Indicators Research*, vol 80, no 79, pp 79–104.

Hantrais, L. (2004) *Family policy matters: Responding to family change in Europe*, Bristol: Policy Press.

Harker, L. (1998) 'A national childcare strategy: does it meet the childcare challenge?' *Political Quarterly*, vol 69, no 4, pp 458–63.

Harker, L. (2006) *Delivering on child poverty: What will it take?* Cm 6951, London: HMSO.

Heath, P. (2009) *Parent–child relations: Context, research, and application* (2nd edn), Columbus, OH: Pierson.

Henricson, C. (2003) *Government and parenting: Is there a case for a policy review and a parents' code?* York: National Family and Parenting Institute.

Henricson, C. (2007) *The contractual culture and family services: A discussion*, London: Family and Parenting Institute.

Henricson, C. and Bainham, A. (2003) *The child and family policy divide: Tensions, convergence and rights*, York: Joseph Rowntree Foundation.

Henricson, C. and Roker, D. (2000) 'Support for parents of adolescents: a review', *Journal of Adolescents*, vol 23, no 6, pp 763–83.

Henshaw, D. (2006) *Recovering child support: Routes to responsibility*, Cm 6894, London: Crown Copyright.

Henwood, K.L. and Procter, J. (2003) 'The "good father": reading men's accounts of paternal involvement during the transition to first time fatherhood', *British Journal of Social Psychology*, vol 42, no 3, pp 337–55.

Hills, J., Sefton, T. and Stewart, K. (eds) (2009) *Towards a more equal society? Poverty, inequality and policy since 1997*, Bristol: Policy Press.

Himmelweit, S. and Sigala, M. (2004) 'Choice and relationship between identities and behaviour for mothers of pre-school children: some implications for policy from a UK study', *Journal of Social Policy*, vol 33, no 3, pp 455–78.

Hirst, P. and Thompson, G. (1999) *Globalisation in question* (2nd edn), Cambridge: Polity Press.

HM Government (2004) *Parental separation: Children's needs and parents' responsibilities*, Cm 6273, London: TSO.

HM Government (2009a) *Next steps for early learning and childcare: Building on the 10 year strategy*, London: TSO.

HM Government (2009b) *Building Britain's future*, Cm 7654, London: Stationery Office.

HM Government (2010) *The Coalition: Our programme of government*, London: HM Government.

HM Treasury (2002a) 2002 *Spending review: Opportunity and security for all, investing in an enterprising society: new public spending plans 2003–2006*, London: The Stationery Office.

HM Treasury (2002b) *Report of the inter-departmental childcare review*, London: The Stationery Office.

HM Treasury (2002c) *Cross-cutting children at risk review*, London: HM Treasury.

HM Treasury (2004) *Child poverty review*, London: Crown Copyright.

HM Treasury (2010a) *Budget 2010*, HC61, 22 June, London: TSO.

HM Treasury (2010b) *Spending Review 2010*, Cm 7942, London: Crown Copyright.

HM Treasury and DfES (2005) *Support for parents: The best start for children*, London: Crown Copyright.

HM Treasury and DfES (2007) *Aiming higher for disabled children: Better support for families*, London: TSO.

HM Treasury, DfES, DWP and DTI (2004) *Choice for parents, the best start for children: A ten year strategy for childcare*, Norwich: HM Treasury.

Hobson, B., Middleton, S. and Beardsworth, A. (2001) *The impact of childhood disability on family life*, York: Joseph Rowntree Foundation.

Holmes, J. and Kiernan, K. (2010) *Fragile families in the UK: Evidence from the Millennium Cohort Study*, available at: www.york.ac.uk/depts/spsw/staff/documents/HolmesKiernan2010FragileFamiliesInTheUKMillenniumCohort.pdf, accessed 3 September 2010.

Home Office (1998) *Supporting families: A consultation paper*, London: Stationery Office.

Home Office (2005) *2005 citizenship survey*, London: Home Office.

Home Office (2006) *Respect action plan*, London: Home Office.

Hooker, H. et al (2007) *The third work–life balance employee survey: Main findings*, Employment Relations Research Series No 58, London: DTI.

House of Commons Children, Schools and Families Committee (2010) *Sure Start children's centres*, Fifth Report of the Session 2009–10, vol 1, HC 130-1, London: TSO.

Hudson, J. and Lowe, S. (2009) *Understanding the policy process: Analysing welfare policy and practice* (2nd edn), Bristol: The Policy Press.

James, A. and James, A. (2008) *Key concepts in childhood studies*, Key Concept Series, London: Sage.

James, A., Jenks, C. and Prout, A. (1998) *Theorizing childhood*, Cambridge: Polity Press.

Jensen, J. (2006) 'The LEGO paradigm and new social risks: consequences for children', in Lewis, J. (ed) (2006) *Children, changing families and welfare states*, Edward Elgar: Cheltenham.

Jensen, J. (2008) 'Writing women out, folding gender in: the European Union "modernises" social policy', *Social Politics: International Studies in Gender, State and Society*, vol 15, no 2, pp 131-53.

JCHR (Joint Committee on Human Rights) (2008) *A Bill of Rights for the UK?*, Twenty-ninth report of session 2007–8, HC-150-1, London: TSO.

Jordan, B. (2007) *Social work and well-being*, London: Russell House Publishing.

Kelley, P., Hood, S. and Mayall, B. (2002) 'Children, parents and risk', *Health and Social Care in the Community*, vol 6, no 1, pp 16–24.

Kempson, E. (1996) *Life on a low income*, York: Joseph Rowntree Foundation.

Kenny, M. (2010) *Developing a civic approach to public services: Time to take pluralism seriously*, London: 2020 Public Services Trust.

Kiernan, K. (2006) 'Non-resident fatherhood and child involvement: evidence from the Millenium Cohort Study', *Journal of Social Policy*, vol 35, no 4, pp 651–99.

Kirby, J. (2009) 'From broken families to the broken society', *The Political Quarterly*, vol 30, no 2, pp 243–7.

Klett-Davies, M. and Skaliotis, E. (2009) 'Mothers, childcare and the work–life balance', in Hunt, S. (ed) *Family trends: British families since the 1950s*, London: Family and Parenting Institute.

Knight, G. and Lissenburg, S. (2004) *Evaluation of lone parent focused interviews: Final findings from administrative data*, London: DWP.

Koffman, L. (2008) 'Holding parents to account: tough on children, tough on the causes of children?' *Journal of Law and Society*, pp 113–30.

Kremer, M. (2007) *How welfare states care: Culture, gender and parenting in Europe*, Amsterdam: Amsterdam University Press.

Labour Party (1997) *New Labour because Britain deserves better*, available at: www.labour-party.org.uk/manifestos/1997/1997-labour-manifesto.shtml.

Labour Party (2001) *Ambitions for Britain*, available at: www.labour-party.org.uk/manifestos/2001/2001-labour-manifesto.shtml.

Labour Party (2010) *A future fair for all*, Labour Party Manifesto 2010, London: Labour Party.

Laming, L. (2003) *The Laming Inquiry into the death of Victoria Climbié*, London: HMSO.

Laming, L. (2009) *The protection of children in England: A progress report*, HC 330, London: Stationery Office.

Land, H. (2002) *Building on sand?*, London: Daycare Trust.

Lareau, A. (2003) *Unequal childhoods: Class, race and family life*, Berkeley, CA: University of California.

La Velle, I., Finch, S., Nove, S. and Lewin, C. (2000) *Parents' demand for childcare*, London: National Centre for Social Research.

Layard, R. and Dunn, J. (2009) *A good childhood: Searching for competing values in a competitive age*, London: The Children's Society/Penguin.

Leira, A. (2002) *Working parents and the welfare state: Family change and policy reform in Scandinavia*, Cambridge: Cambridge University Press.

Leitch Review (2006) *Prosperity for all in the global economy – world class skills: Final report*, London: Crown Copyright.

Levitas, R. (2005) *The inclusive society?* (2nd edn), Basingstoke: Macmillan.

Lewis, G. (2000) *'Race', gender and social welfare: Encounters in a post-colonial society*, Cambridge: Polity Press.

Lewis, J. (1992) 'Gender and the development of welfare regimes', *Journal of European Social Policy*, vol 2, no 3, pp 159–73.

Lewis, J. (2002) 'Individualisation, assumptions about the existence of an adult worker model and the shift towards contractualism', in Carling, A., Duncan, S. and Edwards, R. (eds) *Analysing families: Morality and rationality in policy and practice*, London and New York: Routledge.

Lewis, J. (2003) 'Developing early years childcare in England, 1997–2002: the choices for (working) mothers', *Social Policy and Administration*, vol 37, no 3, pp 219–38.

Lewis, J. (2007) 'Teenagers and their parents: parental time and parenting style – what are the issues?', *The Political Quarterly*, vol 78, no 2, pp 292–300.

Lewis, J. (2009) *Work–family balance, gender and policy*, Cheltenham: Edward Elgar.

Lewis, J. and Giullari, S. (2005) 'The adult worker model family, gender equality and care: the search for new policy principles and the possibilities and problems of a capabilities approach', *Economy and Society*, vol 34, no 1, pp 76–104.

Lewis, C. and Lamb, M.E. (2007) *Fathers and fatherhood: Connecting the strands of diversity*, York: Policy Research Bureau/Joseph Rowntree Foundation.

Lewis, J., Mitchell, L., Sanderson, T., O'Conner, W. and Clayden, M. (2000) *Lone parents and personal advisers*, London: DSS.

Liberal Democrat Party (2010) *Change that works for you: Building a fairer Britain*, Liberal Democrat Manifesto, London: Liberal Democrat Party.

Lindsay, G., Davies, H., Band, S., Cullen, M.A., Cullen, S., Strand, S., Hasluck, C., Evans, R. and Stewart-Brown, S. (2008) *Parenting Early Intervention Pathfinder evaluation*, Research Report DCSF-RW054, London: DCSF.

Lister, R (1997) *Citizenship: Feminist perspectives*, Basingstoke: MacMillan.

Lister, R. (2002) 'The dilemmas of pendulum politics: balancing paid work and citizenship', *Economy and Society*, vol 31, no 4, pp 520–32.

Lister, R. (2003) 'Investing in the citizen-workers of the future: transformations in citizenship and the state under Labour', *Social Policy and Administration*, vol 37, no 5, pp 427–43.

Lister, R. (2004) *Poverty*, Basingstoke: Palgrave.

Lister, R. (2006a) 'An agenda for children: investing in the future or promoting well-being in the present?' in Lewis, J. (ed) (2006) *Children, changing families and welfare states*, Edward Elgar: Cheltenham.

Lister, R. (2006b) 'Children (but not women) first: New Labour, child welfare and gender', *Critical Social Policy*, vol 26, no 2, pp 315–35.

Lister, R. (2010) *Understanding theories and concepts in social policy*, Bristol: The Policy Press.

Lloyd, C. (2009) *2007–8 Citizenship survey: People's views of their local community in England and Wales*, London: Communities and Local Government.

Lohmann, H., Peter, F.H., Rostgaard, T and Spiess, K. (2009) *Towards a framework for assessing family policies in the EU*, OECD Social, Employment and Migration Working Papers No 88, Paris, France: OECD Publishing.

Lonne, B., Parton, N., Thomson, J. and Harres, M. (2008) *Reforming child protection*, London: Routledge.

Lupton, D. and Barclay, L. (1997) *Constructing fatherhood: Discourses and experiences*, London: Sage.

MacDonald, R. and Marsh, J. (2005) *Disconnected youth? Growing up poor in Britain*, Basingstoke, Palgrave Macmillan.

MacInnes, T., Kenway, P. and Parekh, A. (2009) *Monitoring poverty and social exclusion 2009*, London: New Policy Institute.

McKie, L. (2005) *Families, violence and social change*, Buckingham: Open University Press.

Maclean, M. (2002) 'The Green Paper *Supporting Families*', in Carling, A., Carling, A., Duncan, S. and Edwards, R. (eds) *Analysing families: Morality and rationality in policy and practice*, London and New York: Routledge.

Madge, N. (2006) *Children these days*, Bristol: Policy Press.

Madge, N. and Willmott, N. (2007) *Children's views and experiences of parenting*, York: Joseph Rowntree Foundation.

Maher, J. and Saugeres, L. (2007) 'To be or not to be a mother? Women negotiating cultural representations of mothering', *Journal of Sociology*, vol 43, no 1, pp 5–21.

Marshall, T.H. (1950) *Citizenship and social class*, Cambridge: Cambridge University Press.

Matravers, M. (2007) *Responsibility and justice*, Cambridge: Policy Press.

Mayall, B. (2002) *Towards a sociology of childhood: Thinking from children's lives*, Buckingham: Oxford University Press.

Mayhew, E. (2005) 'Demography of childhood', in Bradshaw, J. and Mayhew, E. (eds) *The well-being of children in the UK*, London: Save the Children/University of York.

Mayo, E. (2005) *Shopping generation*, London: National Consumer Council.

Mayo, E. and Nairns, A. (2009) *Consumer kids: How big business is grooming our kids for profit*, London: Constable.

Mead, L. (1997) 'From welfare to work: lessons from America', in Deacon, A. (ed) *From welfare to work: Lessons from America*, London: Institute of Economic Affairs, Health and Welfare Unit.

Melhuish, E., Belsky, J. and Leyland, A. (2008) *The impact of Sure Start local programmes on three year olds and their families*, Research Report/NESS/2008/FR/027, London: HMSO.

Middleton, S., Ashworth, K. and Braithwaite, I. (1998) *Small fortunes: Spending on children, childhood poverty and parental sacrifice*, York: Joseph Rowntree Foundation.

Millar, J. and Gardiner, K. (2004) *Low pay, household resources and poverty*, York: Joseph Rowntree Foundation.

Millar, J. and Rowlingson, K. (eds) (2001) *Lone parents, employment and social policy: Cross-national comparisons*, Bristol: The Policy Press.

Morgan, D. (1996) *Family connections*, Cambridge: Polity Press.

Morris, K., Barnes, M. and Mason, P. (2009) *Children, families and social exclusion. New approaches to prevention,* Bristol: Policy Press.

Moss, P. (2003) *Beyond caring: The case for reforming the childcare and early years workforce*, London: Daycare Trust.

NAO (National Audit Office) (2004) *Early years: Progress in developing high quality childcare and early education accessible for all,* Report by the Comptroller and Auditor General, HC 268 Session, London: National Audit Office.

Neale, J. (2005) 'Children, crime and illegal drug use', in Bradshaw, J. and Mayhew, E. (eds) *The well-being of children in the UK,* London: Save the Children/University of York.

NECTP (National Evaluation of the Children's Trusts Pathfinders) (2007) *Children's Trusts Pathfinders: Innovative partnerships for improving the well-being of children and young people*, Norwich: UEA and London: NCB.

Newburn, T. (2002) 'Young people, crime and youth justice', in Maguire, M., Morgan, R. and Reiner, R. (eds) *The Oxford handbook of criminology* (3rd edn), Oxford: Oxford University Press.

Newman, J. (2001) *Modernising governance: New Labour, policy and society,* London: Sage.

NFPI (National Family and Parenting Institute) (2001) *Listening to parents: Their worries, their solutions*, London: NFPI/MORI.

OECD (2001) *Starting strong: Early childhood education and care*, Paris: OECD.

OECD (2005) *Babies and bosses. Reconciling work and family life, vol 4, Canada, Finland, Sweden and the United Kingdom*, Paris: OECD.

OECD (2009) *Doing better for children*, Paris: OECD.

Official Journal of the Council of Europe (2007) Treaty of Lisbon, 2007/C306/01, vol 50, 17 December 2007, available at: http://eur-lex.europa.eu/JOHtml.do?uri=OJ:C:2007:306:SOM:EN:HTML.

Okitikpi, T. (ed) (2005) *Working with children of mixed parentage*, London: Russell House Publishing.

Olsen, R. and Clarke, H. (2006) *Parenting and disability: Disabled parents' experiences of raising children*, Bristol: The Policy Press.

ONS (Office for National Statistics) (2000) *UK time use survey*, London: ONS.

ONS (2003) *Census 2001*, London: ONS.

ONS (2005) 'Ethnicity: 4 in 5 Bangladeshi families have children', available at: www.statistics.gov.uk/CCI/nugget.asp?!D=1167Pos=1ColRank=1Rank326.

ONS (2008) *The labour force survey*, London: ONS.

ONS (2009) *Social trends 39, 2009*, London: ONS.

ONS (2010a) *Social trends 40, 2010*, London: ONS.

ONS (2010b) *The labour force survey*, London: ONS.

ONS (2010c) 'Marriage registrations in England and Wales remain stable', 11 February 2010, available at: www.statistics.gov.uk/cci/nugget.asp?id=322.

ONS (2010d) *General lifestyle survey 2010*, London: ONS.

ONS (2010e) *Statistical Bulletin: 2010 Annual Survey of Hours and Earnings*, London: ONS.

Orloff, A.S. (1993) 'Gender and the social rights of citizenship: the comparative analysis of gender relations and welfare states', *American Sociological Review*, vol 58, no 3, pp 303–28.

Page, A. with Das, S., Mangabeira, W. and Natale, L. (2009) *School–parent partnerships: Emerging strategies to promote innovation in schools*, London: FPI.

Parton, N. (1991) *Governing the family: Childcare, child protection and the state*, London: Macmillan Education.

Paull, G., Taylor, J. and Duncan, A. (2002) *Mothers' employment and childcare use*, London: Institute for Fiscal Studies.

Penn, H. (2009) *Early childhood education and care: Key lessons from research for policy makers*, Brussels: European Commission.

Penn, H. and Gough, D. (2002) 'The price of a loaf of bread: some conceptions of family support', *Children and Society*, vol 16, no 1, pp 17–32.

Pfau-Effinger, B. (1999) 'Change in family policies in the socio-economic context of European Societies', in Leira, A (ed) *Family change: Practices, policies and values*, Comparative Social Research series, vol 18, Bingley: Emerald Group Publishing Ltd.

Phoenix, A. and Hussain, Y. (2007) *Parenting and ethnicity*, York: Joseph Rowntree Foundation.

Pierson, C. (2006) *Beyond the welfare state: The new political economy of welfare* (3rd edn), Cambridge: Polity Press.

Pierson, P. (ed) (2001) *The new politics of the welfare state*, Oxford: Oxford University Press.

Plaid Cymru (2010) *Think different. Think Plaid*, Manifesto 2010, Cardiff: Plaid Cymru.

Platt, L. (2007) *Poverty and ethnicity in the UK*, Bristol: Policy Press/Joseph Rowntree Foundation.

Pocock, B. (2005) 'Work/care regimes: institutions, culture and behaviour in the Australian case', *Gender, Work and Organisation*, vol 12, no 1, pp 32–49.

Pollard, E.L. and Davidson, L. (2001) *Foundations of child well-being*, UNICEF Education Monograph No 18/2001, Paris: UNICEF.

Powell, M. and Hewitt, M. (2002) *Welfare state and welfare change*, Buckingham: Open University Press.

PricewaterhouseCoopers (2006) *DfES Children's Services: The market for parental and family support services*, London: Pricewaterhouse Coopers.

Pugh, A. (2009) *Longing and belonging: Parents, children, and consumer culture*, London: University of California Ltd.

Pugh, G., De'Ath, E. and Smith, C. (1994) *Confident parents, confident children: Policy and practice in parent education and support*, London: National Children's Bureau.

Quilgars, D., Searle, B. and Keung, A. (2005) 'Mental health and well-being', in Bradshaw, J. and Mayhew, E. (eds) *The well-being of children in the UK*, London: Save the Children/University of York.

Quinton, D. (2004) *Supporting parents: Messages from research*, London: Jessica Kingsley Publishers.

Radford, L. and Hester, M. (2006) *Mothering through domestic violence*, London: Jessica Kingsley Publishers.

Randall, V. (2000) *The politics of child daycare in Britain*, Oxford: Oxford University Press.

Reeve, K. (2008) 'New immigration and neighbourhood change', in Flint, J. and Robinson, D. (eds) *Community cohesion in crisis? New dimensions of diversity and difference*, Bristol: The Policy Press.

Ribbens, J. (1994) *Mothers and their children: A feminist sociology of childrearing*, London: Sage.

Ribbens McCarthy, J., Edwards, R. and Gillies, V. (2000) 'Moral tales of the child and the adult: narratives of contemporary family lives under changing circumstances', *Sociology* vol 34, no 4, pp 785–804.

Ribbens McCarthy J., and Edwards, R. (2002) 'The individual in public and private: The significance of mothers and children, in Carling, A., Duncan, S., and Edwards, R. (eds) *Analysing families: Morality and rationality in policy and practice*, London: Routledge.

Ridge, T. (2002) *Childhood poverty and social exclusion*, Bristol: The Policy Press.

Rodgers, B. and Pryor, J. (1998) *Divorce and separation: Outcomes for children*, York: Joseph Rowntree Foundation.

Rodgers, J.J. (2003) 'Family life, moral regulation and the state: social steering and the personal sphere', in Cunningham-Burley, S. and Jamieson, L. (2003) *Families and the state: Changing relationships*, Basingstoke: Palgrave.

Rose, W. (2009) 'The assessment framework', in Horwath, J. (ed) *The child's world: The comprehensive guide to assessing children in need*, London: Jessica Kingsley Publishers.

Rowlingson, K. and McKay, S. (2005) 'Lone motherhood and socio-economic disadvantage: insights from quantitative and qualitative evidence', *Sociological Review*, vol 53, no 1, pp 30–49.

Sainsbury, D. (2001) 'Gendering dimensions of welfare states', in Fink, J., Lewis, G., Clarke, J. (eds) *Rethinking European welfare*, Buckingham: Oxford University Press.

Sainsbury, R. and Stanley, K. (2007) 'One for all: active welfare and the single age working benefit', in Bennett, J. and Cooke, G. (eds) *It's all about you: Citizen centred welfare*, London: Institute for Public Policy Research.

Scottish National Party (2010) *Elect a local champion*, SNP Manifesto 2010, Glasgow: Scottish Nationalist Party.

Seaman, P., Turner, K., Hill, M., Stafford, K. and Walker, M. (2007) *Parenting and children's resilience in disadvantaged communities*, York: Joseph Rowntree Foundation.

Sefton, T., Hills, J. and Sutherland, H. (2009) 'Poverty, inequality and redistribution', in Hills, J., Sefton, T. and Stewart, K. (eds) *Towards a more equal society? Poverty, inequality and policy since 1997* (2nd edn), Bristol: Policy Press.

Sen, A. (1993) 'Capability and well-being', in Nussbaum, N. and Sen, A. (eds) *The quality of life*, Oxford: Clarendon Press.

SETF (Social Exclusion Task Force) (2006) *Reaching out: Social Exclusion Action Plan*, London: TSO.

SEU (Social Exclusion Unit) (1999) *Understanding social exclusion*, London: SEU.

SEU (2001) *Preventing social exclusion*, London: SEU.

Sevenhuijsen, S.L. (1998) *Citizenship and the ethics of care: Feminist considerations on justice, morality and politics*, London: Routledge.

Sevon, E. (2007) 'Narrating ambivalence of maternal responsibility', *Sociological Research Online*, vol 12, no 2, www.socresonline.org.uk/12/2/sevon.html, doi:10.5153/sro.1527.

Shulruf, B., O'Loughlin, C. and Tolley, H. (2009) 'Parent education and support policies and their consequences in selected OECD countries', *Children and Youth Services Review*, vol 31, no 5, pp 526–32.

Skilton, L. (2009) *Working paper: Measuring societal well-being*, London: ONS.

Smart, C. (2007) *Personal life*, Cambridge: Polity Press.

Smart, C., Neale, B. and Wade, A. (2003) *The changing experience of childhood: Families and divorce*, Cambridge: Polity Press.

Smith, K. (2007) *Millennium Cohort Study: Parenting*, Briefing 5, London: Centre for Longitudinal Studies.

Smith, P.K., Cowie, H. and Blades, M. (2007) *Understanding children's development* (4th edn), Basic Psychology series, Oxford: Blackwell Publishing Limited.

Smith, T. and Lee, C. with Braswell, S., Coxon, K., Smith, G., Sylva, K. and Tanner, E. (2005) *Early stages of the Neighbourhood Nurseries Initiative: Opening the nurseries*, London: DfES.

Social Work Task Force (2009) *Building a safe, confident future, the final report of the Social Work Task Force*, London: DCSF.

Southerton, D. (2006) 'Analysing the temporal organisation of daily life: social constraints, practices and their allocation', *Sociology*, vol 40, no 3, pp 435–54.

Speak, S., Cameron, S. and Gilroy, R. (1997) *Young single fathers: Participation in fatherhood – bridges and barriers*, London: Family Studies Centre.

Speight, S., Smith, R., La Velle, I., Schneider, V. and Perry, J. with Coshall, C and Tipping, S. (2009) *Childcare and Early Years Survey of Parents 2008*, DCSF-RR136, London: National Centre for Social Research.

Stacey, S. and Roker, D. (2005) *Monitoring and supervision in 'ordinary' families: The views and experiences of young people aged 11 to 16 and their parents*, London: NCB.

Stewart, K. (2009) 'Poverty, inequality and child well-being in international context: still bottom of the pack?', in Hills, J., Sefton, T. and Stewart, K. (eds) (2009) *Towards a more equal society? Poverty, inequality and policy since 1997*, Bristol: The Policy Press.

Stiglitz, J., Sen, A. and Fitoussi, J.P. (2009) *Report by the Commission on Measuring Economic Performance and Social Progress*, available at: www.stiglitz-sen-fitoussi.fr.

Sylva, K. and Pugh, G. (2005) 'Transforming the early years in England', *Oxford Review of Education,* vol 31, no 3, pp 11–27.

Sylva, K., Melhuish, E., Sammons, P., Siraj-Blatchford, I. and Taggart, B. (2004) *The Effective Provision of Pre-School Education Project: Findings from the early primary years*, London: DCSF.

Taylor-Gooby, P. (ed) (2004) *New risks, new welfare: The transformation of the European welfare state*, Oxford: Oxford University Press.

UK Children's Commissioners (2008) *Report to the UN Committee on the Rights of the Child*, available at: www.sccyp.org.uk/UK_Childrens_Commissioners_UN_Report.pdf.

UNICEF (2007) *Child poverty in perspective: An overview of child well-being in rich countries*, Report Card 7, Florence: UNICEF Innocenti Research Centre.

Utting, D. (2009) *Assessing and meeting the need for parenting support services: A literature review*, London: Family and Parenting Institute.

Warhurst, C., Eikhoff, E.R. and Haunschild, A. (2008) *Work less, live more? Critical analysis of the work–life boundary*, Basingstoke: Palgrave Macmillan.

Warren, T. (2004) 'Conceptualising breadwinning work', *Work, Employment and Society*, vol 21, no 2, 317–36.

Wattis, L., Yerkes, M., Lloyd, S., Hernandes, M., Dawson, L. and Standing, K. (2006) *Combining work and family life: Removing the barriers to women's progression, experiences from the UK and the Netherlands*, EU Social Fund/Liverpool John Moores University.

White, C., Warrener, M., Reeves, A. and La Valle, I. (2008) *Family intervention projects: An evaluation of the design, set-up and early outcomes*, Research Report DCSF-RW047, London: DCSF.

Williams, F. (1989) *Critical social policy: A critical introduction. Issues of race, gender and class*, Cambridge: Polity Press.

Williams, F. (2004a) *Rethinking families*, London: Gulbenkian Institute.

Williams, F. (2004b) 'What matters is who works: why every child matters to New Labour. Comments on the DfES Green Paper Every Child Matters', *Critical Social Policy*, vol 24, no 3, pp 406–27.

Williams, F. and Churchill, H. (2006) *Empowering parents in Sure Start local programmes*, National Evaluation of Sure Start Report, NESS/2006/FR/018, London: DfES.

Williams, S. (2008) 'What is fatherhood? Searching for the reflexive father', *Sociology*, vol 42, no 3, pp 487 – 502.

Wollny, I., Apps, J. and Henricson, C. (2010) *Can government measure family well-being? A literature review*, London: Family and Parenting Institute.

Women and Work Commission (2009) *Shaping a fairer future: A review of the recommendations of the Women and Work Commission – three years on*, London: Crown Copyright.

Women's Budget Group (2000) *Women's Budget Group's response to the Government's Green Paper: Work and Parents*, available at: www.wbg.org.uk/pdf/Work%20and%20Parents.pdf.

Wright, S. (2009) 'Welfare to work', in Millar, J. (ed) *Understanding social security* (2nd edn), Bristol: The Policy Press.

Yeandle, S., Crompton, R., Wigfield, A. and Dennett, J. (2002) *Employers, communities and family-friendly employment*, York: Joseph Rowntree Foundation.

Index

Note: Page numbers followed by *fig*, *tab* and *n* refer to information in a figure, table and note respectively. There is a list of abbreviations on page vii.